||| ||||| ||| |||| ||||| |||
MW00325454

# THE URANTIA BOO~ ...~~~~~~~~

## URANTIA®

URANTIA FOUNDATION
533 WEST DIVERSEY PARKWAY
CHICAGO, ILLINOIS 60614
U.S.A.

## URANTIA®

®: Registered Mark of URANTIA Foundation

# THE URANTIA BOOK WORKBOOKS

## VOLUME VI

# Bible Study

This series of workbooks originally was published in the 1950s and 1960s to assist those early students who wanted to pursue an in-depth study of *The Urantia Book*. The workbook creators recognized that the materials were imperfect and were far from being definitive works on these subjects. Current students may be able to make more exhaustive analyses due to advances in knowledge and computerization of the text that are available today. Nevertheless, we recognize the enormous effort that went into this attempt to enhance understanding of *The Urantia Book* by some of its earliest students. We think these materials will be of interest to many and are therefore republishing them for their historic and educational value.

*FIRST PRINTING 2003*

# THE URANTIA BOOK WORKBOOKS
## VOLUME VI
## BIBLE STUDY

### The Urantia Book Workbooks

Volume I: Transcripts of Lecture and Discussion of the Foreword and An Analytic Study of Part One of *The Urantia Book*

Volume II: Science in *The Urantia Book*

Volume III: Topical Studies in *The Urantia Book* and A Short Course in Doctrine

Volume IV: The Teachings of Jesus in *The Urantia Book*, The Life of Jesus Compared to the Four Gospels

Volume V: Urantia Doctrine: The Theology of *The Urantia Book*

Volume VI: History of The Bible and A Detailed Study of the Books of The Bible.

Volume VII: Quick Reference Dictionary, Terms and Defined in *The Urantia Book*, and A Keyword Index to the Table of Contetnts

Volume VIII: Worship and Wisdom: Gems from *The Urantia Book*

"URANTIA", "URANTIAN", "THE URANTIA BOOK", and ◎ are the trademarks, service marks, and collective membership marks of URANTIA Foundation.

© 1961, 1962, 1963, 2003 URANTIA Foundation

All rights reserved, including translation, under the Berne Convention, Universal Copyright Convention, and other international copyright conventions.

To request permission to translate or to reproduce material contained in *The Urantia Book Workbooks* or the *The Urantia Book* by any means (including electronic, mechanical, or other—such as photocopying, recording, or any information storage and retrieval system), please contact Urantia Foundation. Copies of Urantia Foundation's current Copyright and Trademark Policies are available upon request.

**ISBN:**
0-942430-94-8

PUBLISHED BY URANTIA FOUNDATION
*Original Publisher since 1955*

533 Diversey Parkway
Chicago, Illinois 60614 U.S.A.
Telephone: +1 (773) 525-3319
Fax: +1 (773) 525-7739
Website: http://www.urantia.org
E-mail: urantia@urantia.org

# Information

URANTIA Foundation has Representatives in Argentina, Belgium, Brazil, Bulgaria, Colombia, Ecuador, Estonia, Greece, Indonesia, Korea, Lithuania, México, Norway, Perú, Senegal, Spain, Uruguay, and Venezuela. If you require information on study groups, where you can obtain *The URANTIA Book*, or a Representative's telephone number, please contact the office nearest you or the head office in Chicago, Illinois.

*International Offices:*

## Head Office

533 West Diversey Parkway
Chicago, Illinois 60614 U.S.A.
Tel.: +(773) 525-3319
Fax: +(773) 525-7739
Website: www.urantia.org
E-mail: urantia@urantia.org

## Canada—English

PO Box 92006
West Vancouver, BC Canada V7V 4X4
Tel: +(604) 926-5836
Fax: +(604) 926-5899
E-mail: urantia@telus.net

## Finland / Estonia / Sweden

PL 18,
15101 Lahti Finland
Tel./Fax: +(358) 3 777 8191
E-mail: urantia-saatio@urantia.fi

## Great Britain / Ireland

Tel./Fax: +(44) 1491 641-922
E-Mail: urantia@easynet.co.uk

## Australia / New Zealand / Asia

Tel./Fax: +(61) 2 9970-6200
E-mail: urantia@urantia.org.au

## Canada—French

C. P. 233
Cap-Santé (Québec) Canada G0A 1L0
Tel.: +(418) 285-3333
Fax: +(418) 285-0226
E-mail: fondation@urantia-quebec.org

## St. Petersburg, Russia

Tel./Fax: +(7) 812-580-3018
E-mail: vitgen@peterlink.ru

*Other books available from URANTIA Foundation:*

The URANTIA Book . . . . . . .hard cover . . . . . . . . . . . . . . . . . . . . . . . . . .ISBN 0-911560-02-5
The URANTIA Book . . . . . . .leather collector (7⁵/₈" x 5³/₄") . . . . . . . . . . . . .ISBN 0-911560-75-0
The URANTIA Book . . . . . . .small hard cover (8⁷/₁₆" x 5¹/₂") . . . . . . . . . . . .ISBN 0-911560-07-6
The URANTIA Book . . . . . . .paperback . . . . . . . . . . . . . . (8⁷/₁₆" x 5¹/₂") . .ISBN 0-911560-51-3
The URANTIA Book . . . . . . .gift-box leather (8⁷/₁₆" x 5¹/₂") . . . . . . . . . . . . .ISBN 0-911560-08-4
The URANTIA Book . . . . . . .softcover . . . . . . . . . . . . . . (8⁷/₁₆" x 5¹/₂") . .ISBN 0-911560-50-5
Le Livre d'URANTIA . . . . . . .hard cover . . . .French . . . . . . . . . . . . . . . . .ISBN 0-911560-05-X
Le Livre d'URANTIA . . . . . . .soft cover . . . .French . . . . . . . . . . . . . . . . .ISBN 0-911560-53-X
El libro de URANTIA . . . . . . .paperback . . . .Spanish . . . . .(8⁷/₁₆" x 5¹/₂") . .ISBN 1-883395-02-X
El libro de URANTIA . . . . . . .hard cover . . . .Spanish . . . . .(8⁷/₁₆" x 5¹/₂") . .ISBN 1-883395-03-8
URANTIA-kirja . . . . . . . . . . .hard cover . . . .Finnish . . . . . . . . . . . . . . . . .ISBN 0-911560-03-3
URANTIA-kirja . . . . . . . . . . .soft cover . . . .Finnish . . . . . . . . . . . . . . . . .ISBN 0-911560-52-1
The URANTIA Book Concordance . . . . . . . . . .English Index . . . . . . . . . . . . . .ISBN 0-911560-00-9
The URANTIA Book . . . . . . . .Audio . . . . . . .English . . . . . . . . . . . . . . . . .ISBN 0-911560-30-0
The URANTIA Book . . . . . . . .CD ROM . . . .English, Finnish, French . . . . . . .ISBN 0-911560-63-7

## The URANTIA Book Workbooks

Forward and Part I . . . . . . . .Paperback . . . .English . . . . . . . . . . . . . . . . .ISBN 0-942430-99-9
Science . . . . . . . . . . . . . . .Paperback . . . .English . . . . . . . . . . . . . . . . .ISBN 0-942430-98-0
Topical and Doctrinal Study . .Paperback . . . .English . . . . . . . . . . . . . . . . .ISBN 0-942430-97-2
Jesus . . . . . . . . . . . . . . . . .Paperback . . . .English . . . . . . . . . . . . . . . . .ISBN 0-942430-96-4
Theology . . . . . . . . . . . . . .Paperback . . . .English . . . . . . . . . . . . . . . . .ISBN 0-942430-95-6
Bible Study . . . . . . . . . . . . .Paperback . . . .English . . . . . . . . . . . . . . . . .ISBN 0-942430-94-8
Terminology . . . . . . . . . . . .Paperback . . . .English . . . . . . . . . . . . . . . . .ISBN 0-942430-93-X
Worship and Wisdom . . . . . .Paperback . . . .English . . . . . . . . . . . . . . . . .ISBN 0-942430-92-1

**Dutch, Korean, Portuguese, and Russian translations also available from Urantia Foundation.**

# INTRODUCTION

Much has already been written regarding the study groups called "The Forum" and "The Seventy". Therefore I will try to confine my remarks more closely to the compiling and printing of several workbooks by Dr. William Sadler to be used in conjunction with *The Urantia Book*.

"The Forum" was the larger of the two groups and met on Sunday afternoons. The Wednesday night group was much smaller, studied in more depth, and was called "The Seventy" as that was the number of its members. Both met at the home of Dr. Sadler at 533 Diversey Parkway in Chicago. Doctor and some others in the group felt that something concrete was needed to train teachers for the future. Workbooks would help the teachers to form classes in the state or country in which they lived and use them to understand and present the concepts and new ideas from the Book in a uniform manner.

For several years members of the Wednesday night group were asked to prepare topical papers and teach the contents to the others in the group thus giving them experience in teaching. Dr. Sadler and his son, Bill, also taught the members of the group the information contained in the Papers of *The Urantia Book*. From the information Dr. Sadler taught at these classes the workbooks were developed for use by the group and for future teachers of the revelation.

The titles of the workbooks were:
Urantia Doctrine;
The Theology of *The Urantia Book*, Part I, Part II, and Part III;
Worship and Wisdom;
The Short Course in Doctrine,
Summary Of The Theology Of *The Urantia Book*;
Science in *The Urantia Book* Volume I (with the collaboration of Alvin Kulieke);
and
The Teachings Of Jesus.

Dr. Sadler possessed a great intellect, which may be one of the reasons he was selected by the Contact Commission to be the recipient of the *Urantia Papers*. He was able to understand and present, in a form that is understandable for others, many of the more difficult concepts and information in *The Urantia Book*. This is a great advantage for students who may be teaching these concepts in the future. The reprinting of these study aids will help many students of *The Urantia Book* gain a more comfortable understanding of the more difficult teachings in the book and an insight into Dr. Sadler's plan for instructing the future teachers of the revelation.

What a legacy has been left to us!

*Katharine*

Katharine Lea Jones Harries

# HISTORY OF THE BIBLE

## TABLE OF CONTENTS

## MAPS

# STUDY OF THE BOOKS OF THE BIBLE

## PART I - OLD TESTAMENT

# THE HISTORY OF THE BIBLE

## BIBLICAL ABBREVIATIONS USED IN THIS VOLUME

### The Old Testament

Gen ....... The Book of Genesis

Ex ......... The Book of Exodus

Lev ........ The Book of Leviticus

Num ...... The Book of Numbers

Deut ...... The Book of Deuteronomy

Josh ....... The Book of Joshua

Judges .... The Book of Judges

Ruth ...... The Book of Ruth

1 Sam ..... The First Book of Samuel

2 Sam ..... The Second Book of Samuel

1 Kings ... The First Book of Kings

2 Kings ... The Second Book of Kings

1 Chron .. The First Book of Chronicles

2 Chron .. The Second Book of Chronicles

Ezra ....... The Book of Ezra

Neh ....... The Book of Nehemiah

Esther .... The Book of Esther

Job ........ The Book of Job

Ps ......... The Book of Psalms

Prov ....... The Book of Proverbs

Eccl ....... Ecclesiastes

Song ...... The Song of Songs

Isa ......... The Book of Isaiah

Jer ......... The Book of Jeremiah

Lam ....... Lamentations

Eze ........ The Book of Ezekiel

Dan ....... The Book of Daniel

Hos ....... The Book of Hosea

Joel ....... The Book of Joel

Amos ..... The Book of Amos

Obad ..... The Book of Obadiah

Jon ........ The Book of Jonah

Nah ....... The Book of Nahum

Hab ....... The Book of Habakkuk

Zeph ...... The Book of Zephaniah

Hag ....... The Book of Haggai

Zec ........ The Book of Zechariah

Mal ........ The Book of Malachi

### The New Testament

Matt ...... The Gospel According to Matthew

Mark ...... The Gospel According to Mark

Luke ...... The Gospel According to Luke

John ....... The Gospel According to John

Acts ....... The Acts of the Apostles

Rom ...... The Epistle to the Romans

1 Cor ..... The First Epistle to the Corinthians

2 Cor ..... The Second Epistle to the Corinthians

Gal ........ The Epistle to the Galatians

Eph ....... The Epistle to the Ephesians

Phil ....... The Epistle to the Philippians

Col ........ The Epistle to the Colossians

1 Thess ... The First Epistle to the Thessalonians

2 Thess ... The Second Epistle to the Thessalonians

1 Tim ..... The First Epistle to Timothy

2 Tim ..... The Second Epistle to Timothy

Tit ........ The Epistle to Titus

Phmon ... The Epistle to Philemon

Heb ....... The Epistle to the Hebrews

Jas ......... The Epistle of James

1 Peter ... The First Epistle of Peter

2 Peter ... The Second Epistle of Peter

1 John .... The First Epistle of John

2 John .... The Second Epistle of John

3 John .... The Third Epistle of John

Jude ....... Jude

Rev ....... Revelation

# PART I
# A SURVEY OF THE BIBLE

# A SURVEY OF THE BIBLE

## 1. THE BIBLE: AUTHORITY AND SIGNIFICANCE

### I. THE BIBLE ESSENTIAL TO CHRISTIANITY

1. From the beginning of Christianity, the Old Testament was accepted as Scripture—the word of God.

2. To understand the relation of the Bible to Christianity means that we must define Christianity, and such a study involves the theologian, historian, archaeologist, and anthropologist.

3. According to *The Urantia Book*, Christianity is the religion *about* Jesus as differentiated from the religion *of* Jesus.

4. The Bible never claims to be an infallible authority. Says Paul in **2 Tim. 3:16**: *"All Scripture is inspired by God and profitable for teaching, for reproof, for correction, and for training in righteousness."*

5. Whatever inspiration is, there must be *degrees* of it. Second Isaiah was more inspired than the First Isaiah.

6. In another place (**Rom. 6:19**) Paul reminds his readers that: *"I am speaking in human terms, because of your natural limitations."*

7. Textual contradictions and other differences make it impossible for us to believe in *verbal* inspiration.

8. Jesus frequently quoted Scripture, but never alluded to it as being inspired. He never called Scripture the *word of God*.

9. Jesus' view of the Scriptures is expressed in his memorable talk with Nathaniel. See *The Urantia Book*, pages 1767-9.

10. The interpretation of Scripture:

    a. *Catholic View*: The church, and only the church, can truly interpret the Bible. And when the church does thus function, the interpretation is *infallible*.
    b. *Protestant View*: Protestants claim that any individual, by aid of the Holy Spirit, can interpret the Bible.

11. The word "Bible" means "little book," but the word itself is not found in the Bible.

## II. HARMONY OF FAITH AND SCRIPTURE

1.  *Incarnation* is the theologic heart of Christianity—and the Bible sustains this doctrine.

2.  *"And the Word became flesh and dwelt among us." John 1:14.* This is the theme song of all New Testament teaching.

3.  Naturally, the next step is the proclamation—*"There is no other name under heaven given among men, by which we must be saved." Acts 4:12.*

4.  While *The Urantia Book* validates the incarnation, it declares the gospel of the kingdom to be "the fatherhood of God and the brotherhood of man."

5.  At Antioch they stressed the humanity of Jesus; at Alexandria, the divinity of the Master.

6.  Docetism taught that Jesus' humanity was but "seeming"—a sort of phantasm.

7.  The Bible could be regarded as an incarnation—a union of the human and the divine.

8.  The divine represents the so-called inspiration; the human accounts for the remarkable diversification—the errors, the contradictions, inconsistencies, etc.

9.  To take away the human element in Scripture would be the equivalent of depriving Jesus of his human nature.

10. Christ's ministry to man did not come to an end at his death on the cross and God's revelation of truth to mankind did not end with the Old and New Testaments.

## III. THE BIBLE AND THE CHURCH

1.  Neither the Old Testament nor Jesus was given just to and for the Jews. Both were a universal bestowal.

2.  The ministry of Christ and the function of revelation are continuous. They are both a part of the eternal purpose.

3.  Christ's incarnation was, in a way, "humanization."

4.  The incarnation of the "Word" in the Bible was also a sort of "humanization" of truth.

5.  The gift of the Spirit was to lead believers "into all truth." Such an experience would go over long periods of time—entail much growth.

6. Since the Bible records were ended almost two thousand years ago—what takes its place in the continued evolution of the church?

## IV. AUTHORITY OF THE BIBLE

1. In the Reformation, the Protestants, in rejecting an infallible Pope, put in his place an infallible book—the Bible.

2. Christ is the only final and absolute authority for the New Testament FAITH.

3. Christ's brotherhood is not authoritarian—the Roman Catholic Church is.

4. To prevent just such a mistake as the Protestants made, Christ left no written records. Only the "word" as it is in Christ is infallible.

5. The Catholic Church does not regard the Scriptures as being infallible— only their interpretation.

6. The Catholics regard "tradition" as being equal to the Bible as authority for doctrine and dogmas.

7. On the whole, the Roman Church has discouraged its lay members from acquiring a knowledge of the Bible.

8. Luther said: "The Bible is the manger in which Christ is laid."

9. The human side of the Scriptures is shown in the inconsistencies and inaccuracies; the divine hand in the revelation of eternal truth.

10. The Bible is inseparably bound up with the whole organism of the Christian faith and experience.

11. The Bible is a "man-selected" group of writing. The Maccabees of the Apocrypha are more scriptural than the Song of Solomon or the book of Esther.

12. In creating the canon of the New Testament it was the intention to include only those writings of apostolic origin.

13. The books of the New Testament were not written as history or biography— they were written solely to propagate the faith.

14. Even Jesus never set himself up as an absolute authority.

15. Paul never claimed inspiration or infallibility. He said: *"Judge for yourselves what I say."* **1 Cor. 10:15**.

16. The belief of Protestants in the literal inerrancy of the Bible, its absolute authority, led to their breaking up into a multitude of sects.

17. The recognition of the fallibility of Scripture in the twentieth century is bringing them together.

18. But this does not mean that every individual should set himself up as the one and only interpreter of the Scriptures.

19. We should look critically upon the Bible when it contradicts the facts of nature—such as the teaching that the earth is flat. (This has nothing to do with genuine miracles.)

20. Symbolism should also be questioned—like the story of Jonah and the whale.

21. Never forget the fact of the "evolution of revelation." Remember also that there have been retrogressions.

22. Do not be misled by the ambiguities of the Bible or by its allegories— such as interpreting the voluptuous Song of Solomon as representing the love of Christ for his church.

23. And do not accept all of the apostolic teachings as the teaching of Christ.

24. The mistaken reporting of Jesus' teaching is shown by the record found in **Matt. 24**. See *The Urantia Book*, p. 1912.

25. Certain portions of the Bible have had a non-Jewish origin. Note the following:

    **Isa. 16, 17.** From a Moabite elegy.
    **Ps. 104.** Sun hymn of Ikhnaton.
    **Prov. 22:17-23:14.** Maxims of Amenomope.
    **Ex. 20-23.** Sounds like Hammurabi.

## V. THE BIBLE AS THE WORD OF GOD

1. Is it proper to speak of the Bible as the word of God? The gospel message was called the word of God. **See Rev. 1:2.** *"Who bore witness to the word of God and to the testimony of Jesus Christ."*

2. Sometimes referred to as *"the word of the cross."* **See 1 Cor. 1:18.**

3. In **Phil. 2:16**, called *"the word of life."* In **Col. 1:5**, called *"the word of the truth."*

4. The gospel of John refers to Christ as "the word." **See John 1:1.** *"In the beginning was the Word, and the Word was with God, and the Word was God."*

5. And in speaking of the incarnation, John says: *"And the Word became flesh and dwelt among us."* **John 1:14.**

6. *The Urantia Book* speaks of the Eternal Son as "the living and divine word." p. 73.

7. Strictly speaking, the Bible should not be called the word of God. Inasmuch as God may be speaking in and through the Bible, it would be qualifiedly the divine word.

8. It was in this sense that the Urantia revelation was spoken of as the "Word made Book."

## 2. THE HEBREW SACRED SCRIPTURES

## THE OLD TESTAMENT

Before sometime around 1000 B.C. there was not much writing among the Jews. Tradition was perpetuated by oral transmission from generation to generation.

### *I. COMPOSITION OF THE OLD TESTAMENT*

1. The Ode of Deborah, commemorating Israel's victory over Sisera (**Judges 5**) is the oldest Old Testament document. Probably composed 1125 B.C.

2. Probably not composed by Deborah. There are two accounts—prose version in **Judges 4** and the poetic version in Chap. 5.

3. Heavy rain and thunderstorms rendered the Canaanite chariots useless—so that they were routed and massacred.

4. Deborah was a wise judge. The Hebrews gave women more recognition in these days than later on in their national history. Deborah was a prophetess as well as a judge.

5. Among the oldest portions of the Old Testament are poems quoted from the lost books of Jashar, Book of the word of Yahweh, etc. See **Josh. 10:12-14**.

6. The oldest Old Testament prose is probably the narrative of the establishment of the kingdom of David.

7. Next come the Elijah stories and the reign of Jehu. 842-815 B.C.

8. The writing of the historical books of the Old Testament began about 600 B.C. They had access to the lost book of "The Acts of the Kings of Judah and Israel." **2 Chron. 25:26**.

9. The story of the kingdoms of David and Solomon. **1 Sam. 16 to 1 Kings 11**.

10. David was shepherd, poet, musician, and warrior. For years a fugitive and outlaw. Became king of Judea and Israel upon the death of Saul.

11. There are two stories of David's being made king.

    a. Anointed king at Hebron. **2 Sam. 2:1-11**.
    b. Elected king. **2 Sam. 5:1-5**.

12. David has a long and eventful reign—subdues the Philistines, Moabites, Zobahites, Syrians, Edomites, and Ammonites.

13. David goes through the rebellion of Absalom and finally sees Solomon on the throne.

14. Solomon reigns 960-922 B.C. He presides over the united kingdom and builds the temple. Marries many wives and establishes far-flung international relations.

15. Has a reputation for being wise. Raises taxes—builds extensively, and all but bankrupts the kingdom.

16. After Solomon's death, the united kingdom breaks up. Wars break out. Jeroboam sets up rival religious system in the northern kingdom.

17. Rehoboam, Solomon's son by an Ammonite princess (**1 Kings 14:21**), carries on an indifferent rule at Jerusalem.

18. Very little is contributed to the Old Testament except some Psalms.

19. The Old Testament was almost one thousand years in taking shape. The "Former Prophets" cover the period from Abraham to the captivity.

20. All sorts of literature are to be found in the Old Testament:

    a. *Legal*—the Pentateuch.
    b. *Historical*—Joshua, Judges, Samuel, Kings, Chronicles, Ezra, Nehemiah, Esther.
    c. *Prophetic*—the major and minor prophets.
    d. *Wisdom*—Proverbs, Job, Ecclesiastes, and the Song of Solomon.
    e. *Devotional*—Psalms.

21. Amos is probably the oldest book in the Old Testament.

## II. GROWTH OF THE OLD TESTAMENT

1. The books of the Old Testament are of composite authorship—few were written by the names they bear. Most of them have been edited and re-edited many times.

2. When writing came into vogue, records were made of many traditions before 1000 B.C.—before the monarchal period:

    a. *War Poems and March Songs*.

       Song of Deborah. **Judges 5**.
       Song of Lamech. **Gen. 4:23**.
       Song of Miriam. **Ex. 15:21**.
       War with Amalek. **Ex. 17:16**.
       Ode to the Ark. **Num. 10:35**.

Taunt Song—Amorites. **Num. 21:27-30.**
Song of the Well. **Num. 21:17.**
Joshua to Sun and Moon. **Josh. 10:12.**

b. *Proverbs and Fables.*

David's proverb. **1 Sam. 24:13.**
Samson's riddles. **Judges 14:14,18.**
Samson's taunt. **Judges 15:16.**
Jotham's fable. **Judges 9:7-15.**

c. *Prophetic Blessings and Oracles.*

Blessing of Noah. **Gen. 9:25-27.**
Blessing of Jacob. **Gen. 49.**
Oracles of Balaam. **Num. 23.**

3. During the times of David, Solomon, and Jeroboam. 1000-910 B.C.:

a. *Poems.*

David's victories. 1 Sam. 18:7.
Sheba's war cry. 2 Sam. 20:1.
David's lamentation over Saul. 2 Sam. 1:19.
David's lamentation over Abner. 2 Sam. 3:33.
Nathan's parable. 2 Sam. 12:1-4.
Solomon's dedication of temple. 1 Kings 8:12.
Blessing of Moses. Deut. 33.

b. *Narratives.*
Founding of the kingdom. I and II Sam. and I Kings.

c. *Laws.*
Book of the covenant. Ex. 20-23.

4. *The 9th and 8th Centuries.*

The Elijah stories. 1 Kings 17-19.
The Omri dynasty. 1 Kings 3:6-9; 20:22.
The Elisha stories. 2 Kings 2-8; 13:14-21.
Yahweh activities. 850 B.C.
Elohist activities. 750 B.C.
Genesis. 850-750 B.C.
Amos. 750 B.C.
Hosea. 745-735 B.C.
Isaiah. 738-700 B.C.
Micah. 715-686 B.C.

5.  *The 7th Century.*

    Deuteronomy published. 621 B.C.
    Zephaniah. 627 B.C.
    Jeremiah. 620—on. B.C.
    Nahum. 615 B.C.
    First edition of Book of Kings. 620-608 B.C.

6.  *The 6th Century.*

    Jeremiah continues. After 585 B.C.
    Habakkuk. 600-590 B.C.
    Ezekiel. 593-571 B.C.
    Holiness code. Lev. 17-26.
    Lamentations. 586-550 B.C.
    Isaiah. 63:7-64:12.
    Second edition of Kings. 560 B.C.
    Revised stories of Joshua, Judges, and Samuel.
    Song of Moses. Deut. 32.
    Isaiah 13:2; 14:4-21.
    Second Isaiah 40-55. 546-539 B.C.
    Haggai. 520 B.C.
    Zechariah 1-8. 520-518 B.C.

7.  *The 5th Century.*

    Parts of Isaiah 59-66.
    Jeremiah 3:14-18.
    Isaiah 34.
    Obadiah.
    Amos 9:8-15.
    Isaiah 11:10-16.
    Malachi. 460 B.C.
    Book of Ruth.
    One story of Ezra 4:8-6:18.
    Joel. 400 B.C.

8.  *The 4th Century.*

    Joel—some parts.
    Isaiah 19:1-15; 23:1-14.
    Proverbs.
    Job.
    Isaiah 24-27.

9. *The 3rd Century.*

   Chronicles. 300-250 B.C.
   Genesis 14.
   I Kings 13.
   Esther.
   Song of Solomon.
   Proverbs 1-9.
   Jonah.
   Isaiah 19:18-25.
   Ecclesiastes. 200 B.C.

10. *The 2nd Century.*

   Daniel. 165 B.C.
   Zechariah 9-11; 13:7-9.
   Isaiah 33.
   Completion of Psalter.

## III. CANON OF THE OLD TESTAMENT

1. The Old Testament represents the growth of almost one thousand years. Only Christians call the Hebrew scriptures the Old Testament.

2. The Hebrews classified the 39 books of their Scripture into four grand divisions.

   a. The Law—Torah. 5 books. The Pentateuch.
   b. The Prophets. 8 books.
      (1) The Former Prophets.
          Joshua, Judges, Samuel, Kings.
      (2) The Later Prophets.
          Isaiah, Jeremiah, Ezekiel.
   c. The Minor Prophets—the Twelve.
   d. The Remainder.
      Daniel, Ezra, Nehemiah, Chronicles.

3. The Old Testament canon was created by a synod of rabbis at Jamnia (near Joppa) in A.D. 90.

4. This was the first "completed" assembly of sacred writings to be formulated by any religion.

## IV. THE OLD TESTAMENT VERSIONS

1. No original manuscripts of either Old or New Testament are in existence today.

2. **The Samaritan Pentateuch.**

   This manuscript is possibly as early as the fourth century B.C. There are 6,000 differences between this text and later Hebrew versions. Only 1,000 are important. One of the oldest of this text is in Paris.

3. **Hebrew Texts**

   One of the oldest is the codex of the Former and Later Prophets, found in the Karaite synagogue at Cairo—written in A.D. 895.

   A complete manuscript of the entire Old Testament is now in Leningrad. A.D. 1008.

   The Dead Sea Scrolls (A.D. 1947) go back to as far as the fifth century B.C. Others to 100 B.C. and A.D. 70.

4. **The Massoretic Texts**

   The Massoretes were a school of textual scholars who devoted themselves to the protection of the Scriptural text.

   They created vowel sounds for the Hebrew text, as well as punctuation. They functioned up to the tenth century A.D.

   The first Hebrew text with vowel sounds was published in A.D. 1488.

5. **Greek Versions**

   The Septuagint—the LXX—is the oldest of the Greek translations. It was completed in 250 B.C. for the Alexandrian library. It may have covered a period of one hundred and fifty years.

   This was the Bible of the apostles, Paul, and the early Christians. It is quoted in the New Testament.

   Several new Greek translations were made in the second and third centuries A.D.

   In A.D. 240 Origen made a six-column comparison of the Greek texts.

6. **The Major Greek Texts**

   *Codex Vaticanus.* In the Vatican library since the fifteenth century. Written at Alexandria in the middle of the fourth century A.D.

   *Codex Sinaiticus.* Found on Mt. Sinai in 1844. Taken to St. Petersburg. Bought by England in 1933. Now in British Museum.

   *Codex Alexandrias.* A fifth century manuscript brought to England in 1624. Now in the British Museum.

   *Codex Ephraemi.* Fifth century manuscript now at Paris.

   NOTE: The first printed LXX was in 1514.

7. **The Latin Versions.**

   The "Old Latin" version originated in Carthage A.D. 250.

   African, European, and Italian versions soon appeared.

   *The Vulgate.* Produced by Jerome A.D. 382. This was a major event and it was many times revised. It was first printed A.D. 1456 and has been the Bible of the Roman Catholic Church ever since Jerome produced it. (Also known as the Douay version.)

   For the first time in over a thousand years the Catholics have recently made a Revised Version of the Vulgate.

8. **Syriac Versions.**

   The Peshitta version was made in the third century, from the LXX—for Christians.

   Bishop Tetta's translation was made in A.D. 616.

9. **The Targums.**

   These are Aram interpretations of the Hebrew text, completed from the fifth to ninth century A.D.

10. **Other Versions.**

    Coptic, Egypt. Fourth century.
    Ethiopia. Fourth century.
    Gothic. A.D. 350.
    Armenian. A.D. 400.
    Georgian. Fifth century.
    Slavonic. Ninth century.
    Arabic. Eighth century.

# 3. CHRISTIAN SACRED WRITINGS

# THE NEW TESTAMENT

## *I. ORIGIN OF THE NEW TESTAMENT*

1.  The early church started out with the present day Old Testament and the Old Testament Apocrypha as its Bible.

2.  The early New Testament collections were written in Greek and consisted of a half dozen separate books.

3.  Paul's letters to the churches—seven—were directed to meet certain definite situations.

4.  The churches were at:

    Rome.
    Corinth.
    Galatia.
    Ephesus.
    Philippi.
    Colossae.
    Thessalonica.

5.  Paul wrote ten letters to these seven churches. They were circulated in one book—Ephesians as the introduction.

6.  In A.D. 95 Clement of Rome wrote a letter to the church at Corinth.

7.  The three gospels, later four, were in a separate book. Dates of writing, according to *The Urantia Book*: Mark A.D. 68, Matthew A.D. 71, Luke A.D. 82, and John A.D. 101.

8.  About A.D. 125 Marcion, a Pontus layman, used the gospel of Luke and Paul's letters as a new Bible.

9.  Athenagoras, of Athens, used the four gospels and Paul's ten letters as "all but Scripture."

10. Theophilus of Antioch (A.D. 180) used the gospels and Paul's letters as "Christian scriptures."

11. **The First New Testament.** The appearance of heretical sects in the second and third centuries demanded that the Christian churches establish an authoritative Scripture.

12. These sects were:

    a.  *Docetism.* Teaching that the humanity of Jesus was a "phantasm."
    b.  *Marcionism.* An over-rigid and drastic church organization.

     c.   *Montanism*. Exaggerated claims for prophetic gifts.

     d.   *Gnosticism*. Denial of Jesus' humanity and other errors.

13.   Content of the first New Testament:

     a.   Irenaeus of Lyons (A.D. 180) says the New Testament contained the four gospels, Acts, Paul's letters, the Peter and John epistles, and the Shepherd of Hennas.

     b.   Tertullian of Carthage (A.D. 197-223) added Jude, but later on rejected the Shepherd of Hennas.

     c.   Hebrews was the last book to gain general acceptance.

     d.   The Alexandrian New Testament also contained I Clement and Barnabas.

14.   The times of Origen.

Serious persecution in A.D. 202 forced Christian leaders out of Alexandria. Origen, 18 years old, became head of the Christian seminary. For fifty years he wrote and taught first in Alexandria and later on at Caesarea. A rich friend published his writings.

15.   Origen accepted Hebrews, but also included Hennas and Barnabas.

16.   Eusebius of Caesarea. He attended the Council of Nicaea in 325. He finished his great church history in 326.

He followed Origen, accepting Barnabas and building up a New Testament just about as we have it today. He rejected Hermas and was doubtful about Revelation.

17.   Athanasius of Alexandria. In 367 he prepared a list of New Testament books: Four gospels, Acts, fourteen letters of Paul, seven general letters, Hebrews, and Revelation. This is just the New Testament as we have it today.

But he did not wholly give up the Shepherd of Hermas until he was seventy years old.

18.   Other early versions. Among these were the Coptic, Syriac, Rabulla, and the Peshitta.

## II. THE WORK OF THE COUNCILS

1.   The councils did not so much form the New Testament canon as give official recognition to its existence.

2.   The synod of Laodicea, 363, recognized the canon as we have it today, except Revelation. It forbade the reading of other writings in the church.

3.   The council of Hippo, 393, accepted Revelation—giving us our present New Testament.

4. The synod of Carthage, 397 (also 419), confirmed the completed New Testament canon.

5. Chrysostom, 407, presbyter of Antioch—later patriarch of Constantinople— rejected the general letters and Revelation.

6. Gregory later accepted the general letters, but not Revelation.

7. The eastern church was divided by Revelation; the western church, by Hebrews.

8. Even today, the Greek church never reads Revelation at church services.

9. Finally, Jerome (382) put both Hebrews and Revelation into his Latin Vulgate translation.

10. Since Pope Damasus of Rome accepted Jerome's Bible, the New Testament of 27 books was finally settled for the western church.

11. So we enter the Middle Ages with the New Testament canon settled in three translations:

    a. *Greek—Latin.*
    b. *Syriac.*
    c. *Ethiopic.*

12. St. Augustine supported the Jerome New Testament.

13. During the Middle Ages many New Testament versions in Germany, Spain, and England presented minor variations.

14. Council of Trent (1546) took *final* action. Once and for all the New Testament canon was adopted.

15. The rejected books became the New Testament Apocrypha.

16. All along, the three controversial books were Revelation, Hebrews, and Hennas.

## III. NEW TESTAMENT VERSIONS

1. Remember: The early Christians had no printed books. Also, the original documents are all gone.

2. The copy of Mark in St. Mark's church at Venice is from Jerome's Vulgate Bible of the fourth century.

3. No two hand-copied manuscripts ever agree completely. These differences are called "variant readings."

4. A gospel of Mark at the University of Chicago contains 181 variants not found in other manuscripts.

5. Two gospels of Mark differ in 873 passages. Two manuscripts of the four gospels disclose 14,040 differences.

6. Some manuscripts present an average of 50 differences per page.

7. These differences are caused by:

   a. Skill of scribes.
   b. Efforts to harmonize.
   c. Removal of heresy.
   d. Attempts at clarification.
   e. Mistakes.
   f. Editorializing.
   g. Skipping lines.
   h. Omissions by error.

8. Illustration of harmonization.

   **Matt. 12:13.** The man with a withered hand. Matt, reads: *"Then he said to the man, 'Stretch out your hand. And the man stretched it out, and it was restored, whole like the other."*

   Early copies of Mark and Luke do not contain *"whole like the other."* But increasingly, later copies contain this addition.

   **NOTE**: *The Urantia Book* (p. 1665) follows the early Mark and Luke— does not contain the later addition.

9. Illustration of removing heresy.

   **Matt. 24:36**. *"But of that day and hour no one knows, not even the angels of heaven, nor the Son, but the Father only."*

   A scribe, believing that Jesus was omniscient, was sure someone had made a mistake, so he changed the text—omitting the words—"nor the Son."

   **NOTE**: Jesus, in making this statement on p. 1915 of *The Urantia Book*, likewise omits "nor the Son." He says: "But the times of the re-appearing of the Son of Man are known only in the councils of Paradise; not even the angels of heaven know when this will occur."

10. Illustration of unification.

    **Luke 23:32**. *"Also other criminals, two, were led away to be put to death with him."*

    The scribes resented the implication that Jesus was a criminal, so they changed it to read: *"Two others also, who were criminals, were led away to be put to death with him."*

    **NOTE**: This passage does not appear in *The Urantia Book.*

11.  Ambiguity.

     Concerning the Lord's Supper in **Matt. 26:27**, it originally read: *"Drink ye all of it."* The scribe changed it to *"Drink of it, all of you,"* as now in the Revised Version.

     *The Urantia Book* (p. 1941) reads: "Take this cup, all of you, and drink of it."

12.  Prejudice against revised versions.

     One bishop burned over 200 copies of a new version of the Bible.

13.  Remember: At the Council of Trent, the Bible was standardized by *majority* vote.

14.  Custom.

     **1 Cor. 13:12.** *"For now we see as in a mirror darkly."* The early church fathers did not like "darkly." It meant "riddles," mystery, "dark sayings," etc. So they just omitted it. But the King James version retains "darkly." Revised Standard Version uses "dimly."

## 4. THE ENGLISH BIBLE

### I. EARLY BEGINNINGS

1   In the third century Origen tells about Christian centers in Britain.

2.   Pope Gregory sent missionaries to England in 597.

3.   In the eighth century the Venerable Bede and Egbert made transla-tions of the Lord's Prayer, Apostles' Creed, and the gospels.

4.   In the ninth century King Alfred promoted further translations.

5.   By the tenth century a dozen psalters were in existence.

6.   In the tenth century the Rushworth gospels appeared.

7.   A Latin psalter appeared in 1320.

### II. THE WYCLIFFE BIBLE

1.   The first complete English Bible was translated by Wycliffe (1324-1384).

2.   Wycliffe died a natural death, but the Council of Constance (1415) ordered his bones and books burned.

3.   The Wycliffe Bible was first published in 1382. It was the only English Bible until the sixteenth century.

4.   In 1250 there was a French translation; in 1416, a German.

### III. TYNDALE'S NEW TRANSLATION

1.   In 1525, at Cologne, Tyndale's New Testament was printed. Later, it was reprinted at Worms.

2.   The British king ordered Tyndale's Bible burned. Packynton, a London merchant, kept the book in circulation by selling copies, at a profit, to the Bishop of London to be burned.

3.   Revisions of this Bible were published in 1534.

4.   Tyndale started to translate the Old Testament, but after imprison-ment in Brussels, he was burned at the stake in 1536.

### IV. MILES COVERDALE'S BIBLE

1.   The first complete *printed* Bible in English was the work of Miles Coverdale, 1488-1568.

2.   This translation was favored by Henry VIII, Cromwell, and Arch-bishop Latimer.

3.  Published in 1535 at Cologne or Marburg.

## V. FIRST LICENSED BIBLE

1.  Published by Thomas Matthew, at Antwerp, in 1538.

2.  Published in both Latin and English.

3.  The Matthew Bible was revised in 1539 and published as the Toveruer Bible. This was the first Bible to be printed in England.

## VI. THE GREAT BIBLE OF 1539

1.  This was known as Cranmer's Bible and was the first authorized English Bible.

2.  This was the first Bible "approved to be read in churches."

3.  In 1546 the English began to burn all Bibles except this "Great Bible," which was largely restricted to the upper classes.

## VII. THE GENEVA BIBLE

1.  In 1557 appears the Geneva Bible, translated by the brother-in-law of Calvin.

2.  This Bible reflects the theology of Calvin and Knox.

3.  It became known as the "Breeches" Bible from the translation of **Gen. 3:7**.

4.  This was the most scholarly and accurate of all English translations up to this time.

5.  This Bible had what might be called "Protestant marginal notes."

6.  This is the first English Bible with complete division into chapters and verses.

7.  This is the first translation to use *italics* to indicate supplied words.

8.  This was the Bible of Shakespeare and the Pilgrim Fathers.

## VIII. THE SECOND AUTHORIZED BIBLE

1.  The Bishop's Bible. Promoted by Archbishop Parker and published in 1568.

2.  The Christian church is at long last publishing a Bible.

3.  This was a "church" project from its inception—translation, publishing, and promotion.

## IX. FIRST ROMAN CATHOLIC BIBLE IN ENGLISH

1. The New Testament in 1582. The Old Testament in 1609. First printed at Rheims.

2. First complete Bible published at Douay in 1633. Long known as the *Douay* Bible.

3. This Bible was designed to get rid of the Protestant "slant" of some versions.

4. Example: **Matt. 6:24**. *"Two masters."* This had been applied to *"two religions."* Christ and Calvin. Catholic and Protestant.

5. This was really a revision of Jerome's Vulgate Bible.

**NOTE**: Only recently have the Catholics brought out their first revision of the Douay Bible.

## X. THE KING JAMES BIBLE

1. This translation was started by the Hampton Court Conference in 1604 and was published in 1611.

2. The King James Version was produced by a corps of 50 translators.

3. But there was strong opposition to a "Revised Bible," as the King James Version was known at that time.

4. The marginal notes were largely left out.

5. The Apocrypha was left in.

6. This was the third authorized Bible in England.

7. It had many misprints:

    a. **Matt. 23:24**. *"At"* for *"out." "Strain at a gnat."*
    b. Archaic words: *"Prevent"* for *"go before."*
    c. *"Damnation"* for *"judgment."*
    d. *"Carriage"* for *"baggage."*

8. For 250 years this version was the Bible of the Protestant world.

9. This version finally left out the Apocrypha.

10. This Bible had a great influence on the English language for over two hundred years.

## XI. THE ENGLISH REVISED VERSION

1. New Testament published in 1881. The whole Bible in 1885.

2. Contained over 30,000 changes.

3. Differences by the American Committee were published in the United States in 1901.

4. The omitted marginal notes were restored largely—in 1898.

## XII. MODERN SPEECH VERSIONS

1. The Fenton Bible. England, 1900.

2. Four Gospels, Spencer, 1898.

3. Ballentine, American idiom. 1898.

4. Twentieth Century New Testament. 1901.

5. Weymouth, British idiom. 1903.

6. Moffatt. 1913. 1923.

7. Goodspeed. 1923. 1931.

8. Smith. 1927.

9. Jehovah's Witnesses, New Testament. 1950.

10. Basic English (children). 1949.

11. Revised Old Testament (Jewish). 1917.

12. Beginning in 1948, Catholic revision of the Douay Bible.

## XIII. REVISED STANDARD VERSION

Published in 1952 by a department of the National Council of Churches.

**NOTE**: In 1961 the English New Testament was published, being the English Committee differences in the Revised Standard Version of 1952. The Old Testament will come later.

## 5. INTERPRETATION OF THE BIBLE

### I. ANCIENT PERIOD

1.  The Greek Septuagint was supposed to be translated by 72 separate men— when they came together, they perfectly agreed.

2.  Scripture was verbally inspired by God.

3.  There were two methods of interpretation:

    a.  Alexandrian. Philo. The allegorical method. The Hellenistic. Later on, the Stoic.
    b.  The traditional or literal Jewish method. The "chosen people."

4.  While in general accepting the Old Testament, Jesus dared to criticize it. He said he came to fulfill—not to destroy the Scriptures.

5.  In *The Urantia Book*, see Jesus' talk with Nathaniel, p. 1767-9.

6.  Jesus makes new interpretations of Scripture in his so-called "Sermon on the Mount."

7.  The book of Hebrews is a new interpretation of much Old Testament teaching.

8.  Early doctrines of the LAW and GRACE.

### II. SECOND CENTURY PROBLEMS

1.  The Jewish and anti-Jewish schools of interpretation.

2.  Tradition and authority:

    a.  Heretics—private teachings.
    b.  Authority of the church.

3.  Alexandria and Antioch:

    a.  Alexandria—Platonist.
    b.  Antioch—Aristotelian.

4.  Schools of interpretation:

    a.  Alexandria—allegorical (Philo).
    b.  Antioch—literal meanings.

5.  Origen leaned to allegory—Paul was a literalist, but dealt in types and anti-types.

6.  Jerome and Augustine:

    a.  Jerome was Antiochean. Translated Hebrew Old Testament into Latin.
    b.  Augustine regarded the Septuagint as "inspired." Looked upon Jerome as a "forger." Followed Origen—allegorical.

Later, Augustine leaned more towards Antioch school.

Jerome was a scholar—Augustine a theologian.

(One of the great debates of this time was whether God had hair and nails.)

Augustine published his "Christian Doctrine" in 397.

Augustine had much to say about figurative and literal language.

7. In 450 Eucherius of Lyons published his handbook on interpretation, "Rules for Allegorical Interpretation."

8. About the same time the Antioch Fathers published their "Introduction to the Sacred Scriptures."

## III. THE MEDIEVAL AND REFORMATION PERIOD

1. It was the Gnostic literature that induced the Christians to complete their assembly of the New Testament.

2. Vincent was a pioneer in:

   a. Authority of Scripture.
   b. Interpretation by the church—tradition.

3. Both Benedict, the monk, and Gregory the Great moved away from the allegory school (Platonic-Philonic) toward the Aristotelian-Antiochean.

4. During the Middle Ages they paid less attention to allegories. The dominant personalities were:

   a. Gregory the Great.
   b. The Venerable Bede.

5. The theme was—the spiritual as opposed to the literal, with due respect to the church fathers.

6. When the prodigal son returned to his "father's house"—the "versions" read: "returned to the church."

7. But allegory persisted—the four wheels of Ezekiel's chariot were: the law, the prophets, the gospels, and the apostles.

8. Even in the tenth century, the allegorical school of interpretation was beginning to give way to the *historical*.

9. For four hundred years the tension between allegory and history increased.

## IV. THE SCHOLASTIC AGE

1. The scholastic era starts with the Franciscans at Oxford and their patron saint is Francis of Assisi.

2. New attention is paid to eschatology and apocalypticism.

3. This movement was at its height about A.D. 1250.

4. Thomas Aquinas, probably the greatest Bible student of all time, was the center of this movement.

5. There is a legend that he memorized the entire Bible.

6. The movement was away from allegories toward *spiritual* interpretations.

7. They went to absurd lengths in symbolism. In **Mark 8:19**, the 5,000 represent men and their five senses.

8. This was the era of the universities.

## V. THE REFORMATION

1. **Luther.**

   a. Denied that the Pope alone could interpret the Bible.

   b. His great discussions had to do with "faith and works."

   c. Said: "The Holy Scriptures can be interpreted only by the Holy Spirit."

   d. Luther says: "Christ is the center of all Scripture."

   e. Luther said his interpretation was "Grammatico-historical."

   f. But he still clung to Origen's allegorical methods.

   g. Luther liked "types"—Noah represents Christ.

   h. Luther begins to create a systematic theology—doctrines. He very much disliked James and Revelation.

2. **Calvin.**

   a. Calvin was the best Bible student of the Reformation.

   b. In his "Institutes" he quoted the Old Testament 1,755 times; the New Testament 3,098 times.

   c. He almost completely neglected the Song of Songs and Revelation.

   d. He wanted to assert the infallibility of the Bible—but was compelled to admit minor errors.

   e. Calvin was worried by the careless way Paul quoted Scripture. **See Eph. 4:8.** *"When he ascended on high he led a host of captives, and he gave gifts to men."* This is **Ps. 68:18**, which reads: *"Thou didst ascend the high mount, leading captives in thy train, and receiving gifts among men."*

f.   If the Bible was "inspired," Calvin thought Paul should have quoted the passage *verbatim*.

g.   He thought the same about **Heb. 2:7** and **Ps. 8:5**.

h.   Calvin thought II Peter was "inferior"—but said it might be explained by Peter's writing it in his "old age."

i.   Calvin interpreted the Bible, in general, in two ways:
    (1)  The sovereignty of God.
    (2)  Predestination of the "elect."

j.   He did recognize the "Progressive Revelation" of God in the Bible.

k.   He largely discarded allegory.

1.   Thus we have the three main divisions of Protestantism:
    (1)  Anglican—Catholic, except for the Pope.
    (2)  Lutheran.
    (3)  Presbyterian.

## VI. INTERPRETATION IN THE MODERN PERIOD

1.   Rise of Biblical criticism, 1650-1800. There were three great groups of influence which led to a re-examination of the Bible:

    a.   The physical sciences:
        (1)  Ptolemaic universe—demolished.
        (2)  Copernicus discoveries. (1473-1543) (The Pope denounced all of this.)
        (3)  Kepler. (1571-1630)
        (4)  Galileo. (1564-1642)
        (5)  Newton—gravitation. (1642-1727)

    b.   Textual study:
        (1)  Valla's "Donation of Constantine."
        (2)  Philosophy of Bacon and Descartes.

    c.   Bibliolatry.
        End of making an idol out of the Bible. Recognition of the progressive character of revelation.
        Liberation from the strait-jacket of orthodoxy.

2.   Cappel, in the sixteen hundreds, was the first textual critic.

3.   Erasmus (1516) had already pointed out how different manuscripts differed in text.

4.   John Mill (1707) began the search for original texts—he all but destroyed belief in verbal inspiration.

5.   The philosophers—Hobbes and Spinoza—attacked the idea that the Bible was "the word of God."

6. The philosophers asserted that the Scriptures were "faulty, mutilated, and tampered with."

7. In 1655 Peyrere said mankind had been created long before Adam. The Inquisition burned him at the stake.

8. A generation later Richard Simon became the father of Biblical criticism. He concluded that the Old Testament did not have its present form until after the Exile.

9. Richard Bentley (1699) was the father of the school of evaluating Scripture by "internal evidence"—as in the two stories of creation in Gen. 1 and 2.

10. Johann Semler was father of the "historical method" of Bible criticism.

11. Gotthold Lessing (1724-1781), a German critic and dramatist, a layman, wrote a book "Nathan der Weise" in 1779. In this work he introduced a new idea—the difference between "the religion of Christ and the Christian religion."

   This is the identical teaching of *The Urantia Book*—the religion of Jesus contrasted with the religion about Jesus.

   Lessing's father was a Lutheran minister. He wanted his son to study theology. But he dabbled in theology, philosophy, and even medicine. He wrote numerous plays, but in his later years took to writing on philosophy and religion.

   This book on "Nathan the Wise" was a play dealing with three principal characters—a Jew, a Mohammedan, and a Christian.

   The government confiscated many of his books and he suffered petty persecutions.

   He was greatly interested in the early history of Christianity and in the philosophy of Spinoza.

   He never attached himself to any particular church or system of philosophic teaching.

12. Bengel (1755) published his historical criticism of the New Testament. This book influenced John Wesley's "Notes on the New Testament."

## VII. LITERARY AND HISTORICAL ACHIEVEMENTS
## 1800 - 1925

1. Schleiermacher dominated much of the thought of this era. While he rejected the uniqueness of the Bible he insisted on a Christocentric faith.

2. In 1864 his "Leben Jesu" insisted on getting religion *directly* from the living Christ.

3. There was an attempt to ascertain the theological intention of the Biblical writers.

4. There was a final unraveling of the various strata of Biblical authorship.

5. There was an improved attempt to find out God's purpose and the *real* history and destiny of mankind.

6. From Amos on down through the prophets they looked for Yahweh's lordship over nature and history.

7. They decided that the "suffering servant" of the Second Isaiah was the Messiah.

8. Discovery of many new fragments of both Old Testament and New Testament led to improved textual criticism.

9. Intensive study of the fourth gospel led to placing its writing early in the second century.

10. At the present time the vogue is the formulation of a Biblical theology.

11. The "total Scripture" school of interpretation:

    a   Determination of the text.
    b.  Literary form.
    c.  Historical situation.
    d.  Author's meaning.
    e.  Relation to total context.
    f.  Background of origin.
    g.  Literal interpretation.

12. "Higher criticism" has about run its course. Common sense has taken over the stage. The time is ripe for the *real* interpretation of *The Urantia Book* to appear.

## 6. HOW TO STUDY THE BIBLE

### I. NATURE AND PURPOSE

1. Who wrote the book under examination—and why?

2. When was it written and what was the background?

3. Remember: The Bible is neither history nor science.

4. The value of comparing the Bible text with *The Urantia Book.*

5. The Bible is essentially an Oriental—at least Levantine—book.

6. Study the meanings of the original text—Greek or Hebrew.

7. The division of Isaiah into three parts is a good illustration of proper technique for studying the Bible.

8. The use of a good Bible dictionary is very helpful. The latest: Harper's Bible Dictionary, by Miller.

9. The great problem is interpretation. What does the text really mean?

10. Look for spiritual help—light. "Thy word is a lamp to my feet." **Ps. 119:105**.

### II. CHRONOLOGY

1. The details of chronology will be considered in the study of Old and New Testament history.

2. The explanation for the extra long lives of ancient personalities is found in *The Urantia Book* p. 857-8. The lunar month of 28 days was called a year. Thus a man living 900 years really lived only about 70 years— "three score years and ten"—a ripe old age for those days.

3. Chronology of the Old Testament books.

   Genesis—1200-450 B.C.
   Exodus—1200-450 B.C.
   Judges—1150-550 B.C.
   I and II Samuel—1000-500 B.C.
   Numbers—850-400 B.C.
   Joshua—850-350 B.C.
   I and II Kings—850-350 B.C.
   Amos—750 B.C.
   Hosea—745-735 B.C.
   Isaiah I (1-39)—740-700 B.C.
   Micah—715-686 B.C.
   Deuteronomy—630 B.C.

Jeremiah—626-586 B.C.

Zephaniah—625-(300) B.C.

Nahum—614-(300) B.C.

Habakkuk—600 B.C.

Job—600 B.C.

Proverbs—600-200 B.C.

Ezekiel—593-571 B.C.

Lamentations—570-450 B.C.

Leviticus—560-450 B.C.

Isaiah II (40-66)—546-400 B.C.

Haggai—520 B.C.

Zechariah (1-8)—520-518 B.C.

Psalms—500-100 B.C.

Obadiah—470 B.C.

Malachi—460 B.C.

Nehenuah—432 B.C.

Ruth—400 B.C.

Joel—350 B.C.

Jonah—350-300 B.C.

Zechariah (9-14)—300-200 B.C.

Song of Solomon—250 B.C.

I and II Chronicles—250 B.C.

Ezra—250 B.C.

Daniel—164 B.C.

Ecclesiastes—160 B.C.

Esther—125 B.C.

(Old Testament Apocrypha—about 180 B.C.)

4.  Chronology of the New Testament books.

Galatians—A.D. 50.

Thessalonian Letters—A.D. 51.

Corinthian Letters—A.D. 53.

Romans—A.D. 56.

Philippians—A.D. 57.

Colossians—A.D. 60.

Philemon—A.D. 61.

Mark—A.D. 68.

Matthew—A.D. 71.

Luke—A.D. 82.

Acts—A.D. 85.

Ephesians—A.D. 95.

Hebrews—A.D. 95.
Revelation—A.D. 96.
I Peter—A.D. 97.
John—A.D. 101.
John's Epistles—A.D. 102.
James—A.D. 125.
Jude—A.D. 125.
II Peter—A.D. 150.
Timothy, Titus—A.D. 160.

## III. CHANGES IN WORD MEANINGS

There follows a list of words. giving their meaning as used in the Bible:

Addicted—to be devoted to something.
Allege—to produce evidence.
Attendance—to pay attention.
Barbarian—any non-Greek-speaking person.
Bowels—heart-felt emotion.
By and by—immediately.
Carriage—what is carried. Not a vehicle.
Clouted—to be patched.
Confection—to smell—not taste.
Conversation—conduct, behavior.
Eminent—refers to physical height.
Fashion—a plan.
Feeble-minded—faint-hearted.
Imagine—to plan an action.
Let—to hinder, impede, or prevent.
Mean—a common person.
Meat—any food.
Passenger—a passer-by, wayfarer.
Prevent—to go before.
Refrain—restrain or check.
Several—separate
Simple—free from guile; blameless.
Sincere—applied to things as well as persons—"sincere milk of the word." 1 Peter 2:2.
Space—applied to time—rather than area.
Suburbs—pastures, common land.
Target—a shield or buckler.
Nain—empty, worthless, foolish.
Worship—applied to human beings as well as to God.

**NOTE**: "The Bible word Book," published by Thomas Nelson and Sons, contains 827 words and phrases which have changed or modified their meanings as used in the King James Version.

## 7. THE OLD TESTAMENT AS LITERATURE

### I. ANCIENT LEVANTINE CULTURE

1.  When the Israelites entered Palestine they found an old and high level of culture. Their culture—aside from religion—was not much above the barbaric level.

2.  Remember: Palestine lay athwart the high roads of ancient world travel and the armies of empire marched back and forth over its hills and valleys.

3.  Nearby peoples—Egypt and Babylonia—had temples, palaces, and wealth— refinement.

4.  The Hebrews were concerned with a national obsession—RELIGION. What is man?

5.  The Canaanites were enjoying a high civilization. They had unusual ability. Their cities were well built.

6.  They originated three systems of writing—two with alphabets. One of these supplanted the writing of Egypt and Babylonia.

7.  One of these—Phoenician—became the written language of the entire Western world.

8.  These Canaanite people had laws, wisdom literature, and a vast religious ritual, as shown by the Ras Shamrah discoveries (1929) on the northern coast of Syria.

9.  The Hebrews were quick to adopt this culture—and even some of their religion.

10. Also remember: The Hebrews did not destroy all these Canaanites as intimated in the Old Testament records.

### II. EARLY HEBREW LITERATURE

1.  Early Hebrew literature was largely poetry. Early fragments were:
    Song of the Well.
    Taunt of Heshbon.
    Boundaries of Moab. (**Num. 21**)
    Song of Miriam.
    Balaam's Oracles (**Num. 23 and 24**)

2.  Stories about the patriarchs were among the early oral literature of the Jews. They were folk traditions.

3.  Poetic tales of conquest—victories over the Philistines. The Song of Deborah. (**Judges 5**)

4.  Samson's exploits. (**Judg. 14 and 15**) Stories in the lost Book of Jashar and the "wars of the Lord."

5.  Jotham's Fable. (**Judg. 9:8-15**)

6.  Many of the Psalms show the influence of Canaanite religious philosophy.

7.  Ezra's reform was an attempt to get rid of many Canaanite infiltrations of the Hebrew religion.

8.  Many shrines to Yahweh were established to combat Canaanite religions, such as at Shiloh, Gilgal, Gibeon, Bethel, and Beer-sheba.

9.  Many rules and regulations were taken over from the Canaanite laws.

### III. LITERATURE DURING THE MONARCHY

1.  Israel's first book of prose was a history—by an unknown historian. **See 2 Sam. 9-20.** A pattern for all historians.

2.  During the time of Solomon there appeared wisdom literature and many songs. (**1 Kings 4:32**) 3,000 proverbs and 1,005 songs.

3.  Isaiah the First carried on during these times. Some of the best of Hebrew literature appeared during these times.

4.  The foundation of the books of Kings appeared. Israel was becoming pen-conscious.

5.  The first book of Psalms was assembled.

### IV. THE LITERARY PROPHETS

1.  Amos and the Second Isaiah were among the first. Deutero-Isaiah represents the apex of prophetic literature.

2.  Ranking high is the Second Zechariah—**Zechariah 9-14**. Most of the prophets were poets.

3.  High in this list are to be found Joel and Habakkuk.

4.  Both Jeremiah and Isaiah the Second saw to it that their spoken sermons were reduced to writing during their lifetime.

5.  The book of Deuteronomy was rediscovered in the temple in 621 B.C. (**2 Kings 22**) It is a strange blend of prophetic and legal literature. It expounds and explains.

6.  Deuteronomy is Israel's first homiletic literature—a book of sermons and laws, characterized by both eloquence and dignity.

7.  Deuteronomy is the most polished and artistic of all Hebrew literature.

## V. THE EXILE AND AFTER

1. The acme of all Hebrew literature—the Second Isaiah—belongs to this period. The basis of three great religions.

2. This is the epoch of great editorial activity—the rewriting of all of the Hebrew sacred literature.

3. Next appears the memoirs of Nehemiah. Still later the books of I and II Chronicles.

4. Psalms is enlarged. Job and the wisdom literature appear.

5. Hebrew books now constitute the greatest literature of all the East.

6. Hebrew writers were masters of the art of gaining and holding human attention. Examples:

   The tragedy of Queen Jezebel. **2 Kings 9:30-35**.
   Abraham's servant going to Mesopotamia for Isaac's wife. **Gen. 24**.
   Joseph's story in Egypt. **Gen. 39-41**.

7. Not only did the Hebrews create the greatest literature of the ancient East, but at the same time it was the greatest *religious* literature of all time— up to the appearance of the New Testament.

## 8. GROWTH OF THE HEXATEUCH

### *I. HEXATEUCH TRADITIONS*

1. The first five books of the Hexateuch were supposed to be written by Moses, the sixth by Joshua.

2. The five books—the Pentateuch—make up the Torah—the Law.

3. It was about 250 B.C. when they began to claim that Moses wrote the Pentateuch.

4. In recent times students of the Hexateuch made certain observations of the Hexateuch—viz.:

    a. Two or more accounts of the same incident.

    b. Numerous inconsistencies.

    c. The evident composite character of the document.

### *II. PARALLEL NARRATIVES*

1. Abraham twice presents his wife as his sister. **Gen. 12:11-14; 20:2-5.**

2. Isaac did the same thing. **Gen. 26:6-11.**

3. Abraham three times receives promise of a son. **Gen. 15:4; 17:16; 18:10.**

4. Three accounts of Sarah and Abraham. **Gen. 17:17-19; 18:12,13; 21:6.**

5. Hagar twice expelled. **Gen. 16:4-14, 21:9-21.**

6. Jacob twice names Bethel. **Gen. 28:19; 35:6,15.**

7. Jacob's name twice changed to Israel. **Gen. 32:28; 35:10.**

8. Name *Yahweh* twice revealed to Moses. **Ex. 3:14,15; 6:2,3.**

9. Moses commissioned twice. **Ex. 3:10-18; 6:11.**

10. Moses twice hesitates to accept. **Ex. 4:10-13; 6:12.**

11. Twice Moses receives Aaron as spokesman. **Ex. 4:14-16; 7:1,2.**

12. Twice the quails are given. **Ex. 16:13. Num. 11:31,32.**

13. Twice water comes from the rock. **Ex. 17:1-7. Num. 20:1-13.**

14. At Sinai, Moses three times commands observance of the feasts.

15. Six times—the keeping of the Sabbath.

## III. INCONSISTENCIES

1. Man and woman created together. **Gen. 1:26,27.** This was after the completion of creation.

   In **Gen. 2:7** man is created first, then the trees and animals; at last woman is made from Adam's rib. **Gen. 2:21,22.**

2. Noah told to take into the ark one pair of animals. **Gen. 6:19,20.**

   In **Gen. 7:2,3** told to take seven pairs of clean animals and one pair of unclean.

3. **Gen. 7:12** records rain on the earth 40 days. In **7:24,** 150 days.

4. In **Gen. 41:34** Joseph advises storing up one fifth of grain. In **verse 35** advises *all* the food.

5. Moses' father-in-law named Reuel in **Ex. 2:18,21.** In **Num. 10:29,** Hobab. In **Ex. 3:1** and other places—Jethro.

6. According to **Num. 2** the sacred tent was in the "midst of the camp." **Ex. 33:7** says it was "outside the camp."

7. In **Num. 13:27** the spies tell Moses Palestine is fertile. In **verse 32** they say it is no good.

8. In **Num. 22:20** God gives Balaam permission to go to the princes of Balak— in **verse 22** God is angry because he went.

9. In **Josh. 2:15** Rahab's house was on the wall of Jericho which collapsed. In **6:22** Joshua directs they bring her out of the house.

10. There are many inconsistencies in the laws.

## IV. CHRONOLOGICAL DIFFICULTIES

1. In **Gen. 12:11** Sarah is an attractive woman—to Pharaoh. **Gen. 17:17** says she was 10 years younger than Abraham, who was 75 (**Gen. 12:4**).

2. **Gen. 25:26.** Isaac was 60 years old when Jacob and Esau were born. In **26:34** Esau is forty years old, so Isaac is 100 years old at this time, when he blesses Jacob on his deathbed. But according to **35:28** he did not die until he was 180—he was 80 years dying?

3. The chronology of Jacob's life is hopelessly mixed up.

4. According to **Ex. 12:40,** the Israelites had been in Egypt 430 years. Putting a number of separate events together it counts up to only 250 years.

5. Thirty-seven years are "lost" in going from Sinai to Kadesh.

6. These, and many others, show that the Hexateuch is the work of more than one man.

## V. BEGINNING OF CRITICISM

1.  In 1753 Astone—a physician—called attention to the alternating use of God and Yahweh in Genesis. This, he claimed, pointed to two authors.

2.  In a hundred years several students claimed that the Hexateuch was a compilation of "fragments."

3.  In 1858 Hupfeld claimed that there were two documents—the Elohim and the Yahweh narratives.

4.  **Graf-Wellhausen Theory**. In 1865 Graf recognized the Elohim document (E) and the Yahweh (J), and claimed that the book found in the temple by Josiah was Deuteronomy (D) and that the editorial additions of the priests during and after the exile represented a fourth (P) factor.

5.  This theory presents four documents:

    a.  The earliest was J, because of the use of the name Yahweh. The tradition of the southern tribes, written about 1000 B.C. Hebron is their center.

    b.  The second document was known as E, because God was called Elohim. This was about 700 B.C. This was following the fall of Samaria and was designed to harmonize the J document with the traditions of tribes having their center at Shechem.

    c.  The third document was Deuteronomy, D. By the sixth century J and E had been conflated. JED was accepted as the Scripture by all Hebrews.

    d.  P represents the Exilic and post-Exilic additions of the priest-hood. This is a fourth century document and makes Jerusalem the center of Jewish life.

6.  The people of the J document entered Palestine from the East—over Jordan. They seemed to know very little about Moses. They know little of Kadesh—Sinai is the center of their history.

7.  In the E document, Yahweh is unknown until revealed by Moses. Hebron is never mentioned. The covenant is given at Mt. Horeb. Kadesh is never mentioned. The Jordan is not crossed at Jericho but at Adamah. After crossing the Jordan they go straight to Shechem.

8.  The purpose of P was:

    a.  To build morale.

    b.  Elevate the priesthood.

c. Preach holiness.

d. Revive the Sabbath.

e. Make Jerusalem the center.

f. Restore circumcision.

# 9. PROPHETIC LITERATURE AND WISDOM LITERATURE

## PROPHETIC LITERATURE

### I. EARLY SPOKEN WORD

1. Hebrews divided their Scriptures into the law, the prophets, and the writings.

2. The prophets were two divisions:

   a. Former Prophets.

      Joshua, Judges, Kings, Samuel.

   b. Later Prophets.

      Isaiah, Jeremiah, Ezekiel, and the 12 minor prophets.

3. Lamentations and Daniel were placed among the "writings."

4. The early prophets were all preachers. Some later wrote out their exhortations.

5. Jeremiah dictated to Baruch. **Jer. 36.**

6. Language of sound was more effective than the language of sight.

7. The early prophets were *ecstatic*. Their behavior was almost orgiastic. There was music, dancing, a frenetic frenzy.

8. Illustration: Saul joins the prophets. Dances—throws a spear at David. Dances with frenzy all day in the nude.

9. The dancing and shouting were like a mad dervish.

### II. TRANSFORMATION OF PROPHETISM

1. The rhythm of dancing was changed to the rhythm of poetry. The cataleptic trance was turned into the more dignified poet.

2. Serious-minded preachers like Hosea, Micah, and Jeremiah began to appear.

3. But the older *visions* persisted even in Isaiah and Amos.

4. The prophets became sort of mediators between man and God.

5. Sometimes the prophecy was written out by the prophet, sometimes by others.

### III. THE EVOLUTION OF PROPHECY

1. The early prophets uttered threats of destruction. Later editors added hope—promises of salvation dependent on repentance.

2. Much of the apparent growth of prophecy was the work of the priest—editors of the captivity.

3. Isaiah the Second is an exception. He presented hope and salvation as a part of his original message.

4. The latter-day prophets began to talk about the end of the world—the triumph of Israel as ruler of all nations.

5. This apocalyptic message was centered in the Messiah who would come to sit on David's throne and rule the world.

6. Prophets were less and less concerned with predicting future events. They dealt more with present predicaments.

7. The prophet was a "man of God"—declaring the "will of God." He was inspired.

8. The five hundred years of the "prophets of Israel" represent the greatest period in the spiritual history of the world.

9. New Testament founders honored the prophets. *"Because no prophecy ever came by the impulse of man, but men moved by the Holy Spirit spoke from God."* **2 Peter 1:21**.

10. The prophets preached holiness, love, and justice, and opposed sacrifices and overmuch ritual.

11. Prophets were not ascetic—they did not separate themselves from the people. And they were patriotic.

12. They were fearless and honest. The later prophets spurned all ecstatic performances.

13. "The sons of the prophets" were counselors and religious teachers—like the evangelists of the Christian era. They had schools at Bethel, Gibeah, Gilgal, and Ramah.

14. There were always to be found false and mercenary prophets.

15. John the Baptist is spoken of as "the last of the prophets."

16. But they still referred to "prophets" during the apostolic days.

17. In both Old Testament and New Testament times there were prophetesses— Miriam, Deborah, Huldah, and Anna.

## THE WISDOM LITERATURE

### *I. WISDOM IN THE NEAR EAST*

1. The "wise men" must not be confused with magicians and astrologers.

2. The Orient had "wise men," but not philosophers. The Greeks and the West had philosophers, but not "wise men."

3. Egypt's Amenhotep was a combination of wise man, philosopher, and religious teacher.

4. Proverbs is typical of the mood and method of the Levantine "wise men."

5. Proverbs ranges from "riddles" to sublime philosophy.

6. Makes large use of plant and animal fables.

7. The "wise men" were "scholars," and really sought to find out the meaning and worth of human life.

8. Egypt and Babylonia had "wise men," but we hear nothing about such in Assyria or Edom.

### *II. WISDOM IN EARLY ISRAEL*

1. The Canaanites had wisdom literature—findings at Ras Shamrah.

2. Israel also had "wise women"—Song of Deborah borders on wisdom literature.

3. When Joab wanted to persuade David to let Absalom come home, he sent to Tekoa for a "wise woman."

4. The "wise woman" suggested going to Abel to seek wisdom—the site of ancient "wisdom schools." **2 Sam. 20:16-22.**

5. The one pure fable of the Oriental type is that of Jotham. **Judges 9:8-15.** Lesson: Respectable persons are too busy for politics, so the reprobates take over.

### *III. WISDOM OF SOLOMON*

1. Typical case: The disputed baby. **1 Kings 3:16-27.**

2 Solomon was astute—and a good psychologist.

3. David was a country man—Solomon was a city man—he knew both the graces and vices of city life.

4. Solomon was a patron of the arts and sciences.

5. They tell us that Solomon authored 3,000 proverbs and wrote 1,005 songs. We have no record of all this—unless in a few Psalms and **Prov. 14.**

6.  Passages ascribed to Solomon—**Prov. 30:18,19; Chap. 24-31.**

## IV. WISDOM BEFORE THE EXILE

1.  Jewish "wise men" were sometimes half humorists and a bit cynical. The Hebrews had three sorts of literature: priest, prophet, and wise man.

2.  Many of the Psalms belong to the wisdom group. **Ps. 15, 24, 19, 16, 49, 73.**

3.  **Ps. 19:2** may be an Oriental riddle. The riddle: *"What is it that speaks by day and night, and yet has no voice?"* Answer: *"The heavens declare the glory of God and the firmament shows his handiwork."*

## V. WISDOM AFTER THE EXILE

A.  **Proverbs**

1.  **Prov. 1** is the symbol of post-Exilic wisdom. *"The fear of the Lord is the beginning of wisdom."*
2.  **Prov. 1-9** is certainly post-Exilic.
3.  Proverbs is a compilation like the Psalms.
4.  There are two sections of Proverbs:
    a.  *The humanist*: Little is said about God. Man is largely the master his mortal destiny. If you want to be happy and prosperous, look to your method of living—be intelligent, industrious, frugal, and moderate.
    b.  *The religious*: Advocates typical Hebrew morality. Be pious, unselfish, and moral.
5.  There are eight divisions of the book.
    a.  Praise of wisdom. **1:7-9.**
    b.  Proverbs of Solomon. **10:1-22:16.**
    c.  Words of the wise. **22:17-24:22.**
    d.  Sayings of the wise. **24:23-34.**
    e.  Proverbs of Solomon. **25:1-29:27.**
    f.  Words of Agur. **30:1-33.**
    g.  Words of King Lemuel. **31:1-9.**
    h.  Praise of a good wife. **31:10-31.**
6.  It was the Hebrew custom to assign proverbs to Solomon and psalms to David.
7.  Proverbs exalts the individual rather than the nation.
8.  **Prov. 22:17-24:22** sounds like the wisdom of Amenemope. 1000-600 B.C. **Ps. 1** and **Jer. 17:5-8** come from the same source.
9.  Proverbs advocates that man is entitled to enjoy material pleasures— perfume, wine, friendship, and married life.

    10. The wise man shuns adultery, usury, fraud, theft, and ill-gotten gains.

    11. Self-interest, rather than moral law, dictates good conduct.

    12. Take an interest in the widow and orphan—even in your enemies'.

B. **Job**

    1. Job is the greatest of Israel's wisdom literature. The question of Job: *"Why do the righteous suffer?"*

    2. Jesus' discussion of Job. *The Urantia Book*, p. 1662.

    3. Job is a challenge of the Egypto-Hebraic doctrine that the righteous and the wicked receive their just deserts here on earth.

    4. Job is an immortal poem about a just soul that suffered, despaired, and battled on until it found peace and salvation.

    5. The book is a great philosophic debate concerning the ever-present but unanswered problem of EVIL.

    6. Job's miserable comforters and their smug orthodoxy did not have the answer.

    7. Job is constructed somewhat on the order of the Greek drama.

    8. Multiple authorship in Mesopotamia. Representative of the Salem school at Kish. See *The Urantia Book*, p. 1043.

    9. Jesus called the book of Job a parable. He said it was "that masterpiece of Semitic literature."

    10. After the failure of theology and the breakdown of philosophy, Job gained his victory by *personal experience*.

    11. Job at last, by faith, reasons himself out of his troubles. He declares: *"I know the way I take; when he has tried me, I shall come forth as gold."*

    12. Job's triumph was complete. He exclaims: *"I know that my vindicator liveth."* (**19:25**) *"Though he slay me, yet will I trust him."* (**13:15**) King James Version.

C. **Ecclesiastes**

    1. This book is a strange mixture of Egyptian pessimism and Greek philosophy.

    2. The author is searching for the "value of human life."

    3. The theme song is: *"Vanity of vanities, all is vanity."*

    4. It is cynicism and pessimism. It presents the theory that all history and nature move in a circle, an ever-revolving and recurring cycle.

    5. The pursuit of pleasure, wealth, and wisdom—all end in futility.

    6. The author harps on the sorry plight of the oppressed, the lonely, the discontented, and the hazards of daily work.

    7. There is much Epicurean philosophy: "Eat, drink, and be merry, for tomorrow we die."

8. Yahweh, the God of Israel, is never mentioned. Elohim is not interested in our daily life. (**5:2**)

9. In **Chap. 8** he equates wisdom with individual education. The book is devoid of the "cosmic viewpoint."

10. Prayer is not mentioned in the entire book.

11. The educated and spiritually-minded reader can't help feeling something of pity for the author.

D. **The Apocrypha**

1. Both Ecclesiasticus and the Wisdom of Solomon continue the presentation of Hebrew wisdom.

2. Ecclesiasticus is shot through with the philosophy of the Stoics.

3. Some of these Old Testament teachings were carried over into the New Testament.

## 10. HISTORY OF ISRAEL'S RELIGION

### I. AGE OF THE PATRIARCHS
*2000 to 1500 B.C.*

1. This was an age of universal restlessness and turbulence throughout the Middle East.

2. The great age of Hammurabi is passing. The Huerians from the Canaanite highlands are over-running the fertile crescent.

3. The Hyksos have invaded Egypt. The Kassites have taken over Babylon.

4. In such a time of international anarchy the Patriarchs lived, and the Hebrew nation was born.

5. The Patriarchs worshiped El Elyon and El Shaddai.

6. Archaeology has contributed much to confirm the Bible record of these times of the Patriarchs.

7. The more recent Mari tablets have in many ways confirmed the Bible story of these times.

8. Their religion was very *real*. Yahweh came to live in their tents. Abraham was called "a friend of God."

9. When they entered Palestine, they set up altars for Yahweh at Shechem, Bethel, Hebron, Beer-sheba, and Penuel.

10. Publication of more of the 20,000 clay tablets found in the Mari Palace, will, no doubt, shed much more light on the times of the Patriarchs.

### II. THE AGE OF MOSES
*1350 to 1250 B.C.*

1. Sources: Yahwist record in the tenth century, the Elohist in the eighth. After that come the priestly records.

2. There is little doubt that Moses was a historic personality. The Moses narrative in *The Urantia Book* is found on p. 1055.

3. The beginnings of Moses' religion are obscure. But he created a religious ceremonial for Israel that culminated in Solomon's temple.

4. In all Israel, there was no outstanding leader between Moses and David.

5. The Hebrews probably entered Egypt under the Hyksos—1750-1560 B.C.

6. Moses may have been influenced by the solar monotheism of Amenhotep (Ikhnaton). This philosophy is presented in **Ps. 104.**

7. Moses killed an Egyptian who had struck a Hebrew laborer, and then fled to the East, where he lived with the Kenites.

8. Moses married Zipporah, the daughter of Jethro. She bore him two sons.

9. While tending sheep Yahweh speaks to him from the "burning bush."

10. Moses returns to Egypt and with his brother Aaron as his spokesman begins plans for the liberation of the Hebrews.

11. Was the Exodus over the Red Sea or the "Sea of Reeds"—the papyrus marsh?

12. The religion of the Israelites begins under miraculous circumstances —the manna and the quails.

13. Hebrew religion starts at Mount Horeb. Yahweh speaks—but not as a nature god. A new Deity appears.

14. But when Moses tarried too long on the mountain, they went back to the worship of the "golden calf."

15. Moses' father-in-law helped him organize the "multitudes." This Kenite clan, with a remnant of the Salem religion, readily accepted the Yahweh revelation. See *The Urantia Book*, p. 1058.

16. Yahweh becomes a "God of history"—the God "who brought you out of the land of Egypt."

17. Yahweh's new covenant was based on his oath to Abraham. From start to finish, the nature of Yahweh was *holiness*.

18. Miriam gets into trouble for criticizing Moses when he marries an Ethiopian (Cushite) woman.

19. In those days they admitted the existence of other gods, but Yahweh was the "God of Israel"—and he was a "jealous God."

20. The battle cry was: "You shall have no other gods before me." **Ex. 20:3.**

21. Yahweh was "all things." He was divine and demonic. Positive and negative. Light and darkness. He created "good and evil."

22. Yahweh must not be represented by any *image*—no idols. Neverthe-less, the Old Testament is strongly anthropomorphic.

23. The ten commandments were the "hub" of all their law. Very early the ark containing the ten commandments became the vital feature of the ritual of the cult.

24. The "tent" or tabernacle became the center of their worship. There was no offering of sacrifices in the wilderness.

25. Moses did not enter the Promised Land, but was allowed to view it from a distance—Mt. Nebo (Pisgah). **Deut. 32:49.**

26. Moses was buried in Moab. He had a "special resurrection." **Jude 9.**

### III. PERIOD OF THE CONQUEST
*1250 to 1020 B.C.*

1. Palestine was a land of many peoples—Huerians, Hittites, Canaanites, and Phoenicians. Most of the early times it was an Egyptian province.

2. Israel's chief enemy was the Philistines.

3. There was much "mixture" between the Israelites and the Canaanites— marriage, religion, and culture.

4. Baal, god of fertility, was the god native to the land. Yahweh proved to be superior to Baal in many ways.

5. But the two gods went along together for a long time. The Israelites worshiped Yahweh as their chief Deity, but also paid some sort of homage to Baal—in order to insure good crops and many cattle.

6. As the Hebrews turned more and more to agriculture, they became tainted with Baalism.

7. Wars, trouble, and the prophets would periodically drive them back to Yahweh.

8. Hosea tells of those who looked to Baal for *"the grain and the wine."* **Hos. 2:8.**

9. Yahweh is the *"mighty God of battles"*—as he helped Gideon. **Ex. 14:14; 15:3.**

10. When things went wrong, Yahweh was not defeated—Israel was defeated.

11. Gradually Yahweh absorbs all of Baal's titles and functions. Yahweh gives rain, grain, and wine. Becomes *"Lord of nature."* **1 Kings 18** and **19, Hos. 2.**

12. Cities of refuge appear and there are many sanctuaries throughout Palestine— Gilgal, Shiloh, Dan, Ophrah, Shechem, Bethel.

13. Eli was head of the sanctuary at Shiloh. The ark was here.

14. There was little government. *"Every man did what was right in his own eyes."* **Judg. 17:6.**

## IV. RELIGION DURING THE EARLY MONARCHY
### 1020 to 922 B.C.

1. Samuel and Saul are the outstanding personalities—king and king-maker.

2. This is the era of the beginnings of prophecy.

3. There is still much of Baal service. Even Saul, in his frustration, sought advice from the "witch of Endor."

4. David brought about some improvement, but morals were not too high—as shown by his affair with Bathsheba.

5. It is difficult to understand just how David could be "a man after God's own heart."

6. Solomon did little to advance religion. The temple was in reality the royal chapel.

7. The religious ritual was more Phoenician and Syrian than Hebrew.

8. At the temple, the brazen sea, the bulls, and other objects were symbols of Baal service.

9. The two pillars, lions, lavers, shovels, basins, and 400 pomegranates all represented surviving symbols of Semitic primitive religions.

10. The Law was attributed to Moses, Psalmody to David, and Wisdom to Solomon.

11. The Hebrews are still suffering from many erroneous things learned in Egypt.

## V. THE DIVIDED KINGDOM
### 922 to 586 B.C.

1. Both kingdoms worshiped the same God. But royal marriages kept Baal worship alive.

2. The prophets begin the battle for return to Yahweh. Says Elijah: "Yahweh is my God."

3. Elijah was the embodiment of nomadic Yahwehism.

4. Elijah appealed to the "earthquake of Horeb," and "the gentle whisper."

5. Elijah built his reform on "the seven thousand who had not bowed the knee to Baal."

6.  Micah was an effective contemporary of Elijah. He was an antagonist of King Ahab.

7.  Elisha follows Elijah, but his career is fraught by much magic.

8.  Next comes Amos with a theology that foreshadows the theology of the Second Isaiah. He comes near preaching a "social gospel."

9.  Amos is the first to preach an international gospel. Yahweh has become the "God of all nations."

10. Now comes Hosea, repeating and adding to the proclamations of Amos. He uses his own domestic troubles as an illustration of Yahweh's relations to Israel.

11. Hosea does not hesitate to declare: "Yahweh has withdrawn from them." **Hos. 5:6**. But he preaches "redemption upon repentance."

12. Next comes Isaiah of Jerusalem, the aristocratic prophet. He turned the messages of Amos and Hosea into proclamations grand and musical.

13. Under Isaiah, Yahweh becomes "the Holy One of Israel." He repeats the judgment, "Yahweh has abandoned his people."

14. Isaiah condemns social injustice and denounces the commercialized priesthood.

15. He tells the Jews they are going into captivity.

16. Micah comes with the final threat of doom and and destruction.

17. Isaiah had declared the temple to be inviolate, but Micah consigns it to destruction.

18. Micah sums up man's duty: *"What does the Lord require of you but to do justice, and to love kindness, and to walk humbly with your God?"* **Micah 6:8.**

19. Finding the book of Deuteronomy in the temple brought about a great reformation. But there were two great errors in Deuteronomy:

    a.  The old doctrine of prosperity due to God's favor, and adversity as the punishment for sin.

    b.  Intensified nationalism.

20. Zephaniah and Habakkuk end this epoch. The one called for a purge of Jerusalem.

21. Habakkuk is better understood by light shed by the Dead Sea Scrolls.

22.  But two more of the major prophets remain to be heard from: Jeremiah and Ezekiel.

23.  Jeremiah logically traced Israel's history from Moses to his day— and pronounced the doom of the nation. He urged surrender to the Babylonians.

24.  He was persecuted and maltreated. He predicted a new kind of "inward revival" in later times after Israel's liberation.

25.  Ezekiel backed up the doom of Jeremiah and revived the "holiness cult." He became the "prophet of hope," and was carried captive into Babylon.

## VI. THE BABYLONIAN EXILE
### 586 to 538 B.C.

1.  The captivity begins with the fall of Jerusalem, 586 B.C. The disheartened pessimism is reflected in the book of Lamentations.

2.  The priests begin the revision of all of Israel's history. They rewrite all the Hebrew literature.

3.  The Hebrews suffer from a sense of national guilt—sin.

4.  The Second Isaiah begins his work and the highest level of prophetic literature is achieved.

5.  The Jewish church—the synagogue—appears. The quest for authority revives the cult of the Law.

6.  The Hebrews begin to think of their "world mission"—their duty to all nations. Hope for deliverance.

7.  For the first time they form definite beliefs about life after death.

8.  Deutero-Isaiah proclaimed hope. *"Behold, the Lord God comes with might, and his arm rules for him; behold, his reward is with him, and his recompense before him."* **Isa. 40:10.**

9.  Judaism is at last fully internationalized. All nations are to share in Yahweh's love and merciful redemption.

10.  In Second Isaiah there appears "the servant of the Lord," foreshadowing the Messiah.

11.  This is the period of the greatest spiritual progress of the Jews.

12.  Samaria and the northern tribes had twice suffered deportation of large numbers to Assyria.

13.  In 539 Babylon fell to the Persians, and Cyrus arranged for the Jews to return to Palestine.

# VII. POST-EXILIC JUDAISM
## *539 to 150 B.C.*

1. The priests did more than to just edit and rewrite the Hebrew scriptures— they added numerous ancient fragments and reduced oral traditions to writing.

2. Judaism is falling under the influence of the Persian period. 538-333 B.C.

3. The priestly code gave importance to:

    a. Avoidance of blood.
    b. Circumcision.
    c. Sabbath keeping.
    d. Holiness as reflected in conduct.

4. The book of Psalms is growing. Great variety. The Hebrews were gifted in music—vocal and instrumental.

5. Psalms range from high hymns of praise to poems of hate and revenge.

6. In the Psalms Yahweh is judge, king, creator, keeper, shepherd, and redeemer.

7. The theme song of the Psalter is God's ETERNITY. But this is not to the neglect of God's love and goodness.

8. God in nature is featured in four Psalms—**8, 19, 29,** and **104.**

9. There is little about sacrifice in the Psalms. See **Ps. 40:6-8.**

10. The Psalter persists in upholding the philosophy of God's prosperity rewards for obedience, and sickness and adversity as punishments for sin.

11. The problem of the meaning of suffering and affliction as wrought out in Job is touched upon in **Ps. 73.**

12. Psalms abound in precious promises—inspired sayings: *"Weeping may tarry for the night, but joy comes with the morning."* **Ps. 30:5.**

13. The wisdom literature was not of a high spiritual order. It was based on "human experience." They were guidebooks for practical living.

14. But their morality was conventional and pious. *"The fear of the Lord is the beginning of wisdom."* **Prov. 15:33.** *(King James Version)*

15. The wisdom books are skeptical as to the orthodoxy of suffering as a penalty for wrongdoing.

16. While the wise man doubts the moral government of the world, still he asserts *"that the souls of the righteous are in the hands of God."* **Wisdom of Solomon 3:1 (Ecclesiasticus).** *(Apocrypha)*

17. The new apocalyptic literature promised salvation by the coming of a "new world"—the kingdoms of men become the everlasting kingdom of God.

18. The book of Daniel was the high point of the "new age" teaching. This was not a Messianic theology—God himself was coming to:

    a. Judge the world.
    b. Resurrect the dead.
    c. Destroy all the wicked.
    d. Set up an everlasting kingdom.

## VIII. THE HEBREW CULT

1. The priests had more of an influence in Jewish religion than would appear from reading the Old Testament.

2. The Canaanite nature cult was all mixed up with the Hebrew religion.

3. From Moses to the Judges the main sanctuary was at Shiloh.

4. Deuteronomy brought in the Holiness cult, which was reinforced by the later priestly code.

5. The Semitic peoples specialized in holy gods, holy places, holy days, holy times, holy things, and holy persons.

6. Before Jerusalem, there were Hebron, Bethel, Shechem, Gilgal, and other holy places.

7. For a long time Baal was worshiped along with Yahweh—at the "high places."

8. Of all holy objects, the ark was the most holy. King Uzziah dropped dead when he touched it.

9. Passover and other feasts were holy seasons. Sabbath was the holy day.

10. Of all things sacred and holy, the Day of Atonement was at the head.

11. Sacrifice was the holy act:

    a. Burnt offerings.
    b. Gift offerings.
    c. Sin offerings.
    d. Vow offerings.

12. Holy persons:

    a.   Priests and Levites.
    b.   Prophets.
    c.   Nazarites.

13. Holy places.

    a.   Temple.
    b.   Synagogue.
    c.   The outlawed "high places."

14. The Hebrew religious ritual evolved through a period of over one thousand years.

## IX. THE MATURE FAITH OF ISRAEL

### A.   THE GOD OF ISRAEL

1.   Israel was Yahweh's chosen people. They believed they were elected.
2.   God delivered them from Egyptian bondage under Moses; from Babylonian captivity under Cyrus.
3.   Yahweh was a God of history, not a God of nature.
4.   He was "God of the Covenant." No other religion had such an origin.
5.   The law and the ritual were based on the covenant.
6.   The covenant was first made with Abraham and renewed under Joshua after entering Canaan.
7.   Yahweh was God of Gods. There might be other gods, but Yahweh was "God of Israel."
8.   Faith in God based on ACTS of God—creative and historical.
9.   God was a person—even though anthropomorphic.
10.  There may have been an evolutionary henotheism, but eventually monotheism arrived.
11.  The holiness of Yahweh was unique—transcending all other gods.
12.  God as a creator was original and unique.
13.  Technique of the revelation of God to the people was new.
14.  Man "made in the image of God"—in no other religion. Basis of Hebrew anthropomorphism.
15.  The concept of sin—the fall of man, somewhat different from all other religions.
16.  A forgiving God—man's salvation—final belief in life after death— the resurrection.

17. The final belief in a new age—the Messiah—the everlasting kingdom.

18. The belief that Israel was intended to be a missionary people to carry the knowledge of Yahweh to all the world was never really put into practice.

19. The Jews never lived up to their obligations as the "chosen people." Instead of going to the world, they withdrew from the world.

B. **HEBREW WORSHIP**

1. Israel rejects pagan magic and demons. (They often went back to these errors.)

2. Hebrews reject heathen festivals—theirs were new and largely original.

3. Special shrines of worship, ending in the temple.

4. Substitution of animal sacrifice for human.

5. New meanings attached to sacrifices.

6. Improved law, literature, and rituals.

7. Clarification of sin, forgiveness, and atonement.

8. The creation of a settled theology and creation of a superior sacred Scripture.

9. The establishment of an enduring world religion.

# PART II
# OLD TESTAMENT HISTORY

Map 2.1: Palestine in the time of the Judges

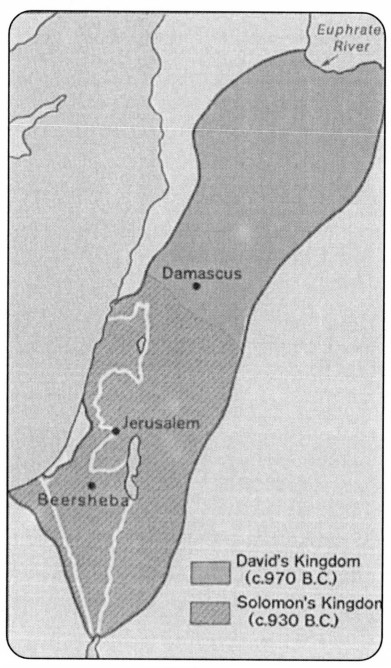

Map 2.2: Expansion of Israel under King David

Map 2.3: The Two Kingdoms

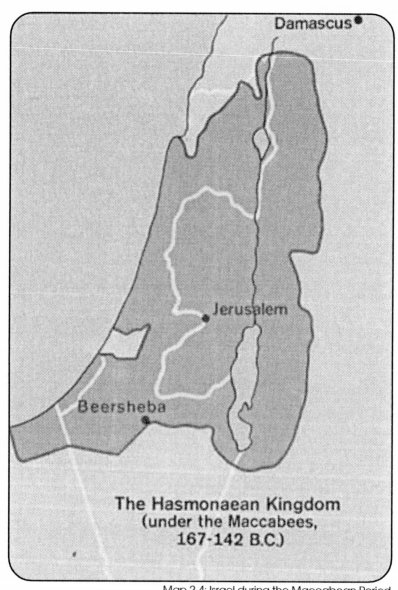

The Hasmonaean Kingdom
(under the Maccabees,
167-142 B.C.)

Map 2.4: Israel during the Maccabean Period

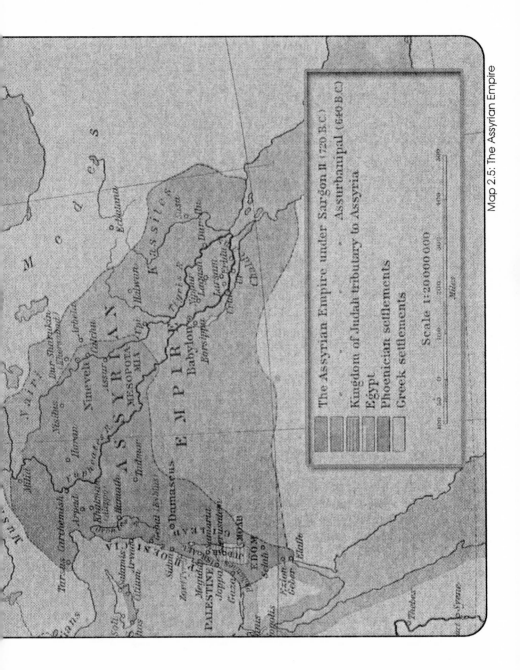

The Assyrian Empire under Sargon II (720 B.C.)
Assurbanipal (640 B.C.)

Kingdom of Judah tributary to Assyria
Egypt
Phoenician settlements
Greek settlements

Scale 1:20 000 000

Map 2.5: The Assyrian Empire

# OLD TESTAMENT HISTORY

## 1. THE ANCIENT ORIENT
### *Before 2000 B.C.*

### *I. FOUNDATIONS OF ORIENTAL CIVILIZATION*

1.   A thousand years before Abraham, civilization was old in the Orient. The Hebrews were latecomers.

2.   6000 B.C.—Jericho—before the age of pottery—was a thriving city. They domesticated animals, had cereal crops, and elaborate irrigation. This was almost 5,000 years before Abraham.

3.   A thousand years later—in the next level—pottery appears. Agriculture and craft specialization are discovered.

4.   By 4000 B.C. colored decorative pottery appears, with human and geometric figures. This pottery is found from Lake Van- south to Kirkuk.

5.   The first city-states appear. We do not know what language they spoke— there was no writing.

6.   The diggers are, of course, bothered by the mystery of the Sumerians. See *The Urantia Book*, p. 875.

7.   They find pottery wheels and the ovens for firing the pottery.

8.   About 3300 B.C. the first writing is discovered. So far, we are unable to read these writings (probably Sumerian[1]).

9.   Aside from *The Urantia Book*, the Sumerians remain the great mystery of all history.

10.   During those times Egypt also enjoyed an advanced culture.

11.   During those times successive waves of "Semites" went forth from Mesopotamia to the north and west.

**NOTE:** The story of the Andite expansion found in *The Urantia Book*, page 889.

---

[1] *Editor's note*: Sumerian cuneiform has since been deciphered and translated.

## II. THE ORIENT DURING THE THIRD MILLENNIUM

1.  Ur was the cultural center of Mesopotamia.

2.  The theocratic city-states were the final stage of Sumerian culture.

3.  At this time, the Sumerians were polytheistic—each city-state had its own god.

4.  The early Semites of Mesopotamia were the Accadians. They adopted Sumerian culture but kept their own Semitic language.

5.  The empire of Accad (2360-2180) was the first real empire. The founder was Sargon of Kish.

6.  The state-center moved from the temple of the god to the palace of the king.

7.  Egypt prospered. The Old Kingdom Pharaohs built the pyramids and other hewn-stone (the oldest) buildings.

8.  Egypt invented hieroglyphic writing. Religion had many ups and downs.

9.  Culture in Palestine was far below that of the Nile and Euphrates. Nevertheless, there were prosperous cities at Jericho, Megiddo, Beth-shan, Ai, Shechem, Gezer, and Lachish.

10. The Canaanites spoke their own language, of which the later Hebrew was a dialect.

11. The Guti overthrew the Accad Empire and a brief "dark age" resulted.

12. Utu-hegal, king of Erech, destroyed the Guti and established the dynasty of Ur (2060-1950). Again Sumerian culture flourishes.

13. But this was the last of Sumerian culture, rule, and language.

14. About this time the Amorite invasion of Palestine began. Many cities destroyed.

15. The Mari empire was next to rule Mesopotamia. There was a long "balance of power" between Mari, Assyria, and Egypt.

16. Numerous groups of Semites infiltrated Palestine during these times.

17. Egypt declined in power and plunged into the "dark ages."

18. Babylon, under Hammurabi, took over. But the Elamites, Assyria, and the Mari were yet to be conquered.

19. Mari (1750-1697) became the ruler of upper Mesopotamia. (Confirmed by recent excavations, yielding thousands of tablets.)

20. The Mari had horse-drawn chariots and the battering-ram. A palace with 250 rooms has been uncovered—one of the wonders of the ancient world.

21. But all this was overthrown by Hammurabi—Babylon took over the empire.

22. Mari was completely destroyed and the god Marduk took over in the new empire.

23. The Hyksos—origin unknown—took over in Egypt. Confusion reigned—a dark age was coming on.

24. The Hittite rule is to come later. But now it is time to go back and pick up the story of Israel during the times of the Patriarchs.

## 2. THE PATRIARCHS

### I. THE PATRIARCHAL NARRATIVES
#### Gen. 12 to 50

1.  These stories are supposed to have been written by Moses. But we know they were penned centuries after Moses' death.

2.  We know that the patriarchal narratives consist of four different sources — J, E, D, and P.

3.  Modern archaeological research has shed much light on, and done much to confirm, the Old Testament story of the Patriarchs.

4.  Excavations of dozens of sites in Palestine confirm the traditions of early Israel. See **Deut. 6:20-25; 26:5-10. Josh. 24:2-13.**

5.  The early traditions and records were probably heroic poems like the Song of Deborah.

6.  It is impossible to reconstruct the patriarchal age, but the little we do know does not contradict the traditional narrative.

7.  Abraham and Lot were heads of large clans.

8.  Abraham was known as the "friend of God."

### II. HISTORICAL SETTING OF NARRATIVES

1.  Abraham is a name known in Babylon. Nahor occurs in the Mart texts. Benjamin was a Mari tribe. Gad and Dan are both found in Mari.

2.  Social customs of the Patriarchs conform to Hittite and Hurrian practices.

3.  They were largely nomads. Lived in tents. Owned no land except for burial grounds.

4.  They were not desert nomads—they did not have camels. Camels did not appear until the times of Gideon.

5.  The patriarchal age lies somewhere between the twentieth and sixteenth centuries B.C..

6.  It is not possible to set an exact date for the Hebrews going into Egypt.

## III. THE HEBREW ANCESTORS

1. Haran—starting point of Abraham's journey—was probably occupied by Huerian clans.

2. Israel probably had multiple ancestors—Canaanites of various origins. Consider Moab, Ammon, and Edom.

3. Abraham's father, Terah, came from Ur of Chaldea.

4. The Arameans also probably find a place among Israel's ancestors.

5. Abraham, Isaac, and Jacob were real people. They were chieftains of semi-nomadic clans.

6. We should remember that the actual events recorded of the Patriarchs were vastly more complex than the Bible narratives.

7. The Patriarchs were not altogether peaceful. Note - the assault of Simeon and Levi upon Shechem. **Gen. 34.** Jacob seizes land near Shechem. Abraham's battles with Chedorlaomer.

8. The religion of the Patriarchs is not well defined. Moses is probably the father of Hebrew religion.

9. See *The Urantia Book* for account of Abraham and Melchizedek. Paper 93, p. 1014.

10. There is no mention of Yahweh until we come to the times of Moses.

11. The God of the Patriarchs was Elohim—the Most High.

# 3. EXODUS AND CONQUEST
## *THE FORMATIVE PERIOD*

## *I. WESTERN ASIA AND EGYPT*

1.  These events took place sometime between 1550 and 1200 B.C.

2.  In 1550 Amosis drove Hyksos into Palestine and Egypt took over the Euphrates territory. Egypt conducted 16 campaigns.

3.  Only serious opposition the Egyptians met was the Hittites. Many local rulers were Indo-Aryans and worshiped Vedic gods—Indra and Mithra.

4.  Amenophis IV changed his name to Ikhnaton, built a new capital, and introduced a monotheistic religion. This was about one hundred years before Moses.

5.  Hittites and others were in revolt and took over Palestine.

6.  The earliest historic reference to Israel tells about King Marniptah fighting the Israelites in Palestine.

7.  Most of the early Canaanites were more properly called Amorites.

8.  There were also many Hurrians and some Indo-Aryans in Palestine. The Horites (Hivites) were non-Semitic.

9.  Among the early inventions of Palestine was the alphabet of the Phoenicians —passed on to Greeks and then to Europe.

10. Later, from somewhere, came the Edomites and the Moabites.

11. Date of the Exodus is in doubt. Probably in the thirteenth century. 1 **Kings 6:1** places the Exodus 480 years before the fourth year of Solomon's reign. This would be in the fifteenth century.

12. For the Moses story, see *The Urantia Book*, p. 1055.

13. Remember that Moses had spent years with Kenites before going back to lead the Hebrews out of Egypt.

14. There are almost two stories about the wilderness wanderings:
    a.  In one, they tarry a long time at Sinai.
    b.  In the other they seem to have spent this time at Kadesh

15. One of these narratives calls the mountain Sinai, the other Horeb.

16. Some students think it possible there were two invasions of Palestine:
    a.  The Kadesh group going in from the south by slow infiltration.
    b.  The Sinai group going over the Jordan from the east after the destruction of Jericho.

17. The conquest of Canaan was gradual and never complete.

## II. FORMATION OF THE ISRAELITES

1. The Hebrews of Palestine were a complex and polyglot people. Moses was part Egyptian and no doubt many Egyptians came along.

2. The Exodus was referred to as a *"mixed multitude."* **Ex. 12:38. Num. 11:4.**

3. There were also Midianites (Kenites) in the group. **Num. 10:29-32.**

4. The wilderness horde may have numbered several thousand, but never 600,000 men of military age—as in **Num. 1:46; 26:51.** Such an army would mean a total population well over two million.

5. In Palestine they freely mixed up with the natives. There was the Gibeonite confederacy. **Josh. 9.**

6. That whole cities came over to the cult of Yahweh is suggested in **Josh. 24.**

7. Remember: Moses' religion was the worship of El Elyon or El Shaddai, until Yahweh revealed himself at the "burning bush."

8. Also remember: That the Jews may have "crossed over," not the Red Sea, but the "Lake of Reeds," near the present town of Suez—the marshy district between Suez and the Great Bitter Lake.

9. Another point: In one place it says the Israelites were cattle raisers. In another place, industrial workers—slaves—brick-makers.

## 4. THE FAITH OF EARLY ISRAEL

### I. RELIGION OF EARLY ISRAEL

1. We first encounter Israel in Palestine as a loose federation of 12 tribes —so-called.

2. The Hebrew confederation was an amphictyony—an association of tribes for the protection of a religious center.

3. The early religion was henotheism. Yahweh was the God of Israel— but there were other gods.

4. The dual record of Israel's faith is shown by the two versions of the Ten Commandments. **Ex. 20. Deut. 5.**

5. Early records of faith:
   a. Song of Deborah. **Judg. 5.**
   b. Blessing of Jacob. **Gen. 49.**
   c. Balaam Oracles. **Num. 23, 24.**
   d. Song of Moses. **Ex. 15:1-18.**
   e. Blessing of Moses. **Deut. 33.**

6. The hub of Israel's faith was the Sinai covenant—they were the "chosen people."

7. Rituals, laws, ceremonies, all cluster around the covenant relationship.

8. They were forbidden to have idols, but they made a fetish out of the "ark of the covenant."

9. In time, "Yahweh alone was God," and then came the "heavenly hosts."

10. Eventually, Israel's faith became monotheistic. It was never polytheistic.

11. The great departure from paganism was the prohibition of Images.

12. Pagan gods were nature gods. Yahweh was a god of creation and history— master of nature.

13. But they did believe that nature was dominated by lower forms of "spirits."

14. Yahweh was neither a sun god nor a fertility god.

15. Somehow they managed to create 12 clans—one for each of Jacob's 12 sons:
    a. Six sons of Lean—Reuben, Simeon, Levi, Judah, Issachar, Zebulun.

    b.   Two by Leah's slave, Zilpah—Gad and Asher.

    c.   Two by his second wife, Rachel—Joseph and Benjamin.

    d.   Two more by Rachel's slave, Bilhah—Dan and Naphtali.

16.    How artificial these 12 tribes were is shown when the loss of the Levites, who ceased to be a secular clan, was compensated by turning Joseph into two clans—Ephraim and Manasseh.

17.    How the amphictyony worked is shown by the Book of Judges.

18.    The presence of the ark determined the central shrine. In the wilderness —the "tent of meeting." Later on—at Jerusalem, the temple.

19.    The priesthood was hereditary.

## II. THE PERIOD OF THE JUDGES

1.    Egypt, Assyria, and the Hittite empires are passing. The Philistines are dominating Palestine—giving the land their name.

2.    The period of the 12 judges (counting Deborah and Barak one) covered about 150 years. Only six of these judges distinguished themselves.

3.    This is a time of adaptation and adjustment for Israel.

4.    The first judge, Othniel, repelled an invasion by unknown forces.

5.    Ehud drove out the Moabite invasion.

6.    Shamgar was not an Israelite, probably a city-king from Galilee, but he repelled the Philistines.

7.    The victory of Deborah and Barak, probably 1125 B.C., was an outstanding event.

8.    The exploits of Gideon (**Judges 6-8**) are well narrated. Domesticated camels first appear in the armies of Israel.

9.    Jephthah and Samson next appear on the stage. And here we find that human sacrifice can still be practiced in Israel.

10.    There was no mechanism for adjusting inter-tribal complaints. The periodic performances of the sheiks were not enough to maintain order and keep the peace.

# 5. ISRAEL UNDER THE MONARCHY

*1030 - 936 B.C.*

## I. SAUL—THE FIRST KING

1. A Philistine victory showed the failure of the amphictyony and led to the formation of the monarchy.

2. The Philistine victory was complete. Israel's army was cut to pieces. Shiloh was destroyed.

3. The Philistines had a monoply of iron—they deprived Israel of all iron.

4. Later the Philistines returned the ark captured at Shiloh to Israelite soil. A plague made them afraid of it.

5. Samuel was the bridge from the old order to the new.

6. Saul was elected king by his army and privately anointed by Samuel at Ramah.

7. Saul was made king because of his victory over Ammon. He also came from a wealthy family.

8. Saul's whole reign was spent at war.

9. Saul was a manic-depressive person and was, therefore, seldom in a normal state of mind. He was slightly paranoid.

10. Saul broke with Samuel and persecuted David.

11. Saul's son Jonathan was a great friend of David.

12. David became an outlaw and organized a private army.

13. After a military defeat, Saul comitted suicide on Mt. Gilboa.

14. This war with the Philistines was started by Jonathan, Saul's son, killing a Philistine official.

15. There are two accounts of Saul in the Old Testament. The older, **1 Sam. 9-14.** More about Saul in the David narratives. **2 Sam. 17:12-31:13.**

16. Remember: Saul had been privately anointed by Samuel, before his army had elected him king.

17. Saul's capital was at Gibeah. The excavation of his capital at Tell-el-Ful (three miles north of Jerusalem) is the oldest datable Israelite fortification .

18. His paranoid tendency caused him to maintain a running feud with David— repeatedly trying to kill him.

19. His suspicion is further demonstrated in his cruel slaughter of the priests of Nob.

20. Saul's mood swings served to inspire Handel's oratorio and Browning's poem.

21. But for his manic-depressive psychotic affliction, no doubt, Saul would have been an outstanding monarch. He had all the personal endowments for such a career.

## II. DAVID BECOMES KING
### 1000 - 961 B.C.

1. For a time David and Esh-baal, son of Saul, were rivals.

2. David was made king at Hebron, undoubtedly with Philistine consent. He took the throne as a vassal of a foreign power.

3. Esh-baal contested the kingship for two years—no open war. He was murdered by two of his officers.

4. David marries daughter of the king of Geshur, an Aramaean state northeast of the Sea of Galilee—in rear of Esh-baal's territory.

5. Next David demands that Saul's daughter, Michal, be returned to him.

6. All Israel is now united under the kingship of David.

7. David finally overthrows the Philistine rule and sets all Israel free.

8. Jerusalem becomes the capital of the united kingdom. Becomes known as the city of David.

9. David transfers the ark to Jerusalem, which now becomes the religious as well as the political capital of the united kingdom.

10. David appoints a new priesthood and further consolidates the state.

11. He extended the conquest of Canaan. David's first major military effort was the Ammonite war under the leadership of Joab.

12. It was about this time that David became involved in the Bathsheba affair and was rebuked by Nathan.

13. David rounded out his territory by the conquest of Moab and Edom. Next he made a conquest of most of Syria.

14. David negotiates a profitable treaty with Hiram, king of Tyre.

15. David now really presided over an empire, but as he grew older, the question of succession became a problem.

16. Now occurred the rebellion of Absalom. **2 Sam. 13-19.**

17. Next came the rebellion of Sheba. **2 Sam. 20.** This was an attempt to take northern Israel out of the kingdom.

18. From tablets recently excavated at Mari, David was known as the "beloved chieftain."

19. David introduced music into the Jewish ritual of worship.

20. The following is an outline of David's career:

   a   *DAVID THE MAN*

      (1) Judean, of Bethlehem. **1 Sam. 16:1-3.**
      (2) Shepherd. **1 Sam. 16:11.**
      (3) Musician. **1 Sam. 16:14-23.**
      (4) Poet. **2 Sam. 1:17-27.**
      (5) Warrior. **1 Sam. 17.**
      (6) Friend of Jonathan. **1 Sam. 18:1-4. 19:1-7.**
      (7) Enemy of Saul. **1 Sam. 18:5-22.**
      (8) Saved by Michal. **1 Sam. 18:22-29.**

   b.  *DAVID A FUGITIVE AND OUTLAW*

      (1) At Naioth, in Ramah. **1 Sam. 19:18-20:42.**
      (2) At Nob. **1 Sam. 21:1-9; 22:11-21.**
      (3) At Gath. **1 Sam. 21:10-15; 27:1.**
      (4) Cave of Adullam. **1 Sam. 22:1.**
      (5) Mizpeh. **1 Sam. 22:3.**
      (6) Forest of Hereth. **1 Sam. 22:5.**
      (7) Keilah. **1 Sam. 23:1-13.**
      (8) Wilderness of Ziph. **1 Sam. 23:14-24.**
      (9) Maon in Arabia. **1 Sam. 23:24-28.**
      (10) Engedi. **1 Sam. 23:29-24:22.**
      (11) Gath (Achish). **1 Sam. 27: 1-5.**
      (12) Ziklag. **1 Sam. 27:6. (1 Chron. 12:1-22)**

   c.  *DAVID KING OF UNITED KINGDOM*

      (1) Anointed at Hebron. **2 Sam. 2:1-11.**
      (2) Abner's counter revolution. **2 Sam. 2:12-4:12.**
      (3) David elected king of Israel. **2 Sam. 5:1-5. 1 Chron. 11:1-3. 1 Chron. 12:23-40.**
      (4) Captures and makes Jerusalem his capital. **2 Sam. 5:6-10. 1 Chron. 11:4-9.**
      (5) Alliance with Hiram, king of Tyre. **2 Sam. 5:11. 1 Chron. 14:1.**
      (6) Makes Jerusalem the religious capital:

        (a)  By transferring the ark. **2 Sam. 6:1-19. 1 Chron. 13:1-14. 1 Chron. 15:1-16:29.**

        (b)  By prayers and preparation. **1 Chron. 21:18-22:5.**

  d.   *PERSONALITIES AND EVENTS IN DAVID'S REIGN*

      (1)  His family. **2 Sam. 3:2-5; 13-16. 1 Chron. 3:1-9; 14:3-7.**

      (2)  The Bathsheba episode. **2 Sam. 11:2-12:25.**

      (3)  Court officials. **2 Sam. 8:15-18; 20:23-26. 1 Chron. 18:14-17. 1 Chron. 27:25-34.**

      (4)  Sons of Saul. **2 Sam. 21:1-14.**

      (5)  Sons of Jonathan. **2 Sam. 4:4; 9:1-13.**

      (6)  Illustrious warriors. **2 Sam. 23:8-12; 18-39. 1 Chron. 11:1-14. 1 Chron. 11:20-47; 27:1-24.**

      (7)  Taking the census. **2 Sam. 24; 1 Chron. 21.**

  e.   *WARS OF CONQUEST*

      (1)  Philistines. **2 Sam. 5:17-25; 21:15-22; 23:13-17; 1 Chron. 11:15-19; 14:8-17; 18:1; 20:4-8.**

      (2)  Moabites. **2 Sam. 8:2; 1 Chron. 18:2.**

      (3)  Zobah. **2 Sam. 8:3; 1 Chron. 18:3,4.**

      (4)  Syrians. **2 Sam. 8:5-12; 1 Chron. 18:5-8.**

      (5)  Edomites. **2 Sam. 8:13,14; 1 Chron. 18:11-13.**

      (6)  Ammonites. **2 Sam. 10:6-11:1; 12:26-31; 1 Chron. 19-20:3.**

  f.   *REBELLIONS*

      (1)  Absalom. **2 Sam. 13-19.**

      (2)  Sheba. **2 Sam. 20:1-22.**

      (3)  Adonijah. **1 Kings 1.**

  g.   *DAVID'S CHARGE TO SOLOMON*

     **1 Kings 2:1-11; 1 Chron. 23:1; 29:20-25.**

**NOTE:** David's throne becomes a symbol of the future hopes of Israel regarding the Messiah: The Messiah was to sit on David's throne and rule the world.

David was not permitted to build the temple, because he had been "a man of war." He was allowed to gather materials for his son Solomon who was directed to build the temple.

## III. THE MONARCHY UNDER SOLOMON
### 960 - 922 B.C.

1. Solomon was a great builder and he became something like an autocratic Oriental ruler.

2. Solomon's foreign policy was one of expansion—by war and by marriage.

3. He greatly expanded Israel's commerce. Trade in copper, horses, and other commodities flourished.

4. This was Israel's golden age of economic prosperity.

5. Solomon built the temple. Jerusalem really became the center of Hebrew worship.

6. But Solomon really did not capture Gezer—it was taken by his father-in-law, the king of Egypt.

7. The monarchy became a burden. Taxes were high. Deficit spending all but ruined the empire.

8. Israel was changing. The dynastic state had left little of the old order.

9. The thousand wives and concubines were a vast departure from the theology of the Davidic kingdom.

10. Political tension in the empire mounted, and there was trouble in sight when Solomon died.

11. You should remember that Solomon was the son of David and Bathsheba.

12. Solomon's wisdom is illustrated by his dealing with the two women and the disputed child.

13. Solomon seems to have been a glamorous and pompous personality, and he loved power.

14. It was a legend that when Solomon was crowned king, he asked not for riches and glory, but only for *wisdom*.

15. His reputation as a *"wise man"* was far-flung. **1 Kings 4:30**. He uttered wise sayings. He was assisted by a corps of court *"writers."*

16. The Queen of Sheba visited him and attested to his wisdom.

17. He seemed to have been a versatile naturalist. **1 Kings 4:33; 10:24**.

18. Later generations regarded him as the author of the book of Proverbs.

19. Solomon could make such extensive conquests at this time because both Egypt and Assyria were in a weakened quiescent condition.

20. Solomon had a navy and carried on a vast overseas trade.

21. He enjoyed a vast revenue from taxation on the extensive caravan trade. He controlled both the land and sea routes.

22. Solomon controlled the frontier routes through Zobah, Damascus, Hauran, Ammon, Moab, and Edom.

23. He maintained a chain of chariot cities with cavalry forces. (These have been excavated at Megiddo and Gezer.)

24 He revived copper mining. He conscripted labor to finish his extensive building projects.

25. He got so in debt to Hiram that he had to cede him 20 towns in Galilee.

26. Gezer was the dowry of the daughter of Pharaoh whom he married.

27. But of all his wives, domestic and foreign, he had only one son— Rehoboam. The later rabbis used this as an argument for monogamy.

28. All of Solomon's foreign wives had their own private chapels and practiced their own religions.

29. Solomon's court was one of luxury and pomp, and it presented an international atmosphere.

# 6. THE TWO KINGDOMS OF ISRAEL
*From the Death of Solomon to Mid-eighth Century*

## I. FIRST FIFTY YEARS OF THE DIVIDED MONARCHY
### 922 - 876 B.C.

1. The division of the kingdom meant the collapse of empire.

2. Both Ammon and Moab set up shop for themselves.

3. Israel and Judah have become second-rate states.

4. The schism was followed by two generations of sporadic warfare, and all this to no conclusion.

5. The first generation:
   a. Rehoboam of Judah, 922-915.
   b. Jeroboam of Israel, 922-901.

6. The Egyptian Shishak invaded Judah—struck with enormous force. Rehoboam paid large tribute.

7. Trouble in Egypt caused Shishak to withdraw.

8. The rival states had internal troubles and kept up their petty warfare.

9. Jeroboam established a new cult to rival that of Jerusalem. He set up shrines at Bethel and Dan.

10. On the death of Jeroboam pandemonium reigned. His son Nadab was assassinated by Baasha. His son Elah was assassinated by Zimri.

11. Zimri took his life when Omri took the throne. It required several years for Omri to establish himself.

12. The internal affairs of Judah were a bit more tranquil. Paganism started by Solomon made more progress.

13. Remember: Rehoboam was Solomon's son by Naamah, an Ammonite princess.

## II. FROM OMRI TO JEHU
### 876 - 842 B.C.

1. The house of Omri brings stability to Israel. He settles things internally and makes peace with his neighbors.

2. Omri's reign was short but he was internationally respected—making alliances with many powers.

3. His son Ahab married the daughter of the king of Tyre—Jezebel. Ahab's sister (or daughter) married Jehoram, son of Jehoshaphat, king of Judah.

4. For a time, Israel and Judah stop their feuding—and present a united front to the world.

5. Omri made an alliance with Ben-hadad of Damascus, but Ahab had to fight these Arameans several times.

6. There was material prosperity. But all was not well—the poor got poorer and the rich got richer.

7. Jezebel brought on a religious crisis. She built a temple for Melquart Asherah. But Jezebel was an aggressive pagan missionary.

8. Prophets of Baal and Asherah enjoyed official status. **1 Kings 18:19.**

9. Elijah began his battle with Jezebel and the prophets of Baal. Though Ahab and Jezebel held on for a time they finally fell.

10. Ahaziah (850-849) and Jehoram (849-842) followed after the fall of Ahab. Trouble in Damascus and Moab destroyed all peace.

11. Elisha makes trouble for the "House of Omri." There was a great revival of Yahwehism.

12. The Rechabites (Kenites) were internal trouble-makers. They followed Nazarite practices.

13. Now came the blood purge of Jehu—842. **2 Kings 9,10.** Jehu entered Jezreel and threw Jezebel out the window. The cult of Baal was destroyed.

14. Things in Judah improved under Jehoshaphat (873-849). He established many reforms. **2 Chron. 19:4-11.**

15. Jehoshaphat's son Jehoram was a Yahwehist—but his queen, Athaliah, was a Baalist. She induced him to kill all his brothers—to exterminate the Omri family.

### III. ISRAEL AND JUDAH
*From Mid-ninth to Mid-eighth Century*

1. Though Jehr founded a dynasty lasting for a century, it was one long reign of *weakness*.

2. Damascus began to encroach upon Israel. They dominated the country and only refrained from invading Judah by receiving a large tribute.

3. Joash and Judah (837-800). Enthroned as a child. (Jehoiada, the chief priest, probably acted as regent.) He was very unpopular—was assassinated and succeeded by his son Amaziah.

4. Things in Israel improved under Jeroboam II (786-746) and Uzziah (783-742). One of the bright and prosperous eras of Israel.

5. But Israel got sick again. Amos and Hosea combat social disintegration. Morals are at a low ebb.

6. Paganism is taking over. The prophets protest in vain. Nevertheless, this is the dawn of the new age of the classic prophets of all Israel.

## 7. DOWNFALL OF THE MONARCHY
*Period of Assyrian Conquest*
*From Mid-eighth Century to the Death of Hezekiah*

### I. THE ASSYRIAN ADVANCE
*Fall of Israel and Judah*

1. With the death of Jeroboam (746) unmitigated disaster overtook the Northern Kingdom.

2. Assyria under Tiglath-pileser III (745-727) went on a rampage. He was the real founder of the Assyrian Empire.

3. Tiglath was not after tribute; he sought permanent conquest.

4. Israel was disintegrating—jealousy, bitterness, and unbridled self-interest prevailed. Israelites turned upon Israelites. **Isa. 9:19.**

5. Much intrigue, many federations, and coalitions were formed, but Assyria overran the whole of Palestine.

6. Pekah's policy brought about the downfall of Israel. Samaria is taken over. **2 Kings 17:1-6.**

7. The last folly of Israel was to depend upon a fragmented Egypt for help. None came.

8. Tiglath forced Ahaz to pay homage to Assyrian gods and make innovations in the temple service. **2 Kings 16:10-18.**

9. Economic and social conditions in Judah went from bad to worse.

### II. HEZEKIAH'S STRUGGLES
*715 - 687 B.C.*

1. Hezekiah remained under Assyria as long as Sargon lived. His strike for independence was favored by Assyria's losing control of Babylon—the rebellion of Merodach-baladan. **2 Kings 20:12.**

2. Hezekiah heeded the warning of Isaiah not to join in the confederation of Egypt, Ethiopia, and others to resist Assyria.

3. These are the times Isaiah walked through the streets of Jerusalem clothed in a loincloth uttering his warnings.

4. Hezekiah instituted sweeping reforms—political, social, and religious. **2 Kings 18:3-6.**

5. He removed the image of Moses' snake from the temple.

6. He tried to enlist the Northern Kingdom in these reforms.

7. Sargon died—his son Sennacherib took over. (705-681). Hezekiah refused to pay tribute. Rebellion began. **2 Kings 18:7.**

8. Hezekiah was aided by uprisings in both Egypt and Babylon.

9. Under the leadership of Tyre, Syria and Phoenicia revolted.

10. Anticipating seige, he dug the famous Siloam Tunnel (**2 Kings 20:20**), bringing water from the Gihon springs.

11. In 701 Sennacherib struck. Babylon was pacified. Tyre was subdued. Babylos, Arvad, Ashdod, Moab, Edom, and Ammon hastened to pay tribute.

12. Hezekiah resisted—was subdued—his land split up—his tribute so high he had to strip the temple of all its royal treasures.

13. The later years of Hezekiah are uncertain. Assyria was in trouble with the Babylos revolt.

14. Egypt assailed Judah. Hezekiah resisted. The prophet assured him Jerusalem would not be taken. **2 Kings 19:29-34. Isa. 14:24-27.**

15. The Assyrians retired—did not take Jerusalem. Hezekiah died—his son Manasseh made peace.

16. The Assyrian army retreated because of a plague of field mice which ate up their equipment. This is referred to as *"the angel of the Lord"* destroying the army. **2 Kings 19:35. Isa. 37:36.**

17. Hezekiah was known as the "praying king."

## III. PROPHETS IN JUDAH

1. Judah has been in real religious trouble ever since Ahaz recognized the Assyrian gods.

2. This is the era of the First Isaiah. For fifty years this prophet dominated the religious atmosphere of Jerusalem.

3. Isaiah is a long story—too extensive for consideration at this time.

4. Isaiah continues from the days of Ahaz over into the times of Hezekiah.

5. At first Isaiah counseled Hezekiah to go along with the Assyrians—later he advised firm resistance.

6. Micah was a contemporary of Isaiah—and a firm supporter.

7. The results of these prophets continued on for generations. They helped to stabilize the Hebrew religion.

8. While Hezekiah's reforms were transient, these prophets formulated an enduring national hope.

9. Is it possible that Jerusalem experienced a second seige by the Assyrians and was delivered by an epidemic which devastated Sennacherib's army?

10. Most students accept the idea of two invasions.

# 8. THE KINGDOM OF JUDAH
*The Last Century*

## I. JUDAH REGAINS INDEPENDENCE
*The Bid of Assyria*

1. Remember: Between the death of Hezekiah and the final fall of Jerusalem one hundred years had passed.

2. The Assyrian Empire was at the time of its greatest expansion and Manasseh became a loyal vassal.

3. Sennacherib was murdered by several of his sons. One, Esar-haddon, consolidated the empire and brought Egypt in line.

4. During a long reign, Manasseh remained a vassal of Assyria.

5. The local shrines of Yahweh were restored. Magic was rampant. Even human sacrifice came back.

6. The voice of prophecy was silenced. The few that did speak branded Manasseh as about the worst king ever to rule Judah.

7. We are entering upon the last days of the Assyrian Empire. The Medes and Persians are coming into power, as well as the Cimmerians and Scythians.

8. Asshur-banapal makes one last heroic effort to save Assyria, spends two years subduing Babylon, wreaks havoc on the Arab tribes, and transplants strangers in Samaria.

9. The Assyrian Empire toppled and fell in less than 20 years.

10. With the end of Assyria, once more Judah was free by default. Josiah ascended the throne and began his reforms.

11. The major reforms of Josiah were:
    a. The temple repairs.
    b. Finding Deuteronomy in the temple.
    c. Repudiation of the Assyrian cult and gods.
    d. Restoration of the Passover.
    e. Destruction of idols.
    f. End of magic practices.
    g. Closing of the Bethel temple.

12. The book of Deuteronomy was the basis of all of the king's later reforms.

13 In the later years of Josiah a new group of prophets arose.

14. Josiah lost his life defending Haran on the battlefield of Megiddo, at the hands of the invading Egyptians.

## II. THE LAST DAYS OF JUDAH

1.  The end of Assyria did not bring full peace to Judah. The death of Josiah marked the end of independence.

2.  Josiah, as an ally of Babylon, tried to stop Nechoh, the Egyptian, at Megiddo. Josiah was killed in this disastrous battle.

3.  Egypt took control of all Palestine (609-605). Next, the Babylonians took over.

4.  Nebuchadnezzar ascended the throne of Babylon. Jehoiakim, king of Judah, became a vassal of Babylon.

5.  Ambassadors of Edom, Moab, Ammon, Tyre, and Sidon gathered in Jerusalem to plan revolt. Jeremiah denounced them.

6.  Zedekiah went to Babylon in a final effort to make peace.

7.  Finally Judah went into rebellion. In January 588 B.C. the Babylonian army arrived for the blockade of Jerusalem.

8.  The walls were breached and the city destroyed. The fleeing Zedekiah was overtaken, blinded, and taken to Babylon.

9.  The Babylonians made Palestine a province, appointing Gedaliah governor. His seat of government was Mizpah.

10. They killed or deported most of the people—leaving only a few farmers alive.

## III. PROPHETS OF THE LAST DAYS

1.  The Hebrew theology was unprepared for the crisis of the captivity. They thought Yahweh had promised David an eternal dynasty.

2.  When Isaiah's promise that Jerusalem would not be taken was fulfilled—they were confirmed in the belief of the inviolability of the temple.

3.  These false hopes drove the nation headlong into suicidal rebellion.

4.  Habakkuk views the Babylonians as the instrument of Yahweh's discipline. **Hab. 1:2-11**.

5.  The tragic Jeremiah did his utmost to show the Jews the true meaning of what had happened.

6.  Both Jeremiah and Zephaniah pointed out the paganism of Manasseh. They intimated that the reforms had been only superficial.

7.  Jeremiah began to preach the nation's funeral oration. **Jer. 11:9-17**. They brought it on themselves by forsaking Yahweh. **Jer. 2:14-17**.

8. The prophets promised that the punishment was only temporary, that deliverance would come from the north.

9. Jeremiah pronounced the belief in Yahweh's eternal protection a fraud— a lie. **Jer. 7:1-15.**

10. By bitter persecution Jeremiah was driven almost to suicidal despair.

11. Ezekiel, in Babylon, among the captives, joined Jeremiah in voicing warnings and admonitions.

12. The prophets doomed Israel for the time being, but they did save it from extinction.

13. The vicissitudes of the worship of Yahweh were shown in the fickle conduct of Israel's kings. Solomon went after the gods of Moabites and Ammonites. Jeroboam set up golden calves at Bethel and Dan. Jezebel, Ahab's Phoenician queen, conducted the worship of Baal. Manasseh reared up altars to the "host of heaven."

14. The Jews are losing their prophets. They are failing to become a missionary people. They are depending on:

    a. Sacramentalism.
    b. Legalism.
    c. Philosophy—wisdom.
    d. Apocalypticism.

## 9. EXILE AND RESTORATION
### 586 - 538 B.C.

## I. THE EXILE PERIOD

1.  The history of this period is found in Nehemiah and Ezra, supplemented by the apocryphal book of I Esdras.

2.  The Babylonian army left Judah a shambles. Battle losses, executions, starvation, and disease almost depleted the country.

3.  Of 250,000, probably 20,000 were left. Samaria was untouched.

4.  The exiles were well treated in Babylon—given considerable freedom. They built houses, farmed, and had some sort of religious life.

5.  There were three deportations—in 597, 587, and 582.

6.  Many Jews fled to Egypt—taking Jeremiah with them. **Jer. 43:7.** Others went to Moab, Edom, and Ammon.

7.  Long had the Jews trusted the dogma that David's dynasty would never end. They even disregarded the prophets.

8.  This was all a great shock to Jewish theology—the dogma of Israel as the "chosen people."

9.  After all, maybe the gods of Babylon were strong and mighty. Their faith was sorely tested.

10. The teaching of Jeremiah and Ezekiel prevailed. Their faith persisted. They lived through it.

11. There was a great revival of Sabbath-keeping—symbol of the covenant.

12. The priests completed their rewriting of the racial records and chronicles.

13. Presently there was born the hope of restoration.

14. Their king, Jehoiakim, who had been imprisoned, was released by Nebuchadnezzar's son.

15. Babylonian power rapidly declined. Cyrus came to power and took over the empire.

16. The Second Isaiah revived hope in Israel. Jews prepared for the restorastion.

17. Yahweh became *"the Lord of History"*— *"Creator of the Universe."* Isaiah hailed Cyrus as the liberating agent of Yahweh.

18. Israel was about to be delivered as in former times they had been delivered from Egyptian bondage.

## II. THE RESTORATION

1. Babylon falls. Isaiah inspires Israel and Cyrus liberates them.

2. The book of Daniel tells the story of the fall of Babylon and the triumph of Cyrus.

3. There are two records of the restoration. **Ezra 1:2-4; 6:3-5.**

4. Cyrus was a new kind of ruler. He favored granting subject peoples cultural autonomy—freedom to have their own religion.

5. Sheshbazzar was followed by Zerubbabel as governor of Judah. The prophets Haggai and Zechariah offered encouragement.

6. The Jews returned in successive waves of dedicated rebuilders. The early arrivals met with bitter disappointment.

7. Cambyses maintained his father's conquests and added Egypt. He continued to foster Jewish restoration.

8. The more prosperous Jews remained in Babylon. The early years were fraught with hardship and frustration. They were greatly hampered by the Samaritans.

9. It required 18 years to lay the foundations for the temple. At last they were aroused and finished the work in four years.

10. Haggai spurred the people to finish the temple. **Hag. 1:1-11.** Zechariah joined in this revival.

11. In March 515 B.C. the temple was finished and dedicated. **Ezra 6:13-18.**

12. But the best things promised by the prophets did not materialize. Judah struggled along—as a sub-province of Samaria.

## 10. REFORMS OF NEHEMIAH AND EZRA
*The Jewish Community in the Fifth Century*

1. These are the times of Ezra, Nehemiah, Obadiah, and Malachi.

2. History runs along with the Jews and the Persian Empire under Darius— which reaches its zenith during this century.

3. Darius won all his wars except against Greece, where he was defeated at Marathon.

4. Jewish communities were well established throughout the Persian Empire.

5. Throughout this century groups of Jews continued to drift back to Palestine. **Ezra 4:12**.

6. There was no end of trouble with the governors of Persia. The southern Edomites harassed them constantly.

7. Under Artaxerxes they began to rebuild their fortifications. **Ezra 4:7-23**.

8. The religious life ran along fairly well. The temple services were in full operation.

9. But the general morale was not good. The Sabbath was neglected. They failed to pay tithes. **Mal. 3:7-10**.

10. Divorce was a public scandal; the poor were oppressed. Intermarriage with the gentiles was common.

11. Nehemiah began a thoroughgoing reorganization of the Jewish community, with the help of Ezra.

12. In Greece, this was the age of Pericles, Socrates, Sophocles, and Phidias.

13. The folly of the Peloponnesian wars left Persia in a more secure position.

14. Nehemiah was attached to the Persian court—he had been the king's cupbearer. He was appointed governor of Judah and authorized to rebuild its fortifications.

15. Nehemiah was a good organizer. In 52 days he had the walls of Jerusalem up. **Neh. 6:15**.

16. But it was two years before all details—gates, towers, etc.—were completed.

17. He was greatly hampered by Sanballat, governor of Samaria. Tobiah, governor of Ammon, also opposed Nehemiah

18. Nehemiah divided his forces into two shifts—one to stand at arms, the other to build.

19. There were only 50,000 people in Judah. Taxes were high. Land-grabbers dispossessed the poor. Nehemiah started far-reaching reforms.

20. Nehemiah had many enemies. He was not only just—but he had a bad temper.

21. Nehemiah ruled 12 years. He then visited Babylon and the Persian court.

22. When he returned he found things in a bad way. Intermarriage, Sabbathbreaking, and all-round religious laxity were the order of the day.

23. It was about this time that Ezra arrived and joined Nehemiah in the task of cleaning up Jerusalem. **Ezra 7:12-26.**

24. Ezra had great help from contributions by Babylonian Jews. Ezra was a priest.

25. Ezra was accompanied by a considerable caravan of Jews. He was ashamed to ask for a military escort.

26. In a public square on an elevated platform, he read the law from daybreak to noon every day.

27. Ezra won the leaders and they brought the people together—and in a downpour of rain they received Ezra's rebuke and admonitions.

28. It was a tough job and a long pull, but Ezra did get some results.

29. Ezra really finished up the reforms started by Nehemiah. Their efforts were effective because they were supported by royal Persian decrees.

30. And Ezra got all of this done in about one year. In some respects, Ezra was the most important person in Israel's history since Moses.

31. The law which Ezra read to the Jerusalem Jews was the new priestly code which had been prepared during the captivity.

32. Now the Jews made a new covenant with Yahweh and the compact was sanctioned by the Persian government.

33. Through adherence to religious law, Israel became a nation—even without statehood.

34. In a sense, this is the way Israel has existed ever since that day.

35. We are not disposed to accept the idea that Ezra arrived in Jerusalem before Nehemiah, even though such a concept may be suggested by a superficial reading of the records of our Old Testament.

# 11. END OF THE OLD TESTAMENT PERIOD
*From Ezra to the Maccabean Revolt*

## I. JEWS DURING FOURTH AND THIRD CENTURIES B.C.

1.  We know very little about the Jews during the fourth century.

2.  At the end of the fifth century, Nehemiah and Ezra completed their work and Artaxerxes I died. The Persian rulers continued friendly.

3.  There was a powerful colony of Jews at Alexandria. Their temple was destroyed and later rebuilt.

4.  Egypt rebelled. Many satraps asserted independence. But Artaxerxes III restored the empire—for the time being.

5.  Persia seemed strong—but was on its last legs. Alexander came to power in Greece.

6.  During the first two thirds of the fourth century, we know little or nothing about Jews in Judah.

7.  The Samaritans build a temple on Mt. Gerizim. They are forever separated from Judah.

8.  Hebrew language is passing—Aramaic is becoming the tongue of Judah.

9.  The Greeks are overrunning all Asia Minor. The Hellenistic period is beginning.

10. Alexander the Great (356-323) is getting ready to take the center of the international stage.

11. Just how and when Judah came under Greek control, we do not know.

12. Alexander made a clean sweep of empire. But when he died the empire was divided four ways.

13. The Ptolemies ruled Palestine for almost a century. They made few changes in the Persian region.

14. The Jews were loyal, and they enjoyed full religious liberty.

15. The Seleucids always claimed the Ptolemies stole Palestine, and Antiochus III, after defeating Egypt, took over all of Asia Minor, including Palestine.

16. He released political captives, ordered return of refugees, and accorded the Jews full religious liberty.

17. This was the Hellenistic era. Everywhere everybody was learning Greek.

## II. RELIGIOUS CRISIS AND REBELLION
### The Jews under the Seleucids

1.  Antiochus III tangled with Rome and was defeated. His successor, Seleucus IV, continued Jewish privileges.

2.  Antiochus IV was another story. His treatment of the Jews drove them into rebellion. He meddled with Jewish religious practices.

3.  Jason bought the high priesthood from Antiochus. A Greek gymnasium was established in Jerusalem.

4.  In three years one Menelus outbid Jason who fled to Trans-Jordan. He began stealing and selling the temple sacred vessels.

5.  Returning from a victorious Egyptian campaign, Antiochus raided the temple— stripping the gold off the structure.

6.  Hearing the rumor that Antiochus had been killed in Egypt, Jason with one thousand men attempted to capture Jerusalem.

7.  The general of Antiochus made a bloody raid on Jerusalem. This was in 167 B.C.

8.  He left a garrison in the city for 25 years.

9.  Antiochus introduced the worship of Zeus and presently forbade the worship of Yahweh.

10. How the Jews reacted to all this is shown in Daniel and the book of Maccabees.

11. Temple sacrifices were suspended. Circumcision was forbidden. The Sabbath was annulled.

12. But the cap of all was in December 167 B.C. when they set up an altar in the temple and offered a swine as sacrifice.

13. Undoubtedly this is the *"abomination of desolation"* spoken of by Daniel. **Dan. 9:27.**

14. And all this culminates in the outbreak of the Maccabean rebellion.

15. Said Antiochus: "I did not want to suppress the worship of Yahweh— I only wanted to unite it with the 'God of Heaven'"—bring it into harmony with Greek religion.

16. The persecutions were drastic and bloody. They would kill Jews for refusing to touch pork.

17. The book of Daniel was written in the midst of all this turmoil and confusion.

18. If you put Antiochus in the place of Nebuchednezzar, you can more fully understand the immediate meaning of Daniel's pronouncements.

19. Daniel is apocalyptic. By this date loyal Jews had begun to believe in the Messiah, the new age—the everlasting and divine kingdom.

20. Now Judas Maccabaeus swings into action—one of five sons of Mattathias, belonging to the Hasidine sect—and inaugurates effective guerrilla war on the enemy.

21. Judas wins first battle with troops of Antiochus. One crushing defeat after another was administered by Judas.

22. One thing which favored Judas was the fact that Antiochus was quite fully occupied by a major campaign against the Parthians.

23. Judas smashed the pagan altars, cleansed the temple, and established the services. Ever since, the Jews have celebrated the feast of Hanukkah in honor of this dedication.

24. The last surviving son of Mattathias was Simon, whose son John succeeded to the high priesthood—and was known as John Hyrcanus.

25. John Hyrcanus was really the last of the great Hasmonaeans. Of John's five sons, Aristobulus imprisoned three brothers and murdered the fourth. But he lasted only one year.

26. The general and increasing confusion in Palestine led Rome to take over.

NOTE: For a review of Hebrew history as presented in *The Urantia Book*, see pages 1071-5.

# 12. JUDAISM AT THE END OF THE OLD TESTAMENT PERIOD

## I. NATURE OF EARLY JUDAISM

1. In the presence of frustration the community reorganized around the LAW.

2. This explains why the Sabbath became such an outstanding feature of Jewish theology.

3. Henceforth, Judah is that remnant of Israel which has rallied around the law and looks forward to the redemption from worldly bondage by the Messianic deliverer—the survival of the everlasting kingdom.

4. The books of Jonah and Joel probably belong to this period.

5. This is an era of theological evolution and reconstruction.

6. The Jews have the Scriptures—and their traditions. Out of these they must build a new philosophy.

7. The canon of Scripture is taking shape. The religion of the law is formulating the cult of the TORAH.

8. The Jews seemed to sense that the age of the prophets had ended. Their future was to be organized around the temple and the law.

9. Twice Yahweh had delivered them from bondage, but their third deliverance had come by means of military conquest.

10. The high priest became an important person in the new Jewish community.

11. It was the LAW rather than the cult that claimed Jewish allegiance.

12. The *scribe* became an important person in the Hebrew religion.

13. The synagogue took a new place in the Jewish community.

14. In the synagogue service the first act was the reading of the law.

15. Presently there came along the new aspect of law—the ORAL LAW.

16. Also now comes into the picture the wisdom feature of the Scriptures.

17. All this means that piety—righteousness—becomes the important feature of religious living.

18. Next come the thousand and one little details of legal restrictions and minute features of obeying the law.

19. They really derived great pleasure from carrying out all these trifling obligations of their ceremonial and moral laws.

20. In the end they arrived at the position of *absolutizing* the law.

21. The Jews were gradually divorcing Yahweh and their religion from *history*.

22. The Jews were becoming legalistic, formal, ceremonial, and increasingly intolerant.

## II. THEOLOGY OF EARLY JUDAISM

1. There were two diverse and contending attitudes among the Jews:
   a. A narrow-minded and intolerant attitude toward all gentiles.
   b. A warm concern for the salvation of the world.

2. This conflict and tension now became real. Stated otherwise it was:
   a. The Jews as the "chosen people"—Yahweh's elect.
   b. Yahweh as the God of all nations—missionary obligations.

3. Israel was surrounded by paganism. Nehemiah and Ezra thought they must protect the remnant of Israel from moral contamination.

4. The Jews succumbed to the idea and the ideal of a "holy people." They surrendered to racial isolationism.

5. Hate of gentiles gained over love for gentiles. Intermarriage was taboo.

6. The idea of the "holy people" grew. More and more the Jews withdrew from all contact with gentiles.

7. Especially they refused to have any dealings with Samaritans.

8. Among the few the sense of world mission was never fully lost, but Judaism never became a missionary religion.

9. They consolidated their theology. Monotheism triumphed. They became more and more eschatological. They persisted in their olden beliefs regarding Providence.

10. There was growth of the concept of angels and intermediaries. Wisdom was exalted. The word of God was all but personified.

11. They wrestled with the problem of evil. Began to charge it up to Satan. Still held to olden concepts of health and prosperity as rewards for righteousness, and sickness and adversity as punishment for sin.

12. Allied with Satan were the fallen angels—demons and evil spirits.

13. Divine justice and rewards after death claimed attention. The majority believed in the resurrection of the dead.

14. They sought to bolster hope for the future and to reinterpret their captivity and restoration.

15. More and more they taught the coming of the Messiah and the new age.

16. The Jews were becoming apocalyptic. They studied anew the book of Daniel.

## III. THE LAST TIMES

1. Presently John the Baptist came. Then began the conflict with Jesus' teachings—and their rejection.

2. Sects and parties were springing up—Israel was becoming divided and weakened.

3. There were:

   a. Pharisees.
   b. Sadducees.
   c. Nationalists.
   d. Hasidim.
   e. Nazarites.
   f. Roman loyalists.
   g. Maccabeans.
   h. Essenes.
   i. Qumrans.
   j. Christians.

4. Then came the revolt against Rome and the END.

# PART III
# NEW TESTAMENT HISTORY

# 1. NEW TESTAMENT GOSPEL

## I. THE GOSPEL

1. The literal translation of gospel means *"bring good tidings."* **Mark 1:3. Rom. 10:15.**

2. The gospel embraced not only events and sayings, but was a portrait of Jesus' bestowal. **Heb. 1:2,3.**

3. When the believer was baptized he confessed that "Jesus is Lord."

4. Love your enemies, and become *"sons of the Most High."* **Luke 6:35.** Love and forgive one another. **Eph. 4:32.**

5. The gospel story is formulated in acts. By Peter—**Acts 4:8-12.** By Paul— **Acts 13:16-41.**

6. In the religion *of* Jesus, and according to *The Urantia Book*, the gospel is: "The fatherhood of God and the brotherhood of man."

7. In the religion *about* Jesus, the gospel message evolved somewhat as follows:

    a. Dawn of the Messianic age. Jesus as the fulfillment of Old Testament prophecy.
    b. Brief account of the ministry, death, and resurrection of Jesus.
    c. Exaltation of the risen Christ—at the right hand of God.
    d. The gift of the Holy Spirit as the sign of Christ's presence.
    e. The second advent of Christ.

8. The result of such preaching on the day of Pentecost confirmed their faith in such a message.

9. The glossolalia of Pentecost is of doubtful authenticity.

10. *"You shall receive power when the Holy Spirit has come upon you."* **Acts 1:8.** Pentecost is really the birthday of the Christian Church.

11. The Spirit was recognized in Old Testament times—see **Judges 14:6.** Now, at Pentecost, the Spirit is "democratized."

12. The church is here. *"And they devoted themselves to the apostles' teaching and fellowship, to the breaking of bread and the prayers."* **Acts 2:42.**

13. These early believers attempted to carry out a communistic plan of living. Later on, Paul was taking up collections to feed the starving brethren at Jerusalem.

## II. THE GOSPEL IN THE GOSPELS

1.  The gospel writers were not presenting history or biography. They were telling a story to confirm faith—"That believing you may have life in his name."

2.  The gospel was the whole of the apostolic message. "All that Jesus began to do and teach."

3.  Said Jesus: *"For the Son of man came to seek and to save the lost."* **Luke 19:10.**

4.  Matthew came along with the idea that the 'Sermon on the Mount" might be the gospel.

5.  "Whosoever will may come" was the keynote of Jesus' teaching. Salvation was a matter of faith.

6.  The fatherhood of God was not a new idea in Israel, but to make use of the fact as the basis of the "brotherhood of man" was a new idea.

7.  There was a new note of comfort in Jesus' teaching. "Come to me all you who are weary and find rest for your souls."

8.  Jesus advised against all fear, anxiety, and worry. His message was one of faith, confidence, and trust.

9.  Jesus knew and freely quoted the Scriptures.

10. He exhorted to doing the will of God—to be perfect even as God is perfect.

11. He healed sickness and restored the disordered mind.

12. He came to "reveal the Father" and "do his will."

13. In the four gospels it is difficult to understand just how Jesus regarded himself as concerned the Messiah. He seldom referred to himself as "the Son of God."

14. The gospel writers seemed to regard Jesus as the Messiah.

15. Jesus' favorite title was "the Son of Man."

16. He asserted his divinity often. "The Son of Man has power to forgive sins." "The Son of Man is Lord of the Sabbath."

17. The gospel writers carry along the notion that the cross was inevitable— that it was God's will.

18. There is much in the gospels to lend support to Paul's later doctrine of the atonement.

19. The New Testament teaches the literal resurrection of Jesus' physical body.

20. The New Testament gives first importance to the cross—the death of Jesus.

21. More and more the resurrection becomes the living core of the gospel.

## III. THE GOSPEL ACCORDING TO PAUL

1. Paul claims to have had a special and personal revelation of "Christ of the Damascus Road."

2. Paul also claims to have received a mandate to preach the gospel to the gentiles.

3. Paul's epistles were largely devoted to:
   a. Defense against attacks made upon his teachings.
   b. Resisting the efforts of Jewish Christians to impose ceremonial demands upon the gentiles.

4. Paul was inclined to ignore the human Christ. **2 Cor. 5:16**.

5. Paul was determined to know only "Christ and him crucified"—the atonement.

6. He was concerned with the "risen and glorified Christ"—the divine Christ.

7. Paul's controversy with the apostles was resolved during his second visit to Jerusalem—when they extended to him "the right hand of fellowship."

8. Paul believed in the "verbal inspiration" of the Scriptures.

9. Paul's conversion is a mystery—also his long isolation afterward. *"I went into Arabia."* **Gal. 1:17**.

10. Paul becomes the philosopher and theologian of the religion *about* Jesus.

11. Paul usually speaks of Christ as "Lord" or "Son of God"—sometimes "Jesus Christ."

12. The keynote of Paul's preaching was "justification by faith."

13. Paul calls his gospel the *"righteousness of God."* **Rom. 1:17**.

14. Paul teaches sonship with God by *"adoption."* **Rom. 8:15**. *(King James Version)*

15. Paul pays little or no attention to Christ's life—he concentrates on his death and resurrection. **1 Cor. 15:3.**

16. Paul had specific ideas about the atonement—being *"redeemed from the curse of the law."* **Gal. 3:13.**

17. Reconciliation through the *"blood of Christ"* means a *"new creation."* **2 Cor. 5:17.**

18. In place of *"the kingdom of God,"* Paul uses *"in Christ"*—a citizen of heaven. **Phil. 3:20.** *(King James Version)*

19. Christ is not only Lord of the individual, but also "Lord of the universe."

20. Paul does not promise a life free from hardship, but does assert "that nothing can separate us from the love of Christ."

## IV. THE GOSPEL ACCORDING TO JOHN

1. As time passes, there is a reaction to Paul's overstressing the divinity of Christ. Hebrews, I Peter, Revelation, and the pastoral epistles all call special attention to the humanity of Jesus.

2. John presents a more balanced picture of both the humanity and the divinity of Jesus.

3. John combines the teachings of the apostles, Paul, and much from the Greeks.

4. Use of "the kingdom of heaven" is not found in John. Already it had resulted in persecutions.

5. The incarnation is a central concept in John. **John 14:9.**

6. The summation of the religion *about* Jesus is found in John 3:16.

7. The incarnation is summed up in **John 14:10.** *"The Father who dwells in me does his works."*

8. Of all the New Testament the gospel of John is the best presentation of both the humanity and the divinity of Jesus.

9. It is interesting to note that the doctrine of the virgin birth is absent in John and in all of Paul's writings.

10. It is in John that Jesus "thirsts" and "weeps."

11. It is in John that we find the "I am" sayings—"I am the bread of life," and so on.

12. John is the most logical, dignified, consistent, and philosophical of all the New Testament writers.

## 2. EARLY CHRISTIAN LITERATURE

### I. MOTIVES FOR WRITING

1. There are three groups of Christian writings:
   a. The 27 New Testament writings.
   b. The Apostolic Fathers.
   c. The New Testament Apocrypha.
2. The New Testament was written in everyday style of Greek. Jesus' oral teaching was in Aramaic.
3. In New Testament times the "letter" was a popular form of communication.
4. One great motive for New Testament writing was to preserve the record for teaching—not to write a history.
5. Luke is the only New Testament writer who evinced anything like an interest in history.
6. Another motive for writing was to make converts—evangelization.
7. Still a third motive was "edification" of believers.
8. In the case of Paul, much of his writing was to combat "errors" and settle disputes.
9. Early New Testament writings were on papyrus. Later on parchment.
10. The arrangement of the New Testament is not chronological. Gospels come first, followed by Acts and Paul's letters to the churches. Then the remainder, followed by Revelation.

### II. NEW TESTAMENT AND APOCRYPHA

1. New Testament students think that the gospel writers had a common source— called Q. This was the notes of the Apostle Andrew. See *The Urantia Book*, P. 1341.
2. Long after Luke wrote "Acts of the Apostles," other writers wrote the acts of Peter, Paul, John, and others.
3. Paul's epistles are the oldest of the New Testament writings— Thessalonians being the oldest.
4. *The Urantia Book* suggests that Paul was "one of the authors of Hebrews."
5. 2 and 3 John, James, Jude, and 2 Peter are late writings and by other authors than those assigned.

6. There was little to choose between 2 Peter and other writings ascribed to Peter which were rejected.

7. Ephesians, after Paul's writing, was revised and edited by a later Christian author.

8. The apocryphal writings most seriously considered by early Christians were:

   1 and 2 Clement
   Epistles of Barnabas, Polycarp, and Ignatius.
   Shepherd of Hermas.
   The Didache.

9. Among the early apologists were:

   Justin Martyr.
   Aristides.
   Tatian.
   Athenagoras.
   Theophilus.

## 3. NEW TESTAMENT LANGUAGE

### I. NEW TESTAMENT GREEK

1.  In the times of Christ, three languages were spoken in Palestine—Aramaic, Greek, and Latin. The official language was Latin.

2.  General interests were:

    a.  Hebrew—The right. Prophets and psalmists.
    b.  Greek—Ideal. Artists and philosophers.
    c.  Roman—Practical. Statesmen, legislators.

3.  In early times, there were many dialects of classic Greek.

4.  KOINE Greek was the common language developed by Alexander's army. By the first century of our era it had become the language of the Roman Empire.

5.  Paul's letter to the Romans was written in Koine Greek. Koine was a simplification of classic Greek.

6.  Koine Greek was the language of Philo and Josephus.

7.  Modern Greek is Byzantine Greek. Came in from the seventh to the eleventh century.

### II. THE NEW TESTAMENT AUTHORS

1.  **HEBREWS**. Of all books in the New Testament, Hebrews attains the highest standard of literary quality of Koine Greek. The style is systematic and very different from Paul. *The Urantia Book* suggests that Hebrews had several authors. See *The Urantia Book*, p. 1024. Paul was probably one of them. See *The Urantia Book*, p. 539, next to last paragraph. The quotation credited to Paul is **Hebrews 12:22**. This is the only New Testament book which refers to Melchizedek.

2.  **JAMES**. Along with Hebrews, James is at the top of literary excellence. It is distinctly Jewish, but in excellent language. There are no Hebraisms. The book exhibits great literary skill in alliteration and syllable formation.

3.  **LUKE AND ACTS**. Luke, the physician (**Col. 4:14**), was the most versatile of all New Testament writers. The preface to the gospel of Luke (**1:1-4**) is the most perfect of Greek composition, comparing with the preface of Herodotus. Luke uses 750 words not found elsewhere in the New Testament. Many times his words indicate the medical viewpoint—Peter's mother-in-law had a *high* fever. A man was *full* of leprosy. Professional pride caused him to leave out—"and

she was no better," in the case of the woman who had "suffered many things from many physicians." Luke avoids foreign words. He never uses "rabbi," always "master." But as a true reporter he often retains Jewish idiom—like "and it came to pass." In Acts he employs the more elegant Greek.

4.  **1 PETER.** 1 Peter shows more classical Greek than any other New Testament writing. There is little or no vernacular Koine. There is here such an "elegant touch" as to suggest that such refined nicety is beyond the literary ability of the Galilean fisherman whose Aramaic brogue betrayed him. The dignity and elevation of this epistle suggests that it might have been dictated to, and revised by, Peter's secretary, Silvanus. **1 Peter 5:12.**

5.  **MARK.** Mark is an example of the nonliterary Koine. There is a lack of polish in Mark's colloquial style which is somewhat covered up when put in English. He is very repetitious. Of 45 verses in the first chapter, 35 begin with "and." Twelve of 16 chapters begin in the same way. Mark had a small vocabulary. Of 1290 words he uses, only 80 are peculiar to him, as compared with the other gospels. But there is a freshness and vigor along with great brevity that marks him as an "artistic genius."

6.  **REVELATION.** Of all New Testament books, Revelation is on the lowest literary level of Koine Greek. Dionysius of Alexandria called the Greek of Revelation barbaric. The writer seems to think in Aramaic while writing in Greek. Nevertheless, the book is filled with powerful sayings. One explanation of these peculiarities of Revelation may be its frequent revisions and distortions. See *The Urantia Book*, p. 1555.

7.  **MATTHEW.** Matthew's Greek is better than Mark's, but not so good as Luke's. It is smoother than Mark's, but more monotonous than Luke's. Matthew has 95 personal expressions, as compared with Mark's 41 and Luke's 151. Matthew has a penchant for grouping things by threes or sevens:

Three divisions of genealogy.
Three temptations.
Three illustrations of righteousness.
Three commands.
Three miracles of healing.
Threefold "Fear not."
Three parables of sowing.
Three parables of warning.
Three prayers in the Garden.

Three denials by Peter.
Three questions by Pilate.
Seven clauses in the Lord's prayer.
Seven demons.
Seven parables.
Seven loves.
Seven baskets.
Forgiving not seven times.
Seven brothers.
Seven woes.

8. **JOHN**. John's gospel has a simplicity and grandeur which is unrivaled by any other book of the New Testament. John's vocabulary is less than that of the other gospels, but far more impressive and majestic. He makes effective use of fundamental words, such as: truth, light, world, sin, judgment, and life. His construction is sometimes almost "child-like." A stylistic peculiarity of John is combining negative and positive expressions: "He confessed and denied not." "Should not perish, but have everlasting life." He writes pure Greek, but the Semitic viewpoint is always appearing. There are two other peculiarities. He writes in short weighty sentences. "I am the light of the world." "Jesus wept," the shortest verse in the Bible. The other, a peculiar circular or spiral-motion type of reasoning. See **John 8:38-44**.

9. **EPISTLES OF PAUL**. Paul had a characteristic style, though his letters vary greatly. Now and then he almost reaches the high level of Plato. He likes to ask and answer supposed questions or objections. Most of his epistles were dictated. The Timothy and Titus letters are a bit different from the other epistles. If Paul had known his letters were to become part of "the word of God"—inspired Scripture—he would have edited them more carefully, as someone later on did edit and polish up Ephesians.

10. **2 PETER**. The style of II Peter is very different from that of I Peter. The Greek is awkward, but is greatly improved by translation into English. Important words are frequently repeated. If these differences are due to different secretaries, then Peter gave his secretaries much freedom of expression. Most scholars think II Peter was written early in the second century.

11. **JUDE**. The style of Jude is better than II Peter, but is very much like that of the second chapter of II Peter. Jude likes to express himself in triads. It is good idiomatic Koine Greek.

12. **LANGUAGE OF JESUS**. Jesus taught in good everyday Aramaic. Many Aramaic words and phrases are carried over into New Testament records. The Jews were fond of puns and many of Jesus' sayings were on this order. The saying about "straining out gnats and swallowing the camel" was a pun—the Aramaic words for gnat and camel made a jingle.

## III. INTERPRETATION OF NEW TESTAMENT LANGUAGE

1. Three influences determine the interpretation of New Testament Greek:
   a. Influence of Old Testament usage.
   b. Everyday Koine usage.
   c. Special meaning given to words by early Christian usage.
2. Discovery of Egyptian papyri in the nineteenth century taught translators how to understand Koine Greek.
3. Illustration: Jesus' statement about being unable by anxious thought to add one cubit to his stature. What Jesus really said: "Add to your span of life."
4. The Old Testament is the lexicon of the New Testament. Many New Testament words can be understood only by Old Testament usage. Law in Greek means statute—in Old Testament usage it means revelation—God's will.
5. In Hebrew the word "parable" covers "sayings" as well as "stories."
6. Christianity created new words and phrases, such as "in Christ."
7. The word "grace" takes on new meaning in New Testament theology.
8. The word "peace" comes to mean vastly more in Christian religion than formerly.
9. "The world and the flesh" comes to have new meanings in Christianity. Other words having new meanings were: life, faith, save, meek, election, and kingdom of God.

## 4. GROWTH OF THE GOSPELS

### I. THE SYNOPTIC PROBLEM

1. There is a considerable gap between Jesus' Galilean Aramaic and the Greek of the gospels.

2. Also, the Jesus teaching has passed from Jewish hands to the gentiles.

3. Paul cites two definite traditions which had been passed on to him:
   a. **1 Cor. 11:23-25.** The Lord's supper.
   b. **1 Cor. 15:3-8.** The resurrection.

4. Luke refers to "already written records." The Q manuscript (Andrew's notes).

5. Because of "resemblances" Matthew, Mark, and Luke have been called the "Synoptics."

6. Use of written sources produces agreement; of oral tradition, disagreement.

7. Augustine first pointed out this problem of resemblances and differences in the gospels.

8. The generally accepted solution:
   a. Mark is first of the four gospels.
   b. In addition to Mark, Matthew and Luke had another Greek documents.
   c. But there is enough additional matter to indicate still other sources of material.

### II. THE MARCAN SOURCE

1. Of 661 verses in Mark, 610 are in either Matthew or Luke— majority in both. Of 88 paragraphs in Mark only three are missing in both Matthew and Luke.

2. The order of sections in Mark is repeated in Matthew or Luke. Even the order of sentences in telling a story compares.

3. Fifty-five per cent of Luke's language is from Mark. Matthew repeats 59 per cent.

4. There is an agreement as concerns the use of "unusual language." Even peculiar sentence construction reappears.

5. All the evidence indicates that the Q document was in many ways like Mark.

6. It is fair to conclude that Matthew and Luke depended upon three sources:

    a. Mark.
    b. Q manuscript.
    c. Other sources.

## III. THE ADDITIONAL SOURCES

1. The Q manuscript furnishes for Matthew and Luke a considerable body (over 200 verses) of Jesus' sayings.

2. Matthew and Luke tell identical stories about:

    The temptation.
    The centurion's son.
    Sermon on the Mount.
    Lord's prayer.

3. The use of *identical* words in Matthew and Luke indicate the existence of Q.

4. Luke differs more from Mark than Matthew. Luke either had other writings or else he made his own record of oral traditions.

5. Matthew contains a striking series of Old Testament quotations not found in Mark or Luke.

6. There are several stories peculiar to Matthew:

    Coin in fish's mouth.
    Dream of Pilate's wife.
    Guard at the tomb.

7. It is generally believed (including in the *The Urantia Book*) that Mark is the gospel according to Peter. But the language is not that of Peter.

8. In Paul's preaching he appeals to:

    The Scriptures.
    His personal experience.
    Tradition—common knowledge.

9. Paul's traditions differ in some respects from the narratives of the Synoptic gospels.

10. Form criticism is more recent in origin. It concerns the "form" of the narrative as indicating date of origin. But the various scholars are not very well agreed on the basis of interpretation.

## *IV. BESIDES THE SYNOPTICS*

1. Aside from the passion narrative and four or five stories, the fourth gospel is wholly different from the Synoptics.

2. John even differs regarding the day of the crucifixion. *The Urantia Book* confirms John's record.

3. It is likely that each of the larger churches had a body of tradition of its own. Maybe also some written notes.

4. John's gospel is such a body of tradition associated with Alexandrian Greek philosophy.

5. There was the tradition of Rome, Antioch, Ephesus, and Jerusalem.

6. Much of the mythical tradition is contained in the final records of the Apocrypha.

## 5. NEW TESTAMENT TIMES
### THE GRECO-ROMAN WORLD

## I. THE HELLENISTIC AGE

1. The Hellenistic age extends from the death of Alexander to the founding of the Roman Empire.

2. Armies, salesmen, colonists, artists, and philosophers spread the "spell of the Greek spirit" throughout the world.

3. Hellenistic culture and language spread all over the Roman Empire. It was: "the importance of the individual."

4. Mesopotamia and Egypt were in decline. Egypt became a Roman province at the battle of Actium, 30 B.C.

5. Athens became the cultural center of the Empire.

6. Alexander left the Jews unmolested—they were practically independent.

7. When Alexander died, the Greek Empire fell apart.

## II. MORALITY AND PHILOSOPHY

1. The Jews compared the morals of the gentiles with Sodom and Gomorrah. Early Christians held about the same opinion.

2. Paul took a dim view of "heathen" morals. He harped on sexual depravity.

3. Homosexuality was not looked down on by the Greeks. Plato almost idealized the practice.

4. Paul, like the Jews, looked upon homosexuality with horror. **1 Thess. 4:3-8. Col. 3:5. Eph. 5:3. Gal. 5:19.**

5. Prostitution was tolerated all over the gentile world—even became a part of their religious ceremonials.

6. Slavery was general—human life was cheap. Crucifixion and burning at the stake were common among the Romans.

7. Christianity took a strong stand against all this—even tried to improve the status of the slave.

8. Rome granted religious freedom—except for persecutions now and then of Jews and Christians.

9. Philosophy was an important aspect of Hellenic culture. The Greeks were seeking for ultimate truth.

10. In the Orient the cultural leaders were prophets—Moses and Zoroaster.

11.  Plato's theory of ideas—the true reality—intrigued Christians. It was like the idea of the material being the shadow of the heavenly reality.

12.  Christians shared in Plato's search for "absolute truth" as the pattern for living.

13.  Plato's belief in immortality of the soul charmed Christians— although Plato did not believe in survival of the physical body.

14.  Aristotle, Plato's pupil and tutor of Alexander, taught that every object was composed of substance and attributes.

15.  Motion, he taught, proves the existence of a "prime mover." This prime mover is infinite and is what religionists call God.

16.  Thomas Aquinas taught that the doctrine of transubstantiation in the Lord's Supper was based on Aristotle.

17.  Epicureanism was an attempt to ignore both science and religion— the simple fulfillment of natural desire. But it was not a sensual philosophy.

18.  Stoicism was widespread during this period. Paul was something of a Stoic —"I have learned in whatsoever state I am therewith to be content."

19.  Marcus Aurelius was a Stoic, also Seneca. They dwelt on unity and reason.

20.  Reason was the world-soul. Man's intelligence is a fragment of universal and living reason.

21.  All men are sons of God—the universal brotherhood. They sought to ignore emotion.

22.  Evil is but the belief of ignorance. Conscience is the voice of "Divine Reason"—somewhat like Jeremiah's doctrine of God's law written on the heart. **Jer. 31:33.**

23.  Stoicism was a religious naturalism—rationalistic pantheism. But it did produce a valiant sort of ethics.

### III. RELIGION

1.  Paul talks to the Stoic and Epicurean philosophers at Athens on the "unknown God." They were never hostile toward religion.

2.  The Greeks had an elaborate polytheism. Zeus was chief diety, with headquarters on Mt. Olympus.

3. On the Acropolis, Athena, goddess of wisdom, had her temple—the Parthenon. Many of the columns are still standing.

4. Hades was god of the underworld. He was a brother of Zeus. At death, the soul or shade went to Hades.

5. Eleusinian mysteries had to do with the cult of eternal life—immortality. It was a Greek sacrament about the God who died and rose again.

6. The cult of Dionysus (Bacchus) honored the god of wine. The theater presented comedy and tragedy.

7. Apollo, god of medicine, brought punishment and even death. He was the inspiration of poets and prophets.

8. From all over the Greek world they came to Delphi to consult Apollo—the oracles.

9. Aesculapius—the divine physician—son of Apollo—was the great healer. This healer god had a daughter—Hygeia—goddess of health.

10. Today the symbol of medicine is the staff of Aesculapius with a serpent entwined about it.

11. Mithra—god of soldiers—a long-time contemporary of Christianity, along with Isis, Egyptian god of Immortality.

## IV. HELLENISTIC JUDAISM

1. The Second Isaiah had been leading the Jews away from nationalism toward universalism.

2. In Egypt there was a revolt against Jerusalem. The Jews built a temple on the island of Elephantine, whose ceremonials were like those of the Jerusalem temple.

3. A third temple was built by the Samaritans at Shechem. This temple was destroyed by John Hyrcanus in 129 B.C.

4. At the time Antiochus tried to destroy the temple services at Jerusalem (167 B.C.), the Samaritans named their temple on Mt. Gerizim for Zeus.

5. Even Paul attended the temple ceremonials when he was in Jerusalem.

6. But after A.D. 70 Jewish religious life was centered in the synagogue. This is the era of Jewish eschatology—belief in the coming of the Messiah and the "new age."

7. The Egyptian Greeks wanted the Scriptures in their own tongue. This led to the translation, at Alexandria, of the Hebrew Bible into Greek.

8. Both Jews and Christians all over the Greek-speaking Roman world could now read the Scriptures in Greek.

9. These were the Old Testament scriptures that were read by Jesus and his apostles.

10. Greek thought was making inroads into Jewish thought. See the wisdom literature—Job, Proverbs, and Ecclesiastes—as well as the wisdom of Solomon.

11. Philo, at Alexandria, began to make allegories out of the Old Testament. Example: When the heaven and earth were created, it means "mind and sense perception."

12. Early Christians, at the Alexandria school, were influenced by Philo—including Clement and Origen.

13. Greek art gained ground among Jews. Synagogues are elaborately decorated with Bible scenes.

14. Anti-Semitism is aroused by the refusal of Jews to be assimilated—their racial isolation.

15. Jews suffered persecution in both Egypt and Rome.

16. The early Christians were persecuted in Rome because the Emperor regarded Christianity as a Jewish sect. Later they suffered because they clung to the idea of "the kingdom of heaven."

## 6. PALESTINE DURING NEW TESTAMENT TIMES

### I. FROM ALEXANDER TO POMPEY

1. Samaria and Idumea were attached to Judea; Perea was attached to Galilee.

2. Under Alexander, Palestine was relatively free—independent, except when Antiochus attempted to destroy "Jewish superstitions."

3. The Hasmonaean revolt was successful beyond anticipation. Israel was expanded in territory.

4. The people did not like military priests—a five-year civil war broke out.

5. Alexandra, Jannaeus's widow, brought peace.

### II. UNDER ROME

1. Hyrcanus joined with the Arabs to besiege his brother at Jerusalem, and Rome took over. Independence was gone forever.

2. Samaria and Galilee were attached to Syria. Israel's neighbors hailed the Romans as a deliverer.

3. The Romans were very tolerant of local customs and granted full religious liberty.

4. The walls of Jerusalem were rebuilt and it was granted Joppa as a seaport.

5. Herod became king of Judea. This Idumean received the title "King of the Jews."

6. Caesarea became the capital and both Judea and Samaria were rebuilt.

7. Palestine was divided into three administrative parts:
   a. Galilee and Perea—Antipas.
   b. Districts north and east of Galilee given to Philip.
   c. Archelaus had Samaria and Judea—and Idumea.

8. The Zealots were an old party and never ceased to make trouble.

9. There were three religious parties:
   a. Pharisees—the progressive or liberal party.
   b. The Sadducees were the fundamentalists.
   c. The Essenes were the isolationists—the ascetic cult.

10. The Zealots were the "home rule" political party.

11. The worst trouble with Rome came when Gaius (37-41) wanted to put his statue in the "holy of holies" in the temple at Jerusalem.

12. The Jews kept looking for the Messiah, while they rejected Jesus. In A.D. 132 they accepted Bar Cocheba and started a new revolt against Rome.

13. After this the Sanhedrin was restored to power. Taxes were collected by salaried agents. Only customs were "farmed out" to publicans.

14. After Archelaus, Judea was ruled by procurators, Pilate being the fifth of that order to govern Judea.

15. Agrippa, grandson of Herod, was the last of the procurators. He was the most popular of all Roman governors.

16. At last another semi-Jewish king sat on David's throne—at least for three years.

17. At last (A.D. 66) the full-stage revolt against Rome broke out. It ended in A.D. 70 when Titus took Jerusalem and "not one stone of the temple was left upon another."

18. Christians, having been forewarned by Jesus, fled to Pella. But the Jews never forgave them for thus forsaking Jerusalem.

## III. THE LAW AND ITS INTERPRETATION

1. The Jews took their religion very seriously. Through Moses, God— Yahweh— had given them his law.

2. This law—the Torah—was a revelation of God's will. Their whole religious duty was—"Cease to do evil; learn to do good." **Isa. 1:16,17**.

3. The temple (synagogue) was a symbol of the LAW.

4. The Jews had priests at Jerusalem, but no fixed ministers at the synagogues.

5. The oral law soon became as binding as the written law:
   a. Midrashim—running commentary on the law.
   b. Mishnah—the classified or codified oral law.

6. The final compilation of the oral law was the Talmud.

7. Of 4,500,000 Jews, only 700,000 dwelt in Palestine. There were more Jews in Alexandria than in Jerusalem.

8.  Jewish "hope" crystallized in two directions:

    a.  The Messianic hope—a mighty king sitting on David's throne and ruling the world.

    b.  Eschatology—the coming of Yahweh—destruction of the world. Judging the quick and the dead. The resurrection. The new heavens and the new earth. The universal kingdom of righteousness.

# 7. HISTORY OF THE EARLY CHURCH

## *THE PRIMITIVE CHURCH*

1. The crucifixion scattered the followers of Jesus to the four winds. It was their belief in the fact of the resurrection that finally brought them together at Jerusalem.

2. How, when, and why they gathered in Jerusalem—we do not know. We just find them there.

3. On the day of Pentecost we find 120 believers assembled in an upper room at Jerusalem. **Acts 1:15.**

4. The promised Spirit comes, and they go out to preach—Peter taking the lead.

5. The "speaking with tongues"—glossolalia—was utterance of certain arbitrary sounds—not a definite language. Paul is supposed to have had this "gift."

6. Joel had foretold of this "pouring out of the Spirit."

7. This day marks the birth of the Christian church, with its thousands of baptisms.

8. Organization was simple. The resurrected Jesus was Lord—and would soon return. This belief in the second advent was the main reason for their giving up all private property.

9. They had no creed—each believer was free to make his own interpretation of the gospel.

10. The creed was simple—"Jesus is Lord"—Paul recognized this. See **Rom. 10:9. 1 Cor. 12:3. Phil. 2:11.**

11. They had just two sacraments—baptism and the Lord's Supper.

12. Jesus had not insisted on baptism—but since he was baptized by John—it became a rite of the church.

13. Remember: They expected Jesus' return—any day, week, or month.

14. But trouble developed. Jesus' coming was delayed. The "common property" was exhausted, Poverty stared them in the face.

15. Presently, the new church had to separate from Judaism. The Jews began persecutions.

16. The Jerusalem church was largely composed of Hellenized Jews— many from all about the Roman Empire.

17. There was serious trouble between the native Jewish Christians and the Hellenist converts. Stephen was leader of the Greeks.

18. Stephen was dragged out during his trial and stoned to death. Paul saw all of this. **Acts 8:1**.

19. While the Jews allowed the native Christians to remain, they drove the Hellenists out of Jerusalem. Thus they carried the gospel all over the gentile world.

20. There were large churches at Antioch, Damascus, and Rome. Paul was on his way to Damascus when he saw his vision.

21. The Jews confined their labors to Palestine. They could not get away from the notion that Jesus would return soon. They, in error, kept repeating a supposed saying; *"You will not have gone through all the towns of Israel, before the Son of man comes."* **Matt. 10:23**.

22. Agrippa (A.D. 42) began the persecution of Christians. James was put to death.

23. Peter was yielding leadership to James, the Lord's brother. Paul and James held opposite positions regarding the gentiles. Peter tried to stand between them.

24. But friction persisted. Finally Paul and Barnabas went up to Jerusalem for a finish fight. They finally reached a compromise. Paul was allowed to "go his way", and preach his gospel. The two accounts of this meeting don't fully agree. **Acts 15. Gal. 2**.

25. For many years the church went forward in two camps. The Jerusalem church became poverty stricken and Paul took up collections in his gentile churches to help them.

26. As the revolt against Rome agitated Jerusalem, the Christians were very unpopular as they resisted the war-fever. Before the end they all fled to Pella.

27. The Jerusalem church was short lived, but it assembled and preserved the writings which later on became the New Testament.

28. It is unfortunate that we have so little of record concerning the latter days of the Jerusalem church. But they did render a valuable service during the formative period of Christianity.

## 8. THE LIFE OF PAUL

1.  Saul was born in Tarsus. Paul was his Latin or Roman name—his father was a Roman citizen. He did not change his name from Saul to Paul because of his conversion.

2.  Paul was a "Pharisee of the Pharisees"—he was familiar with the philosophy of the Stoics and the Cynics. He also understood the pagan religions. **Acts 23:6.**

3.  Like most Jewish boys, he was taught a trade—tent-making, and he worked at it, on and off, much of his life. **Acts 18:3.** (He was an expert weaver of goat's hair.)

4.  His conversion took place around A.D. 32, when he was about 30 years old. His death—A.D. 64 or 65. He was an active missionary about 33 years.

5.  Paul was present at Stephen's death—the first martyr of the new religion.

6.  Paul early became associated with Barnabas, from Cyprus.

7.  There were many gentile believers even before Paul began his work—but no strong churches.

8.  Paul means "small"—no doubt he was a small person.

9.  Paul had been a pupil of the renowned Gamaliel at Jerusalem.

10.  Paul leaned much toward Philo's allegorical type of Scripture interpretation. **1 Cor. 10:1-11. Gal. 4:22-31.**

11.  On the road to Damascus, to arrest Christians, Paul says he met Jesus, and he became a believer on the spot.

12.  At Damascus, Ananias, a believer, instructed Paul and helped him escape the Jews.

13.  Perhaps the best account of Paul's conversion is found in **Acts 9:1-19.**

14.  His first public effort was to preach about Jesus in the Damascus synagogue.

15.  After a sojourn in Arabia, Paul returns and preaches in Damascus.

16.  Creating hostility in Damascus, he escaped, going to Jerusalem. He had a sister in that city.

17.  About this time he seems to have done some preaching in his home town—Tarsus.

18. About eight years have elapsed when he establishes himself in Antioch. Barnabas is already located there.

19. Barnabas takes a "collection" for the Jerusalem believers from Antioch.

20. Paul and Barnabas, with John Mark, start their first missionary journey, going to Paphos, capital of Cyprus, where the Roman proconsul, Sergius Paulus, was converted.

21. John Mark was a cousin of Barnabas.

22. They go from Paphos to Perga, where for some unknown reason, John Mark leaves them, returning to Jerusalem.

23. Paul looked upon John's conduct as desertion. **Acts 15:38.**

24. They taught in the synagogue at Pisidian Antioch, but the Jews rejected them.

25. They went to Iconium, where they had great success. But a great dissension arose in the city.

26. They went to Lystra, where the man born lame was healed, and the citizens thought two Greek gods had come among them.

27. But the Jews produced an attack on the missionaries, and they fled to Derbe. They made many converts.

28. They decided to stop here—to retrace their steps and build up the churches they had established.

29. New troubles developed. Jews came down to Antioch from Jerusalem, insisting that the only way to enter the Christian church was through Judaism.

30. Paul and Barnabas went to Jerusalem to settle this dispute. This was their second, trip—14 years after the first.

31. Peter came to their defense. The Jerusalem council decided that the only requirement of gentiles would be to abstain from:

Blood.
Food offered to idols.
Things strangled.
Fornication.

32. Peter visited Antioch and ate with gentiles, but, when confronted by the Jerusalem Jews, backed down.

33. Paul and Barnabas decided to undertake the second missionary tour. Barnabas wanted to take John Mark—Paul said no. So Barnabas and Mark left Paul to make the journey alone.

34. Paul then decided to take Silas from Jerusalem. They visited the churches established on their first trip. At Lystra they met Timothy, who joined them for the rest of the tour.

35. We know little about this trip until they reach Troas. Here Paul had a dream, hearing, "Come over to Macedonia and help us."

36. They went at once to Philippi, where the gospel was first preached in Europe. Here they were beaten and thrown in prison. (The jailer and his family were converted.)

37. But they had been in Philippi long enough to found a strong church. Paul later wrote one of his epistles to them. Here, Lydia, a business woman, became the first European convert to Christianity.

38. Paul took ship to Athens; Silas and Timothy remained in Berea. Paul did not have much success at Athens, and soon went on to Corinth.

39. At Corinth they met with great success. Silas and Timothy joined Paul here. Timothy told Paul of trouble at Thessalonica and Paul sent his letter, I Thessalonians, to the church. This was the spring of A.D. 50. In a few weeks he sent his second letter.

40. They spent 18 months in Corinth and then went to Syria, stopping off at Ephesus. Paul then went to Antioch, stopping at Caesarea on the way.

41. This second journey covered over two years, A.D. 49-51. Paul had a good rest and sent his epistle to the Galatians.

42. Before long, Paul was ready to start his third journey. The first stop of any length was at Ephesus. He taught in the synagogue and at the school of Tyrannus for two years. (Apollos, a Hellenist of Alexandria, had already started the work here. This is where Aquila and Prisca were converted.)

43. Paul talked about "fighting with wild beasts." Was it figurative, or was he arrested and put in the arena with wild animals?

44. There was trouble at Corinth. Paul sent Timothy, then went himself. Soon he went by ship to Tyre. He went down the coast and over to Jerusalem.

45. Some Jews stirred up trouble for Paul and in the uproar, the Romans arrested Paul. Being a Roman citizen, they sent him to Caesarea, where Felix kept him in custody for two years.

NOTE: Somewhere along here Luke joined Paul's party, for he writes in Acts in the first person.

46. Festus was now the ruler. When Paul was brought before him for a second trial—he appealed to Caesar.

47. Paul spoke before Agrippa, and his sister from Jerusalem visited him.

48. Paul sailed for Rome. The ship, it being autumn, got into serious trouble off the coast of Crete. In **Acts 27:1-28:13** Luke records one of the most famous shipwreck stories in all history.

49. The ship was storm-tossed for two weeks; finally the passengers were landed at Malta.

50. Paul, not being a criminal prisoner, was given much liberty and did much missionary work.

51. There is a legend that while here Paul contracted malaria—that this was his "thorn in the flesh." Other traditions attributed his trouble to epilepsy or chronic eye trouble.

52. While in Rome awaiting his trial, Paul wrote Colossians, Philemon, and Philippeans.

53. The book of Acts ends abruptly. Paul had been a prisoner in Rome for two years. We really don't know what happened to Paul. Following are the possibilities:

    a. He may have been tried, convicted, and executed.
    b. He may have been tried and acquitted.
    c. The case may never have come to trial, because of the loss of papers at the time of the shipwreck.

54. The early church fathers all agree that Paul was tried and convicted.

55. Paul may have been acquitted and arrested the second time during the Nero persecutions of 64 and 65.

56. Paul had been a valiant warrior—everywhere he went he left loyal friends and fierce enemies. He was a man of conflict, but he was a stalwart Christian.

57. He was the master theologian of Christianity—its chief philosopher. He was something of a self-supporting missionary. He never "ate any man's bread." He was truly the "apostle to the gentiles."

# 9. THE POST-APOSTOLIC AGE

## I. PALESTINE

1. In A.D. 62 James, head of the Jerusalem church, was stoned. Soon afterward the church moved to a gentile city—Pella.

2. In July 64 Nero blamed Christians for the burning of Rome, and bloody persecutions began.

3. The church was plagued by internal problems as well as by external troubles. Gentile Christianity was more vulnerable to heresy.

4. Peter's preaching and Paul's letters were the traditional backbone of the early Christian church.

5. After the passing of the apostles and the members of Jesus' family, sects and heresies began to appear.

6. "False prophets" sprang up everywhere. There were two wings of Jewish Christians:

   a. The fundamentalists were the Ebionites.
   b. The liberals were the Nazarenes.

7. The Ebionites rejected the gospel of Matthew.

## II. SYRIA

1. After A.D. 70, Antioch became the headquarters of the Christian church. Here, also, the Gnostics had their stronghold.

2. And it was at Antioch that Jesus' followers were first called "Christians."

3. Antioch produced Ignatius, the first known martyr, after the apostles.

4. The gospel of Mark was widely circulated—and accepted—at Antioch. Later, both Matthew and Luke were accepted.

5. Peter was the traditional authority of the church at Antioch. Even the apocalyptic "Gospel of Peter," was widely read in the Syrian churches.

6. Bishop Sarapion of Antioch at first accepted the "Gospel of Peter," but later on fully rejected it.

7. But the Syrian churches were beset by a combination of idolatrous polytheism and Jewish ceremonialism.

8. Next comes Docetism—denying the material existence of Jesus. He was "not born of woman"—could not suffer pain or death.

9. Then comes Gnosticism, a combination of Jewish, pagan, and Christian terminology. Gnostic teachers from Antioch spread over Asia Minor, Egypt, and Rome.

10. Ignatius, bishop of Antioch, wrote letters to all the churches and to Polycarp, bishop of Smyrna. He sought to augment the authority of the bishops—to fight heretics.

11. He circulated a manual on church government known as the "Teaching of the Twelve Apostles."

### III. ASIA MINOR

1. Ephesus was the center from which the gospel spread throughout Asia Minor.

2. Everything could be found at Ephesus—superstition, frauds, quackery, tension, conflict, and heresy. Disciples of Peter or Paul.

3. Paul's letters were first brought together at Ephesus.

4. Among the Jerusalem leaders coming to Hierapolis was Philip—one of the seven (**Acts 6:5**) and his four daughters—prophetesses.

5. Marcion—a Docetist—spread his "error" from Asia Minor to Rome. Finally expelled from the Rome church.

6. Marcion accepted only Paul's letters and the gospel of Luke. He drove the churches to adopt a creed.

7. Then came the Montanist schism—the "Phrygian frenzy."

8. Feb. 22, A.D. 156, marks the date of the martyrdom of Polycarp— the companion of those who "had seen the Lord."

### IV. GREECE

1. There was always some sort of trouble with the church at Corinth. **1 Cor. 1:10.** Even the church at Rome sent them a rebuking letter. 1 Clement. (Apocrypha)

2. The Athens church might waver, but the church at Rome was always steady.

3. In general, the Grecian churches made progress and, in spite of their ups and downs, prospered.

### V. EGYPT

1. The "Epistle to the Hebrews" and the so-called "Epistle of Barnabas" were addressed to Egyptian Christians.

2. Gnosticism spread throughout Egypt. God became the "Philosophical Absolute."

3. They also circulated a "Gospel According to the Egyptians"—being the gospel of a sect, the Encratites.

## VI. ROME AND WEST

1. Rome spread the gospel to the west, using the gospel of Mark—presenting Jesus in "action"—rather than as a preacher.

2. Rome was getting interested in church discipline—how to do penance, how to deal with apostates, etc.

3. A minor prophet, Hermas, brother of Bishop Pius, exerted considerable influence. His work "The Shepherd of Hermas" came close to getting into the New Testament canon.

4. Justin became a lay professor of philosophy—and an able defender of the "faith" before his martyrdom.

5. Justin did much writing against Marcion and other heretics—including reincarnation.

# STUDY OF THE BOOKS OF THE BIBLE

# Part One

# BOOKS OF THE OLD TESTAMENT

# GENESIS

## I. OUTLINE—BRIEF

| | TOPIC | CHAPTER:VERSE |
|---|---|---|
| 1. | Creation | 1,2 |
| 2. | The Fall | 3-5 |
| 3. | The Deluge | 6-9 |
| 4. | The Nations | 10,11 |
| 5. | Abraham | 12-20 |
| 6. | Isaac | 21-27 |
| 7. | Jacob | 28-36 |
| 8. | Joseph | 37-50 |

## II. OUTLINE—COMPLETE

| | TOPIC | CHAPTER:VERSE |
|---|---|---|
| 1. | Creation | 1:1-2:3 |
| 2. | Creation of Man | 2:4-25 |
| 3. | The Fall of Man | 3:1-24 |
| 4. | Beginnings of Civilization | 4:1-26 |
| 5. | Descendants of Adam | 5:1-28 |
| 6. | Beginning of Agriculture | 5:29-32 |
| 7. | Sons of God and Daughters of Men | 6:1-4 |
| 8. | The Flood | 6:5-9:19 |
| 9. | Last Days of Noah | 9:20-29 |
| 10. | Descendants of Noah | 10:1-32 |
| 11. | Confusion of Tongues | 11:1-9 |
| 12. | Descendants of Shem | 11:10-26 |
| 13. | Genealogy of Abraham | 11:27-32 |
| 14. | The Call of Abraham | 12:1-8 |
| 15. | Abraham in Egypt | 12:9-13:1 |
| 16. | Abraham and Lot | 13:2-18 |
| 17. | The War of the Kings | 14:1-24 |
| 18. | Covenant with Abraham | 15:1-21 |

# III. PURPOSE

1. To tell the story of "beginnings."

2. More especially, to tell about the beginnings of Israel. The call of Abraham.

3. To portray man's relation to God.

# IV. AUTHORSHIP

1. Genesis is a compilation. Individual authors are unknown.

2. There were four major contributors and probably numerous editors.

3. The contributors were:

    A. $J^1$—the Judah or Yahwist Document.
    B. $J^2$—a second Yahwist Document.
    C. **E**—the Ephraim or Elohist Document.
    D. **P**—the Priestly Document.

4. Dates:

    1. $J^1$—850 B.C.
    2. $J^2$—750 B.C.
    3. **E**—700 B.C.
    4. **P**—500-450 B.C.

# V. $J^1$—A YAHWIST DOCUMENT

1. The original and primitive material is in **Chapters 2-4**.

2. Tells how man was expelled from the Garden and took up agriculture. **3:23**.

3. Cain—a fugitive—became a wanderer—beginning of nomadism. (There are two records of Cain—not to mention getting a wife.)

4. In **9:20** it says Noah was the first tiller of the soil. (There are also two accounts of Noah.)

5. The **J** documents are the traditions of the southern Israelites, with headquarters at Hebron. They are the Kadesh or Mt. Horeb tribes who penetrated Canaan from the south. (Hebron was one of the cities of Caleb and was also known as Kirjath-arba.)

6. Tells of the "mighty" and the "Nephilim." For more light on Nephilim, see *The Urantia Book* p. 856.

7. In $J^1$ Abraham is associated with Hebron.

8. The Deborah song—the earliest Old Testament document—is a $J^1$ contribution.

9. This author deals with Sodom and Lot—and the misbehaving daughters of Lot (origin of the Moabites and the Ammonites).

10. Isaac, patriarch of the northern tribes, at Beer-sheba, becomes the son of father Abraham. Abraham, 100—Sarah, 91. (Isaac was a more important person than the Old Testament record indicates.)

11. The East-Jordan tribes are taken into the Abraham fold. This embraces the Jacob traditions—for Jacob was the father of the East-Jordan tribes. (Jacob is a much more real person as compared to Isaac. There are three strands in his story.)

12. Now comes the story of Esau and Jacob. (Some parts of this story are difficult to accept.)

13. Next, the story of Jacob, Laban, and his daughters. (Jacob is a queer combination of the honest and the dishonest—the clever and the stupid.)

14. $J^1$ portrays the Israelites as "clever" and the Canaanites as "stupid."

15. $J^1$ explains how Judah became head of things over his three older brothers.

16. This author has Joseph sold into Egyptian slavery by his brothers.

17. The $J^1$ story of creation presents many features of the Babylonian myths of creation. It also resembles some of the Egyptian myths.

18. It also elaborates the Ishmael story.

19. Presents Joseph buried at Shechem—another narrative buries him in Egypt.

**Note:** This was during the Hyksos occupation of Egypt and they were favorably disposed toward strangers.

## VI. $J^2$—ANOTHER YAHWIST DOCUMENT

1. This document is prompted by the crisis of David's moving his capital from Hebron to Jerusalem.

2. Still more was it prompted by the disruption of the kingdom of David and Solomon.

3. $J^2$ is a supreme attempt to maintain the "unity of Israel."

4. $J^2$ presents many myths, legends, and traditions of which $J^1$ was wholly ignorant.

5. First, there was a Canaanite version of a Babylonian creation myth and a story about the Garden of Eden. They most artistically revised both of these stories.

6. $J^2$ presents man as an agriculturalist from his expulsion from the Garden. $J^1$ had man come up from cultureless nomadism to agriculture. In order to resolve this dilemma, they make use of the story of Cain and Abel.

7. $J^2$ introduces the story of the flood as presented in the former document, but makes Noah a new hero.

8. He elaborates the story of Jacob and Rachel, and how he discovers that she is his cousin.

9. $J^2$ identifies one of the three strange visitors to Abraham as Yahweh.

10. He explains Jacob's becoming heir to the "promise," because Esau sold his "birthright."

11. $J^2$ was worried over some of $J^1$'s narratives—he thought they were too lax in morals and their treatment of sex offenses. So he proceeded to edit five of them:

    A.   Jacob outwitting Laban.
    B.   Rachel's theft of the teraphim.
    C.   Judah and Tamar.
    D.   Seduction of Dinah.
    E.   Joseph and his master's wife.

12. A new and elaborated story of Isaac's marriage. An attempt to show that Jacob's wives were not Canaanites, but of Abraham's stock. All to keep "pure" the Israelite blood.

13. $J^1$ had said Isaac was the founder of Beer-sheba. Now $J^2$ comes along and says Abraham founded Beer-sheba. He also carries over a story of Isaac to Abraham—representing his wife as his sister.

14. $J^2$ endeavors to present Beer-sheba as of equal rank with Hebron as a religious shrine.

15. $J^2$ adds the story of Ishmael and the Ishmaelites.

16. The story of Jacob at Bethel is illustrative of the attempt of $J^2$ to bring the $J^1$ record into agreement with the traditions of the north.

17. Not many additions were made to the J story before it was conflated with a new document.

## VII. E—THE EPHRAIM OR ELOHIST DOCUMENT

1. In the Moffatt Bible these different sources of Genesis are printed in different style types.

2. When several documents are "put together"—"fused," the result is called a CONFLATION. The person who does this is known as a REDACTOR.

3.  There is no trace of the E document in the first eleven chapters of Genesis.

4.  The E document always uses Elohim for God. It makes no mention of Yahweh.

5.  It begins the narrative with Abraham—**Chapter 12**.

6.  E deals with the Horeb traditions. These tribes worship Elohim, were long camped at Kadesh, and got their law at Mt. Horeb.

7.  The author of E was a northerner.

8.  According to E, Beer-sheba was Abraham's only dwelling place. No reference is ever made to Hebron.

9.  He locates the story of Abraham's imperiling his wife in Egypt, and a parallel story about Isaac in Gerar.

10. E is always concerned with rehabilitating the moral reputation of the patriarchs.

11. The drastic rewriting of the story of Jacob and Laban. Instead of one rogue trying to outwit another, he depicts Jacob as the innocent victim of Laban's duplicity.

12. Joseph is kidnapped by a passing caravan, instead of being sold into slavery by his brothers.

13. E omits the story about Joseph putting his cup in Benjamin's sack.

14. The E author was averse to so much sex in the Scriptures. He cut out the following sex stories:

    A.  Lot and his daughters.
    B.  Seduction of Dinah.
    C.  Judah and Tamar.
    D.  Joseph and his master's wife.

15. E omits the story of Jacob's wrestling at the Jabbok—probably because of the theological difficulties it occasioned.

16. The cult of "Humanism" is appearing. The only story of Abraham peculiar to E is the testing of his faith in the "sacrifice of Isaac."

17. E tells a more humane story about Hagar and Ishmael.

18. Now comes the conflation of documents—combined $J^1$ and $J^2$ with E—and this was the Hebrew scripture until after the exile.

# VIII. P—PRIESTLY DOCUMENT

1. Now comes the time, during the Babylonian exile, when the priests undertake a drastic revision, a complete rewriting, of the whole of the Hebrew scriptures. This is the **P** document, and its purpose was:

    A.  Boosting of morale—augmentation of national pride.
    B.  Rebuilding of Jerusalem.
    C.  Restoration of the temple with its sacrifices and ceremonials of worship.
    D.  Confirmation of the concept of the "chosen people."
    E.  Adjustment of the new idea of the synagogue to the central temple worship.
    F.  Establishment of Abraham as the father of Israel, Moses the Deliverer, and David the founder of an everlasting dynasty.
    G.  Bringing the Scriptures up to date—to effect a more expert conflation of their revision with the already combined writings of **J** and **E**.

2. The outstanding purpose of **P** is to associate Abraham exclusively with Hebron and Moses with Mt. Sinai.

3. Revision of the creation story. **Gen. 1:1-2:3**. May be tainted with some Babylonian myths, but is austere in its grandeur.

4. The primeval "watery chaos" is left out. The "Spirit moving over the face of the deep" sounds like a Babylonian story.

5. Change of the "firmament, covering of heaven." as a solid substance.

6. Purpose of the heavenly bodies to regulate time, and the idea of deity consultation, "let us" make man.

7. **P** compresses eight creative acts into six days, in order to provide for the establishment and hallowing of the Sabbath.

8. **P** omits the story of the fall of man—in its place, presents the genealogy extending from Adam to the flood.

9. In the story of the Patriarchs, omits all reference to sanctuaries and altars.

10. In the history of Israel, no sacrifices are offered to Yahweh until Moses receives such instructions at Mt. Sinai.

11. **P** omits all stories reflecting unfavorably on the moral character of the founding fathers.

12. **P** is the framework of the present book of Genesis.

13. **P** represents many improved features of Genesis. "Man is made in the image of God."

14. **P** tells a new or enlarged story about:

    A.  Creation. **1:1-2:3.**

    B.  The flood. **Parts of Chap. 6 and 9.**

    D.  Abraham buys land. **23.**

    E.  The ten genealogies.

    F.  The Sabbath. **2:3.**

    G.  Forbidding blood. **9:3-6.**

    H.  Circumcision. **17:22-27.**

15. The **P** document stresses revelations to Adam, Noah, Abraham, and Moses.

# IX. THE TEACHINGS OF GENESIS

1. Remember that **E** was trying to free the Patriarchs from the charge of moral laxity.

2. Also remember: There always were two distinct groups of Hebrews. The Yahwists and the Elohists. The Judahites and the Ephraimites. The Northern and the Southern. The Hebron and the Beer-sheba groups. The Mt. Sinai and Mt. Horeb tribes. And even in later times, the Jews and the Samaritans.

3. That God is PERSONAL. That he is all-powerful—and that he is the CREATOR.

4. That God is divine—and that his acts are all purposeful. He is the God of history.

5. It was the task of $J^1$ to transform the Yahwism of the desert into the monotheism of a God-serving nation—of all mankind.

6. $J^2$ strove for spiritual unity. He adapted Babylonian myths to Yahwism. He made the religion of Israel different from all other religions.

7. The redactor of the **J** and **E** documents, in order to promote unity, must have retained many documents that were morally repugnant to him.

8. There were many motives behind the **P** editors:

    A.  Again, first among the motives was unity.

    B.  But, most of all, it was the intention to exalt the temple services and the priesthood at Jerusalem.

    C.  They also wanted to root out myths and falsehoods. (We do not know how many they removed—we only know what they retained.)

    D.  They wanted to overcome the tendency toward "localism" and "nationalism"—even the nationalism of Deuteronomy.

E. They really wanted the Jews to accept their mission to the gentiles. You see, they had lived among gentiles and had learned even to like them.

F. Last, but not least, they wanted to enthuse the Jews to rebuild Jerusalem and re-establish themselves in Palestine.

G. And they wanted to improve and harmonize the Hebrew scriptures.

9. When trying to improve the Genesis record, they were always afraid to remove the older and primitive records. Hence, so many dual documents. Two accounts of creation—two accounts of the creation of man and woman.

10. The whole message of Genesis is "In the beginning—God." No matter how mythical or symbolic the language—the TRUTH is there.

11. When properly regarded, Genesis affords no ground for a conflict between science and religion. Genesis is neither science nor history.

12. In Christian theology, the fall of man becomes relevant. Says Paul: *"For as in Adam all die, so also in Christ shall all be made alive."* **1 Cor. 15:22.**

## X. SELECTED TEXTS

1. **Creation.** *"In the beginning God created the heavens and the earth."* **1:1.**

2. **Image of God.** *"Then God said, 'Let us make man in our image.'"* **1:26.**

3. **Voice in the Garden.** *"The Lord God called to the man, and said to him, 'Where are you?'"* **3:9.** (See *The Urantia Book* p. 842-3.)

4. **The curse.** *"In the sweat of your face you shall eat bread."* **3:19.**

5. **Brother's keeper.** *"Then the Lord said to Cain, 'Where is Abel your brother?' He said, 'I do not know; am I my brother's keeper?'"* **4:9.**

6. **Enoch's translation.** *"Enoch walked with God; and he was not, for God took him."* **5:24.**

7. **The Nephilim.** *"The Nephilim were on the earth in those days... when the sons of God came in to the daughters of men."* **6:4.**

8. **The rainbow.** *"I set my bow in the cloud, and it shall be a sign... never again... a flood to destroy all flesh."* **9:13,15.**

9. **Confusion of language.** *"Let us go down, and there confuse their language, that they may not understand one another's speech."* **11:7.**

10. **Melchizedek and Abraham.** *"After his return from the defeat of Chedor-laomer...Melchizedek king of Salem brought out bread and wine...and Abraham gave him a tenth of everything."* **14:17-20.** (See *The Urantia Book* p. 1020.)

11. **Abraham's faith**. *"And he believed the Lord; and he reckoned it to him as righteousness."* **15:6**.

12. **Circumcision**. *"You shall be circumcised in the flesh of your foreskins, and it shall be a sign of the covenant."* **17:11**.

13. **The pillar of salt**. *"But Lot's wife…looked back, and she became a pillar of salt."* **19:26**.

14. **Jacob's ladder**. *"And he dreamed that there was a ladder set upon the earth, and the top of it reached to heaven; and behold, the angels of God were ascending and descending on it!"* **28:12**.

15. **Mizpah**. *"Therefore he named…the pillar Mizpah, for he said, 'The Lord watch between you and me, when we are absent one from the other.'"* **31:49**.

16. **Joseph in Egypt**. *"Joseph was governor…and Joseph's brothers came, and bowed themselves before him."* **42:6**.

# Exodus

## I. OUTLINE—BRIEF

## II. OUTLINE—COMPLETE

## III. PURPOSE

1. Exodus means to the Old Testament what the Gospels mean to the New Testament.

2. To tell the story of Israel's departure from Egypt.

3. To reveal the power and purpose of Yahweh in the deliverance of his "chosen people."

4. To narrate the organization of the "multitude" into a social and religious community.

## IV. AUTHORSHIP

1. Moses did not write Exodus. There were several authors and many editors, but as persons they are unknown.

2.  In addition to our old friends **J**, **E**, and **P**, we have a new contributor, **D**—representing the Deuteronomic cult.

## V. HISTORY OF THE SOURCES

1.  The book grows out of a wealth of well preserved oral traditions.

2.  While both **J** and **E** run along throughout Exodus, they do a much better job of tying together the two narratives.

3.  **J** and **E** cannot be as easily separated in Exodus as they were in Genesis.

4.  The **E** document introduces Elohim in **3:5** and continues to use it throughout the book.

5.  To **J** the holy mountain is Sinai; to **E** it is Horeb.

6.  **E** calls Moses' father-in-law Jethro; **J** does not give his name in Exodus, but elsewhere calls him Hobab.

7.  The lines separating **J**, **E**, and **P** are most clearly shown in the narration of the plagues.

    A.  **J** sends the plagues directly from God—though natural causes may play a part. Moses simply announces them. **J** also tells about the "east wind" at the Red Sea.

    B.  **E** exalts Moses—and his wonder rod. The Egyptians recognize Moses as a great leader.

    C.  **P** gives high honors to Aaron—the priesthood.

    D.  The Deuteronomic notes are not numerous.

8.  Exodus's redactor did a good job in the conflation of the document.

## VI. EXODUS AS A HISTORY OF ISRAEL

1.  All authorities today accept Moses as a historic personality, regardless of any and all myths associated with his career.

2.  The history of Egypt contains no record of the Hebrew exodus.

3.  **J** begins his story with Moses killing the Egyptian overseer. **E** begins with the birth of Moses.

4.  **J** says the Hebrews were "cattle breeders"; **E** makes them slaves or "pensioners."

5.  **E** makes much of the miraculous power of Moses' rod; **J** blames everything on Pharaoh's "hardening his heart."

6.  **P** is the only one telling the story of the tabernacle.

7. There is doubt about the Pharaoh of the exodus. Some think it was Rameses II, but it was most likely Seti I—the new king "who did not know Joseph."

8. **J** and **P** call the mountain *Sinai*. **E** and **D** call it *Horeb*.

**Note:** In general, Bible scholars are inclined to think the two names may possibly refer to the same mountain.

9. It is interesting to note that in the early Hebrew writings God is never spoken of as Father.

## VII. THE PLAGUES OF EGYPT

1. The plagues were *"God's great act of judgment."* **7:4**. This is the view of **P**.

2. The different strands sort out as follows:

   A. **J** narrates seven—the fourth and fifth are wholly his.

   B. **P** is present in five accounts, the third and sixth are wholly his. The first illustrates **P**'s tendency to make it a real calamity.

   C. Five are from **E** in part or in whole. The ninth is probably wholly his.

3. In **P** God always gives Moses the command: *"Say to Aaron."* **7:19–8:5**. Aaron then uses the rod.

4. In **J** Moses goes alone before Pharaoh. His demand: *"Let my people go, that they may serve me."*

5. In **E** Moses uses the rod. He ends a plague with: *"and he did not let the children of Israel go."*

6. These plagues may be symbolic rather than historic. Some of these conditions could have arisen from natural causes.

## VIII. THE KENITES

1. They were a religious clan belonging to the Midianites. Jethro was their high priest.

2. They had a high civilization—varied vocations—metal workers, etc. They also had a well developed religion.

3. For the whole story of the Kenites see *The Urantia Book* p. 1056.

4. Moses had a good Egyptian education before he joined up with the Kenites. See *The Urantia Book*, p. 1055. He knew the *"wisdom of the Egyptians."* **Acts 7:22**.

5. The priest Jethro was also known as Reuel. **2:18**.

6. Moses married Jethro's daughter, Zipporah, and had two sons. **18:3**.

7. It was while tending Jethro's flocks that Moses had his experience of the "burning bush" and received Yahweh's commission to lead Israel out of bondage.

8. Moses was a stammerer and Aaron was assigned to serve as his spokesman.

9. It was Moses' shepherd's staff (rod) that became the wonder worker in Egypt.

10. Miriam, Moses' sister, criticized him for marrying an Ethiopian (Cushite).

## IX. THE SINAI COVENANT

1. As Yahweh made a personal covenant with Abraham, so he now renews that covenant with the "children of Abraham" at Sinai.

2. They are not sure about the exact location of Sinai. Three different mountains have been designated. The majority opinion locates it near the old Egyptian copper mines—where Count Tischendorf found the manuscript of Codex Sinaiticus in 1844 at the monastery of St. Catherine. This mount is about 5,000 feet above sea level. The region abounds with peaks 8,000 feet above sea level.

3. It was here at Sinai that the polyglot horde of Israel became a nation, a church, a partially civilized community.

4. The wilderness problem is: How could they spend so much time at Sinai and be camped so long at Kadesh?

5. Here Moses got the Ten Commandments. Here they fell to worshipping the "golden calf," and Moses, after breaking the tablet, had to get a second tablet.

6. Here they got the "ethical" Ten Commandments (**Ex. 20:1-17**) to take the place of their former "ritual" Ten Commandments (**34:10-26**).

7. The vast body of laws given at Sinai is a part of the Sinai covenant.

8. There is a remote resemblance between the Hebrew Code and the Code of Hammurabi. In all probability both the Hebrew and the Hammurabi codes were founded on older Assyrian or Hittite codes.

9. Associated with Sinai are the stories of the manna and the quails, water from the rock, the war with Amalek, and the high point of Moses on the mountain.

## X. SIGNIFICANCE OF THE TABERNACLE

1.   The latter part of Exodus is devoted to directions for making and operating the tabernacle.

2.   At Shiloh and in Solomon's Temple, the ark had been the symbol of God's presence.

3.   This whole story about the tabernacle seems to have originated with the priests during the exile.

4.   It is a singular fact that the tabernacle is not mentioned in the *The Urantia Book*.

5.   The whole plan of the tabernacle is based on Solomon's Temple. Of course, it has been both the Hebrew and Christian view that Solomon's Temple was built after the plan of the olden tabernacle.

6.   The priests did make one great change. They transferred the significance of the creation from the ark with its law and symbols of magic to the "mercy seat" above the ark.

7.   Thus the worship was directed away from "legalism and works" to "faith and trust" in divine love and mercy.

8.   This led to the "Day of Atonement" as the apex of the Jewish system of worship.

9.   The concept of God was growing—Yahweh was becoming a transcendent Deity.

10.   The **P** writers wanted to associate the covenant with Abraham rather than with Moses and Sinai, but the rabbis would not have it. And the rabbis won.

11.   Usually, the struggle has been between the priests and the prophets.

12.   Exodus is not a history. Its concern is not so much with the past as with the *present*.

13.   The real purpose: To make Israel *"a kingdom of priests and a holy nation."* **19:6.**

14.   Exodus is one of the most complicated books in the Bible. When you read Exodus you are listening to many voices telling many stories at different times. You try to make it all meaningful as you do your best to "put it together."

15.   Learn how to find the nuggets in Exodus—not just the mistakes and complications.

16.   The book may say that "the Lord hardened Pharaoh's heart," but we know that later on they arrived at superior ideas of Deity—and the prophets presented a majestic and transcendent Father in heaven.

## XI. SELECTED TEXTS

1. **The new king**. *"Now there arose a new king over Egypt, who did not know Joseph."* **1:8**.

2. **Finding Moses**. *"Now the daughter of Pharaoh came down to bathe at the river...She saw the basket among the reeds...When she opened it she saw the child."* **2:5,6**.

3. **With Jethro**. *"And Moses was content to dwell with the man, and he gave Moses his daughter Zipporah."* **2:21**.

4. **The burning bush**. *"And the angel of the Lord appeared to him in a flame of fire out of the midst of a bush; and he looked, and lo, the bush was burning, yet it was not consumed."* **3:2**.

5. **I AM**. *"God said to Moses, 'I AM WHO I AM.'"* **3:14**.

6. **Moses' stammering**. *"But Moses said...'I am not eloquent...I am slow of speech.'"* **4:10**.

7. **Before Pharaoh**. *"Moses and Aaron went to Pharaoh and said, 'Thus says the Lord, the God of Israel, "Let my people go, that they may hold a feast to me in the wilderness."'"* **5:1**.

8. **Hardening Pharaoh's heart**. *"'But I will harden Pharaoh's heart... Pharaoh will not listen to you.'"* **7:3**.

9. **Moses' reputation**. *"The man Moses was very great in the land of Egypt."* **11:3**.

10. **The Passover**. *"'It is the Lord's passover. For I will pass through the land of Egypt that night, and I will smite all the first-born in the land.'"* **12:11,12**.

11. **Consecration of first-born**. *"The Lord said to Moses, 'Consecrate to me all the first-born...both of man and of beast.'"* **13:1**.

12. **The pillar of cloud**. *"The pillar of cloud by day and the pillar of fire by night did not depart from before the people."* **13:22**.

13. **The salvation of the Lord**. *"And Moses said to the people, 'Fear not, stand firm, and see the salvation of the Lord...for the Egyptians whom you see today, you shall never see again.'"* **14:13**.

14. **Drying up the Red Sea**. *"Then Moses stretched out his hand over the sea; and the Lord drove the sea back by a strong east wind all night, and made the sea dry land."* **14:21**.

15. **The manna**. *"Then the Lord said to Moses, 'Behold, I will rain bread from heaven for you; and the people shall go out and gather a day's portion every day.'"* **16:4**.

16. **Water from the rock.** *"Behold, I will stand before you there on the rock at Horeb; and you shall strike the rock, and water shall come out of it, that the people may drink."* **17:6.**

17. **The Ten Commandments.** *"Then God spoke all these words saying, 'I am the Lord your God...You shall have no other gods before me.'"* **20:1-3.**

18. **Moses gets the law.** *"The Lord said to Moses, 'Come up to me on the mountain, and wait there; and I will give you the tables of stone, with the law and the commandment.'"* **24:12.**

19. **Moses on the mountain.** *"And Moses entered the cloud, and went up on the mountain. And Moses was on the mountain forty days and forty nights."* **24:18.**

20. **The tabernacle.** *"And let them make me a sanctuary, that I may dwell in their midst."* **25:8.**

21. **The priesthood.** *"'And you shall put them upon Aaron your brother, and upon his sons with him, and shall anoint them and ordain them and consecrate them that they may serve me as priests.'"* **28:41.**

22. **God repents.** *"And the Lord repented of the evil which he thought to do to his people."* **32:14.**

23. **The tent of meeting.** *"Now Moses used to take the tent and pitch it outside the camp...and he called it the tent of meeting."* **33:7.**

24. **Finished tabernacle.** *"Thus all the work of the tabernacle of the tent of meeting was finished; and the people of Israel had done according to all that the Lord had commanded."* **39:32.**

25. **The pillar of fire.** *"Throughout all their journeys the cloud of the Lord was upon the tabernacle by day, and fire was in it by night, in the sight of all the house of Israel."* **40:38.**

# LEVITICUS

## I. OUTLINE—BRIEF

## II. OUTLINE—COMPLETE

## III. PURPOSE

Leviticus is the Hebrew law book—the manual of ritual and the code of regulations for the daily living of the Israelites.

## IV. AUTHORSHIP

1. Moses did not write Leviticus.

2. Leviticus is an exclusive **P** document. It was written by the Hebrew priests during the exile or soon thereafter. 500-450 B.C.

## V. RELIGIOUS SIGNIFICANCE OF LEVITICUS

1. Of all the books of the Bible, Leviticus would be of least interest to the average reader.

2. Leviticus "grew" from the days of Moses to the exile. Such a book is not written at one time by any one person. Like all law books, it accumulates over long periods of time.

3. The key word of the book is "holiness."

4. There is very little narrative in the book—it does tell about a blasphemer's being stoned to death.

5. And it does promulgate the high command: "Love your neighbor as yourself."

6. That Leviticus represents long periods of time is shown by many contradictions, such as the year beginning in the autumn in one place, and at spring time in another.

7.  In Israel, as in all nations, common law is a growth over centuries.

8.  It is interesting to note that five fragments of Leviticus were found among one batch of Dead Sea scrolls.

9.  The whole Mosaic system was an effort to substitute animal sacrifice for human sacrifice.

10. It may be easy to understand why a book like Leviticus should be in a Jewish Bible, but why should it be in a Christian Bible? The answer is simple—the early Christians adopted the whole Old Testament—Leviticus and all.

11. A Protestant would have much the same feeling if he would try to make sense out of the "Pontifical Ceremonies"—the handbook of Roman Catholic ceremonial usages.

12. The bringing of the "first fruits" in a basket to the priest was a profound religious experience to a devout Israelite. We should try to see these things as they saw and felt them.

13. The ceremony of the Day of Atonement may seem like a primitive affair to us. But view it as described in the Apocrypha (**Ecclus.[Sirach] 50:5-21**) and you will learn how a pious Jew was moved to the depths of his soul.

14. You can also get something of the feelings of the Hebrew worshiper by reading some of the **Psalms**, for example, **42, 84**, and **150**.

15. Then there is the value of really knowing just how the olden Hebrews practiced their religion.

16. Don't overlook the symbolic and dramatic aspects.

## VI. THE OFFERINGS

1.  **Cereal offering.** This type of offering is associated with Melchizedek— it even goes back to the days of Cain and Abel. Also known as the "meat" offering, and the "meal" offering. Usually accompanied by either a trespass or burnt offering. It was made with oil, honey, and salt. Offered uncooked with incense; cooked, without incense. In some ways it was like a "remembrance" supper.

2.  **Peace offering.** This was the "thanks" offering. Rendered as in the fulfillment of a vow. Often followed by a fellowship meal. It was the most common type of sacrifice.

3.  **Sin offering.** This was the general sacrifice for sinfulness—not necessarily conscious sin. Not associated with a common meal. Destroyed outside the camp.

4.  **Trespass offering.** This sacrifice had more to do with social offenses and property rights, broken pledges, guilt feelings, "conscience complex."

5.  **Burnt offering.** Offered every day by the priest for all Israel. The fire for the burnt offering was never permitted to go out. It was supposed to have originally been "kindled by the Lord."

6.  **The Day of Atonement.** First, the high priest and his fellow priests must make atonement for themselves. Then both sin and burnt offerings for the people were performed. Then comes the casting of lots to determine the goat for Israel and the "scapegoat" or the goat of Azazel—to carry the sins of Israel out into the wilderness.

    Azazel is mentioned in the book of Enoch as the "leader of evil spirits."

## VII. LEVITICUS AND THE NEW TESTAMENT

1.  The passage most often quoted by Jesus was **19:18**. *"You shall love your neighbor as yourself."* Five times quoted by Jesus and two times by Paul.

2.  Jesus understood and respected Old Testament laws. He told the leper whom he healed to go and show himself to the priests "as Moses had appointed."

3.  Said Jesus: *"If you would enter life, keep the commandments."* **Matt. 19:17**.

4.  The book of Hebrews pays most attention to rituals, pointing out that these things are "types" of what was fulfilled in Christ.

5.  Paul uses the concept of the temple of God (**26:12**) as basis for calling man's body *"a living temple."* **2 Cor. 6:16**.

6.  If you want to get good out of Leviticus, try to see it as the devout Jew saw it when he engaged in worship.

7.  Always remember: The better you understand the Old Testament, the better you can understand the New Testament.

## VIII. SELECTED TEXTS

1.  **Pleasing odor to the Lord.** *"'And the priest shall take from the cereal offering its memorial portion and burn this on the altar...a pleasing odor to the Lord.'"* **2:9**.

2.  **Divine fire.** *"And the fire came forth from before the Lord and consumed the burnt offering."* **9:24**.

3.  **Animal foods.** *"'These are the living things which you may eat...Whatever parts the hoof and is cloven-footed and chews the cud, among the animals, you may eat.'"* **11:2,3**.

4. **Swine.** *"'The swine, because it parts the hoof and is cloven-footed but does not chew the cud, is unclean to you.'"***11:7.**

5. **Sea food.** *"These you may eat, of all that are in the waters. Everything... that has fins and scales...you may eat.'"* **11:9.**

6. **The insects.** *"'Among the winged insects that go on all fours you may eat those which have legs above their feet...the locust... cricket... and the grasshopper.'"***11:20-22.**

7. **Other unclean animals.** *"'These are unclean to you... the weasel, the mouse, the great lizard... the gecko, the land crocodile, the lizard, the sand lizard, and the chameleon.'"***11:29,30.**

8. **Holiness.** *"'You shall therefore be holy, for I am holy.'"* **11:45.**

9. **Childbirth.** *"'If a woman... bears a male child, then she shall be unclean seven days... She shall continue for thirty-three days...If she bears a female child, then she shall be unclean two weeks... and continue... for sixty-six days.'"* **12:2-5.**

10. **Diagnosing leprosy.** *"'The priest shall make an examination, and if there is a white swelling...it is a chronic leprosy.'"***13:9-11.**

11. **Unclean houses.** *"If the disease breaks out again in the house, after he has taken out of the stones and scraped the house and plastered it...it is a malignant leprosy in the house; it is unclean. And he shall break down the house...and he shall carry them forth out of the city.'"***14:43-45.**

12. **Discharges.** *"'When any man has a discharge from his body, his discharge is unclean... If a woman has a discharge of blood for many days, not at the time of her impurity... she shall be unclean.'"***15:2,25.**

13. **The atonement.** *"'And Aaron shall lay both his hands upon the head of the live goat, and confess over him all the iniquities of the people of Israel, and all their transgressions, all their sins; and he shall put them upon the head of the goat, and send him away in the wilderness.'"***16:21.**

14. **Eating blood.** *"'If any man...eats any blood, I will set my face against that person.'"***17:10.**

15. **Homosexuality.** *"'You shall not lie with a male as with a woman; it is an abomination.'"***18:22.**

16. **Love your neighbor as yourself.** *"'You shall not take vengeance or bear any grudge against the sons of your own people, but you shall love your neighbor as yourself.'"***19:18.**

17. **Spiritualism.** *"'If a person turns to mediums and wizards, playing the harlot after them, I will set my face against that person, and will cut him off from among his people.'"***20:6.**

18. **Mediums.** *"'A man or a woman who is a medium or a wizard shall be put to death; they shall be stoned with stones.'"* **20:27**.

19. **Blasphemy.** *"'He who blasphemes the name of the Lord shall be put to death; all the congregation shall stone him.'"* **24:16**.

# Numbers

## I. OUTLINE—BRIEF

## II. OUTLINE—COMPLETE

## III. AUTHORSHIP

1. Moses was not the author. He is usually spoken of in the third person.

2. He would not call himself the meekest man on earth. 12:3.

3. Three quarters of the book is by **P**, with contributions by **J** and **E**. But little of **D** is present.

## IV. CONTENTS

1. Part I at Sinai occupies 19 days.

2. Part II—Paran and wilderness, 38 years.

3. Part III-Moab, five months.

4. One poem comes from a lost book—"The Word of Yahweh."

5. Called "Numbers" because of the census. In Hebrew Bibles the book is called "The Wilderness."

## V. HISTORICAL VALUE

1. The book is a wonderful portrait of human nature—the good and the bad. At one point they really wanted to *"choose a captain, and go back to Egypt."* **(14:4)**

2. Don't make too much out of historical fact. What shall it profit a man to know all the facts, but miss the meaning?

3. The chronological problem:

    A. At Sinai. It would require years and years to do all that was done at Sinai—not 19 days—to build the tabernacle and to organize the social and religious life of the Israelites.

    B. At Kadesh. There is much evidence that the Israelites camped at Kadesh for many years—not just five months.

    C. The thirty-eight years. The wilderness wanderings for 38 years are difficult to understand. Little or nothing is narrated to account for this long period.

4. And all of this leads to the theory that there were two groups of Israelites:

    A. The Sinai group, camped for years at Sinai, and going through Moab, to enter Canaan over the Jordan and by way of Jericho under Moses and Joshua.

    B. The Kadesh group, camped for many years at Kadesh, and entering Canaan from the south—and doing so by gradual and peaceful penetration.

5. While the Jews claimed that Yahweh was God of Israel, they also recognized that Chemosh was the god of Moab. **(21:29)**

6. At first Moses would go into "the tent of meeting" and talk with Yahweh. Later on, Yahweh was a remote and holy Deity. Only the high priest, once a year, could come near him in the Most Holy Place. **(3:10)**

7. Numbers, in a way, is an addition to Exodus—completes the story of deliverance of Israel from the Egyptian bondage.

## VI. SELECTED TEXTS

1. **Test for marital fidelity**. *"And the priest shall take holy water...and some of the dust that is on the floor of the tabernacle and put it into the water...May this water...make your body swell and your thigh fall away...And when he has made her drink the water, then, if she has defiled herself and has acted unfaithfully against her husband, the water that brings the curse shall enter into her and cause bitter pain, and her body shall swell...But if the woman has not defiled herself...Then she shall be free."* **5:16,22,27,28**.

2. **The benediction**. *"The Lord bless you and keep you: The Lord make his face to shine upon you, and be gracious to you: The Lord lift up his countenance upon you, and give you peace."* **6:24-26**.

3. **The guiding ark**. *"And the ark of the covenant of the Lord went before them three days' journey, to seek out a resting place for them. And the cloud of the Lord was over them by day, whenever they set out from the camp."* **10:33,34**.

4.  **The quails.** *"'O that we had meat to eat:We remember the fish we ate in Egypt for nothing, the cucumbers, the melons, the leeks, the onions, and the garlic; but now...there is nothing at all but this manna."* **11:4-6.**

    *"And there went forth a wind from the Lord, and it brought quails from the sea...And the people rose all that day, and all night, and all the next day, and gathered the quails...And the Lord smote the people with a very great plague."* **2:31-33.**

5.  **Miriam's leprosy.** *"Miriam and Aaron spoke against Moses because of the Cushite woman whom he had married...And the Lord heard it. Now the man Moses was very meek."* **12:1-3.**

    *"And the anger of the Lord was kindled against them...and when the cloud removed from over the tent, behold, Miriam was leprous, as white as snow."* **12:9,10.**

6.  **Spying out the land.** *"So they went up and spied out the land...They...cut down...a branch with a single cluster of grapes, and they carried it on a pole between two of them...At the end of forty days they returned from spying out the land."* **13:21,23,25.**

    *"But Caleb...said, 'Let us go up at once, and occupy it; for we are well able to overcome it.' Then the men who had gone up with him said, 'We are not able to go up against the people...There we saw the Nephilim... and we seemed to ourselves like grasshoppers.'"* **13:30,31,33.**

7.  **Milk and honey.** *"'If the Lord delights in us, he will bring us into...a land which flows with milk and honey.'"* **14:8.**

8.  **Only Caleb and Joshua see Canaan.** *"Not one shall come into the land... except Caleb...and Joshua."* **14:30.**

9.  **Sabbath-breaking.** *"They found a man gathering sticks on the sabbath day... And the Lord said to Moses, 'The man shall be put to death.'"* **15:32,35.**

10. **Penalty of rebellion.** *"And the Lord said...'Get away from about the dwelling of Korah, Dathan, and Abiram'...And as he finished speaking...the earth opened its mouth and swallowed them up."* **16:23,24,31.**

11. **Aaron's rod.** *"The rod of Aaron...had sprouted and put forth buds, and produced blossoms, and it bore ripe almonds."* **17:8.**

12. **Tithes.** *"'To the Levites I have given every tithe in Israel for an inherit- ance.'"* **18:21.**

13. **Balaam's ass talks**. *"Then the Lord opened the mouth of the ass, and she said to Balaam, "What have I done to you, that you have struck me these three times?'...Then the Lord opened the eyes of Balaam, and he saw the angel of the Lord standing in the way, with his drawn sword in his hand."* **22:28,31**.

14. **Brutal slaughter**. *"'Kill every male among the little ones, and kill every woman who has known man by lying with him. But all the young girls who have not known man by lying with him, keep alive for yourselves.'"* **31:17,18**.

# Deuteronomy

## I. OUTLINE—BRIEF

## II. OUTLINE—COMPLETE

## III. AUTHORSHIP

1. The original core of the book was by **J** and **E.**

2. The **D** contribution. The author of the book as we have it today was **D**, an educated and eloquent member of the Deuteronomic cult, which sought to harmonize and co-ordinate the teachings of the priests and the prophets.

3. **P.** The overall conflation of the book was by the exile priests, but their contribution was of minor importance.

## IV. CHARACTER AND SIGNIFICANCE

1. The addresses of Moses are no doubt based on authentic traditions.

2. This book is a declaration of the faith of Israel. It is unique among all the books of the Old Testament.

3. Deuteronomy is a book of sober, earnest, and moving eloquence. Nothing in Jewish literature can compare with it, except the writings of the Second Isaiah.

4. In this book are found those positive forms for the commandments as stated by Jesus: *"You shall love the Lord your God with all your heart."* **6:5.**

5. Deuteronomy possesses an evangelical tone that resembles the gospel ring of the New Testament.

6. Religion in this book far transcends the legalistic ceremonials of Exodus and Leviticus.

7. Deuteronomy is quoted 83 times in the New Testament and alluded to many times. Only six New Testament books fail to mention Deuteronomy.

8. Deuteronomy may be a "Law book" but it is also a book of "preaching." The **D** author was a "Preaching lawyer."

9. Deuteronomy is the first Bible book that teaches—*"We Love God because he first loved us."*

10. It deals with both cultic and economic affairs—but with a theologic background.

11. Egypt taught a perfect creation and that Pharaoh was an incarnate God. Mesopotamia taught a prolonged and violent creation, and the king as a mortal ruler chosen by God.

12. Israel taught a new concept—a perfected creation by a personal God, who also chose his people and their rulers.

13. Israel taught that God started man out with a monogamous family. The doctrine of the "fall of man" was unique in Jewish philosophy.

14. Deuteronomy first clearly presents Yahweh as a redeemer—a savior. It is the Old Testament gospel.

## V. DEUTERONOMY IN THE NEW TESTAMENT

| *JESUS* | *NEW TESTAMENT WRITERS* |
|---|---|
| Matt. 4:4. Deut. 8:3 | Acts 3:22. Deut. 18:15,18. |
| Matt. 4:7. Deut. 6:16. | 1 Cor. 9:9. Deut. 25:4. |
| Matt. 4:10. Deut. 6:13. | 2 Cor. 13:1. Deut. 19:15. |
| Matt. 5:31. Deut. 24:1. | Gal. 3:13. Deut. 21:23. |
| Mark. 12:30. Deut. 6:5. | Rom. 10:6-8. Deut. 30:12,14. |

## VI. STRUCTURE AND STYLE

1. The second sermon is the core of the book. The first and third addresses, together with the appendices, were added later.

2. Moses is the expounder. *"The Lord spoke to Moses, saying, 'Speak to the children of Israel.'"* In only one case does God speak directly to Aaron.

3. Deuteronomy covers the whole life of Israel—and ends up with the blessings and curses—depending on obedience or disobedience.

4. Deuteronomy is the best organized of all the Old Testament writings. It represents the over-all editorship of *one man*.

5. Of all Old Testament books Deuteronomy presents a homogeneity of style. It is a new style of flowing and impressive oratory.

6. There is no end of well balanced clauses, sustained rhythm. But it is never monotonous or prolix.

7. Among characteristic words or expressions, attention may be called to:

    A. **Love**. God's concern for his people. Love as used by Hosea and in the Psalms.

    B. "Hear, O Israel."

    C. "The Lord, the God of your fathers."

    D. "To go after other gods."

    E. "To hearken to the voice of the Lord."

    F. "To walk in God's ways."

    G. "That it may be well with thee."

H. "Which I command thee this day."

I. "That the Lord may bless thee."

J. Uses Horeb instead of Sinai.

8. In some places Deuteronomy sounds like the style of Jeremiah.

9. In many ways the style of Deuteronomy is more like that of **E** than of **J**.

## VII. THE REFORMS OF KING JOSIAH

1. In **2 Kings 22 and 23** we learn that when King Josiah was repairing the temple his workmen found a "book of the law." This was in 621 B.C.

2. This new-found "book of the law" was some portion of the present book of Deuteronomy.

3. Josiah used this new-found book as the basis of his reforms, destroying all places of sacrifice outside of Jerusalem. There were many sites of paganism throughout Palestine.

4. Many priests and Levites were left stranded. A few went to Jerusalem.

5. The king had Deuteronomy read to the people—believing it to be the work of Moses.

6. This was about the time of the death of Asshurbanipal—Assyria was passing, Egypt was weak, and Josiah was able to stop paying tribute and assert his independence.

7. Josiah destroyed the idols and overthrew the altars. But his reforms were not long-lasting.

8. About one hundred years before Josiah's reforms, Hezekiah had carried out similar reforms.

9. These were the times when Jews all over Palestine were granted permission to slaughter animals for food, without the services of the Levites at the altars.

10. Up to this time, all animals were first offered as sacrifices, and then portions eaten for food.

11. Deuteronomy was something new in sacred writings. It exalted the priesthood and upheld the temple in Jerusalem as the *only* place for sacrificial worship. At the same time it rang with the tone of the prophets—albeit, Moses was its central figure.

## VIII.THEOLOGY

1. The primary demand of Deuteronomy is Loyalty to Yahweh.

2. *"The Lord is God; there is no other besides him."* **4:35.**

3. Never before did a God take a *"nation for himself."* **4:32-34.**

4. Yahweh is not only a gracious and loving God—but also a *jealous* God.

5. The land belonged to God. They must obey God "that their days may be long in the land."

6. The reasons for choosing Israel were *mysterious*—only that Yahweh had promised the Patriarchs.

7. The second major thought in Deuteronomy is that God has directed the destinies of Israel. *"When they did wrong, he punished them. When they did right, he delivered them."*

8. God made use of even secular nations as his agents in dealing with Israel.

9. Throughout Deuteronomy we are taught that "God directs history."

10. Deuteronomy teaches us that war—when instigated and directed by Yahweh— is a *holy war.*

11. There is a somber and terrible earnestness about the book of Deuteronomy.

12. There is a humanitarian aspect to many of the social laws of Deuteronomy. Revenge was ruled out.

13. The greatest of all sins was *idolatry.* The worship of other gods destroyed the concept of Israel as "a peculiar people."

## IX. SELECTED TEXTS

1. **Total killings**. *"'We captured all his cities…and utterly destroyed every city, men, women, and children.'"* **2:34.**

2. **Moses views the land**. *"'Go up to the top of Pisgah and lift up your eyes… and behold it…for you shall not go over this Jordan.'"* **3:27.**

3. **Finding God**. *"'You will seek the Lord your God, and you will find him, if you search after him with all your heart and with all your soul.'"* **4:29.**

4. **The Ten Commandments. 5:6-21.**

5. **The great commandment**. *"'You shall love the Lord your God with all your heart, and with all your soul, and with all your might.'"* **6:5.**

6. **The chosen people**. *"'You are a people holy to the Lord your God; the Lord your God has chosen you.'"* **7:6.**

7. **Blessing and curse.** *"'I set before you this day a blessing and a curse: the blessing, if you obey the commandments...and the curse, if you do not obey the commandments.'"* **11:26-28.**

8. **Eating blood.** *"'You shall not eat the blood; you shall pour it out upon the earth like water.'"* **12:16.**

9. **False prophets.** *"'If a prophet arises among you...and gives you a sign... and the sign...comes to pass, and if he says, "Let us go after other gods" ...you shall not listen to the words of that prophet.'"* **13:1-3.**

10. **Seven-year release.** *"'Every seven years you shall grant a release...Every creditor shall release what he has lent his neighbor.'"* **15:1,2.**

11. **The poor.** *"'The poor will never cease out of the land; therefore...you shall open wide your hand to your brother, to the needy, and to the poor.'"* **15:11.**

12. **Newlyweds.** *"'When a man is newly married, he shall not go out with the army or be charged with any business; he shall be free at home one year, to be happy with his wife.'"* **24:5.**

13. **Muzzling the ox.** *"'You shall not muzzle an ox when it treads out the grain.'"* **25:4.**

14. **Secret things.** *"'The secret things belong to the Lord our God; but the things that are revealed belong to us and to our children.'"* **29:29.**

15. **Joshua's commission.** *"The Lord commissioned Joshua...and said, 'Be strong and of good courage; for you shall bring the children of Israel into the land which I swore to give them: I will be with you.'"* **31:23.**

16. **Primitive ideas.** *"'I...am he, and there is no god beside me; I kill and I make alive; I wound and I heal; and there is none that can deliver out of my hand.'"* **32:39.**

# JOSHUA

## I. OUTLINE—BRIEF

## II. OUTLINE—COMPLETE

# III. AUTHORSHIP

1. When it comes to the determination of authorship, Joshua is the most difficult and complex of all the books of the Old Testament.

2. **J, E, D,** and **P** can all be traced through the book, but **D** is predominant.

3. The **P** contributions appear most in the last half of the book.

4. Joshua, a tribal hero of Ephraim, was magnified into the leader of all Israel and author of this book.

5. Joshua is a Deuteronomic book. This same Deuteronomic style runs through Joshua, Judges, Samuel, and Kings.

6. It would seem to be the work of one individual, not the production of a group.

# IV. HISTORICAL ASPECTS

1. Joshua takes up the history of Israel on the east bank of the Jordan where Numbers left them.

2. Archaeology has lent much evidence to prove the correctness of Joshua. These excavations are at Jericho, Bethel, Lachish, and Debir.

3. According to Joshua, the Israelites cross the Jordan, take Jericho, and then cut a swath right through the middle of Palestine. Then they subdue the south and then the north.

4. But, in other places, the record confirms the fact that this conquest was not complete. Jerusalem was not conquered until the times of David. (See **Judges 1.**)

5. Excavations show that many Canaanite cities suffered two or even three total destructions.

# V. THE RELIGIOUS MESSAGE

1. From a religious standpoint, Joshua represents the story of God's dealings with his people.

2. The authors use the medium of history to hammer home their points.

3. When we face the religious aspects of Joshua our problem is: How can you reconcile Yahweh's holy wars—injunction to destroy all men, women, and children—with the ethical teachings of the Old Testament and the teachings of Jesus Christ?

4.   Yahweh claims dedicated obedience, because of the following:

A.   His covenant with Abraham.

B.   He delivered them from Egyptian slavery.

C.   He led them into the promised land.

5.   The New Testament analogue is found in **1 Peter I:4**. *"An inheritance which is imperishable, undefiled, and unfading."*

(This book formed a part of a greater whole which embraced the Deuteronomic narratives extending from the times of the conquest to the kingdom.)

## VI. SELECTED TEXTS

1.   **Joshua's mandate**. *"'As I was with Moses, so I will be with you; I will not fail you or forsake you. Be strong and of good courage.'"* **1:5,6.**

2.   **Spying out Jericho**. *"'Go, view the land, especially Jericho.' And they went, and came into the house of a harlot whose name was Rahab, and lodged there."* **2:1.**

   *"Then she let them down by a rope through the window, for her house was built into the city wall."* **2:15.**

3.   **Passing over Jordan**. *"And while all Israel were passing over on dry ground, the priests who bore the ark...stood on dry ground in the midst of the Jordan, until all the nation finished passing over."* **3:17.**

4.   **Taking Jericho**. *"And the Lord said to Joshua, 'See, I have given into your hand Jericho, with its king and mighty men of valor.'"* **6:2.**

   *"'You shall march around the city...once...for six days.'"* **6:3.**

   *"On the seventh day they...marched around the city...seven times."* **6:15.**

   *"The people raised a great shout, and the wall fell down flat."* **6:20.**

   *"But Rahab the harlot...and all that belonged to her, Joshua saved."* **6:25.**

5.   **The sin of Achan**. *"And they fled before the men of Ai."* **7:4.**

   *"And Achan answered Joshua, 'Of a truth I have sinned...When I saw among the spoil a beautiful mantle...I...took them...they are hidden in the earth inside my tent.'"* **7:20,21.**

6.   **Ambush of Ai**. *"The ambush rose quickly out of their place...they ran and entered the city and took it; and they made haste to set the city on fire."* **8:19.**

7.   **Deception of Gibeon**. *"The inhabitants of Gibeon...acted with cunning, and went...and took worn-out sacks...patched sandals...and worn-out clothes; and all their provisions were dry and moldy."* **9:3-5.**

8.  **The sun stands still.** *"Then spoke Joshua...'Sun, stand thou still at Gibeon'...And the sun stood still, and the moon stayed, until the nation took vengeance on their enemies."* **10:12,13.**

9.  **Victory claims.** *"Then the whole congregation of the people of Israel assembled at Shiloh, and set up the tent of meeting there; the land lay subdued before them."* **18:1.**

10. **Nature of Yahweh.** *"Joshua said to the people, 'You cannot serve the Lord, for he is a holy God; he is a jealous God; he will not forgive your transgressions or your sins.'"* **24:19.**

# JUDGES

## I. OUTLINE—BRIEF

## II. OUTLINE—COMPLETE

## III. AUTHORSHIP

1.  This is one of the five Deuteronomic books, and the second book in the group of the "Former Prophets."

2.  The original book was by **J** and **E**, based on oral tradition and probably the written records of two lost books—"Jashor" and "The Wars of the Lord."

3. All of this was thoroughly rewritten by an able and devout Deuteronomist.

4. There is very little of **P** in the book of Judges as we now have it.

## IV. COMPOSITION AND STRUCTURE

1. The judges were both military leaders and civil rulers.

2. Judges is a collection of a large number of independent stories. It contains the "Song of Deborah," the oldest Old Testament document.

3. The latter part of Judges may seem like pure fiction, but no doubt these tales were based on well-founded oral tradition.

4. Repetitions suggest that some parts were copied from written records. **Judg. 1:10-15** reads almost verbatim like **Josh. 15:13-19. Judg. 1:27,28** just like **Josh. 17:11-13. Judg. 2:6-10** like **Josh. 24:28-31**.

5. Every crisis is introduced by the same formula: *"The people of Israel did evil in the sight of the Lord."*

6. There are five reasons given as to why the Jews did not fully exterminate the Canaanites:

   A. Strong fortifications and military experience.
   B. Willingness of Israel to make alliances with the Canaanites.
   C. Yahweh punishing Israel for their sins.
   D. Testing Israel's faithfulness.
   E. Training Israel in the art of war.

7. Most attention is paid to the six major judges.

8. The period of the judges covers a little over 400 years.

## V. THE JUDGES

Othniel. **3:7-11**
Ehud. **3:20**
Barak and Deborah. **4:5,6**
Gideon. **6:1-8:32**
Abimelech. **8:33-9:57**
Tola. **10:1,2**
Jair. **10:3-5**
Jephthah. **11-12:7**
Ibzan. **12:8-10**
Elon. **12:11,12**
Abdon. **12:13-15**
Samson. **13:24-16:31**

## VI. THE PERIOD OF THE JUDGES

1.  Judges covers the period extending from Joshua leading the Israelites into the promised land to Saul, their first king.

2.  Othniel, first judge to lead Israelite forces against their enemies, brought an end to the Moabite invasion and oppression.

3.  Of Shamgar (a minor judge), we learn only that he repulsed the Philistines.

4.  Deborah and Barak led the tribes in the battle against Sisera on the plain of Esdraelon.

5.  Gideon repulsed the Midianite invasion. This was the first use of camels against Israel.

6.  Abimelech tried to be a king for three years. He was overthrown by an internal rebellion. This was the real beginning of the Yahweh-Baal conflict.

7.  Jephthah repelled the Ammonite oppression.

8.  The tall tales of Samson have to do with the ever-recurrent exploits of the Philistines.

9.  The Song of Deborah illustrates the dynamic zeal of the Yahwist of these times.

10. The ethics and morals of these days were not high. Men were clever and treacherous and murdered on the slightest provocation. Samson visited a harlot.

11. Whatever other attributes Yahweh may have, he is still a *jealous* God.

12. The philosophy of Judges is still the old Jewish concept: obey God and prosper, disobey and suffer.

(The morals of the time can be judged by the story of the concubine's dying of mistreatment and then being cut up and the parts sent abroad in the land as a call to avenge the outrage.)

## VII. SELECTED TEXTS

1.  **Death of Joshua.** *"And Joshua...died at the age of one hundred and ten years."* **2:8.**

2.  **Victory of Deborah and Barak.** *"And the Lord routed Sisera...and his army...and Sisera alighted from his chariot and fled...And the army of Sisera fell by the edge of the sword; not a man was left."* **4:15,16.**

3.  **Song of Deborah. 5:1-31.**

4.  **Victory of Gideon.** *"And the three companies blew the trumpets and broke the jars, holding in their left hands the torches...and they cried, 'A sword for the Lord and for Gideon!'"* **7:20**.

5.  **Jephthah's vow.** *"Jephthah made a vow to the Lord...'If thou wilt give the Ammonites into my hand, then whoever comes forth from the doors of my house to meet me...shall be the Lord's, and I will offer him up for a burnt offering.'"* **11:30,31**.

    *"Then Jephthah came to his home at Mizpah; and behold, his daughter came out to meet him."* **11:34**.

6.  **Samson's defeat.** *"She made him sleep upon her knees; and she called a man, and had him shave off the seven locks of his head...and his strength left him."* **16:19**.

    *"Then he bowed with all his might; and the house fell upon the lords and upon all the people that were in it."* **16:30**.

# Ruth

## I. OUTLINE

## II. AUTHORSHIP

1. Author unknown. Probably some liberal-minded Jew of the post-exilic period.

2. In the Hebrew canon it was placed among the "writings"—along with Song of Solomon, Ecclesiastes, Lamentations, and Esther.

3. Probably written sometime in the 5th Century B.C.

## III. THE PURPOSE

1. Probably included in the Jewish canon of sacred scriptures because the grandson of Ruth's child was David, king of Israel.

2. The main purpose of this story is to counteract the attitude of Ezra and Nehemiah against mixed marriages.

3. It is the ideal "short story." It is a "friendship" story; there is no villain.

4. It is a rare story of friendship between two women—like that of David and Jonathan, among men.

5. It counteracts the popular notion of difficulty in getting along with mothers-in-law.

6. It is a story of irresistible charm.

7. The heroine is brave, determined, loyal, and sagacious.

8. The book exemplifies the teaching of Paul: *"There is neither Jew nor Greek."* **Gal. 3:28.**

## IV. THE STORY OF RUTH

1. Ruth forsakes her people to go with Naomi, who has lost her husband and two sons.

2.   Naomi is welcomed at Bethlehem.

3.   Ruth joins the gleaners to get food.

4.   Naomi sends Ruth to Boaz by night.

5.   The marriage—and Naomi adopts the child.

## V. SELECTED TEXTS

**Ruth and Naomi**. *"But Ruth said… 'Where you go I will go, and where you lodge I will lodge; your people shall be my people, and your God my God.'"* **1:16.**

# SAMUEL

*(Before the Septuagint, First and Second Samuel formed one book.)*

## I. OUTLINE—BRIEF

## II. OUTLINE—COMPLETE
### *1 SAMUEL*

### *2 SAMUEL*

### III. AUTHORSHIP

1.    Samuel did not write the book.

2.    The early book was of dual authorship—**J** and **E**. Note:

    A.    Saul is anointed king privately by Samuel, and twice in public.

    B.    Saul is twice deposed from the throne.

    C.    David is introduced twice to Saul.

    D.    David twice offered a daughter of Saul in marriage.

E.   David twice escapes Saul.

F.   David three times makes a covenant with Jonathan.

G.   Goliath is slain by David and by Elhanan.

3.   The book was thoroughly overhauled and rewritten by **D**.

4.   Samuel is one of the most brilliantly written histories of ancient times— 500 years before Herodotus

5.   **D** and **P** turned Samuel, a village seer, into a "mighty prophet."

6.   Samuel is a masterpiece of history, psychological insight, literary style, and dramatic power.

Note: Field Marshal Allenby, when in Palestine in 1918, examined the battle-field account of Jonathan's attack on the Philistine garrison (**1 Sam. 14:1-23**) and was able to identify the crag *"on the north in front of Michmash, and the other on the south in front of Geba."* He pronounced Jonathan's strategy as sound.

## IV. HISTORICAL VALUE

1.   Evidence of repetition and duplication, not already noted, show that the Deuteronomic redactor failed to iron out these contradictions:

A.   The Ziphite treachery to David is told two times.

B.   Two stories of David's escape from Nob.

C.   Two conflicting accounts of Saul's death.

D.   Two stories of the war against Amalek.

2.   It will be helpful in understanding the rather sudden change in Saul's character to recall that he was a manic-depressive.

3.   There are three types of history:

A.   *Narrative type.* To record a good tale.

B.   *Didactic type.* To treat events as a storehouse for moral teaching.

C.   *Scientific type.* To ascertain the facts.

4.   The types A and B characterize the writing of most Old Testament history.

5.   Samuel may not be accurate history, but it is a good source book.

## V. THEOLOGY

1.   The theology of Samuel is just about as primitive as that of Joshua and Judges. But there is some indication of growth.

2.   Note the following reminders of primitive theology:

A.   Sacred stones. **1 Sam. 7:12.**

B.   Sacred trees. **1 Sam. 14:2.**

C.   Sacred hills. **1 Sam. 10:5.**

D.   Blood revenge. **2 Sam. 3:27.**

E.  The taboo. **1 Sam. 21:4.**

F.  The vow. **1 Sam. 14:24.**

G.  Propitiatory sacrifice. **1 Sam. 26:19.**

H.  Necromancy. **1 Sam. 28.**

3.  It has been suggested that the Semites had a genius for religion but the Jews were specialists.

4.  The Jewish religion had many things in common with all man-made religions.

5.  At first the Jews shared many things with primitive paganism, but they evolved—they experienced growth.

6.  The Hebrews had revelation. There arrived the prophets.

7.  When Saul could not get comfort from the prophets, he went back to necromancy—he consulted with the witch of Endor.

8.  There was a great deal of lottery in Hebrew theology—finding out about the divine will by casting lots.

9.  The early prophets were associated with "ecstatic frenzy." In some ways this was like the dancing dervishes.

10.  Plato regarded all prophets as being afflicted with some sort of "divine madness."

11.  In Jewish religion, the ecstatic trance played the part that "speaking with tongues" played in the early Christian religion.

12.  Paul warned the church at Corinth that there were many more valuable spiritual gifts than "speaking with tongues."

13.  Both Samuel and Nathan were types of "advanced" prophecy. They functioned without either ecstatic frenzy or trance-visions.

14.  On special occasions Samuel had visions, but Nathan did not.

15.  The nations around Israel had their tribal gods:

A.  Chemosh—god of Moab.

B.  Melek—god of Ammon.

C.  Dagon—god of the Philistines.

16.  But unlike these tribal gods, Yahweh continued to grow—evolved into the God of all creation—"King of Kings and Lord of Lords."

17.  Now and then Israel would revert to nationalism, as in the case of Nehemiah and Ezra.

18.  We all have trouble with the ethics of Yahweh, who could order the complete extermination of whole peoples, but that was common practice among Semites.

19. The Hebrews still clung to their olden concepts of Providence—Yahweh, God of history, Lord of life and death. All success is the reward of virtue.

20. The concept of the chosen people—election of Israel—is still predominant. The sons of Eli did not reform because it was "the will of God to kill them."

21. The Hebrew theology is pervaded with the idea of a whole, nation suffering because of the sin of one individual.

22. Later on both Jeremiah and Ezekiel tried to modify this concept of punishing the innocent for the sins of others.

## VI. SELECTED TEXTS
### *1 SAMUEL*

1. **Samuel grows up.** *"Now the boy Samuel continued to grow both in stature and in favor with the Lord and with men."* **2:26.**

2. **Eli hears bad news.** *"'Israel has fled before the Philistines, and there has also been a great slaughter... Your two sons also...are dead, and the ark of God has been captured.'"* **4:17.**

3. **Return of the ark.** *"'Send away the ark of the God of Israel, and let it return to its own place, that it may not slay us and our people.'"* **5:11.**

4. **Clamor for a king.** *"'You are old...now appoint for us a king to govern us like all the nations.'"* **8:5.**

5. **Saul anointed.** *"Then Samuel took a vial of oil and poured it on his head, and kissed him and said, 'Has not the Lord anointed you to be prince over his people Israel?'"* **10:1.**

6. **Obedience vs. sacrifice.** *"'Behold, to obey is better than sacrifice, and to hearken than the fat of rams.'"* **15:22.**

7. **God repents.** *"And the Lord repented that he had made Saul king over Israel."* **15:35.**

8. **God sends evil spirit.** *"The Spirit of the Lord departed from Saul, and an evil spirit from the Lord tormented him."* **16:14.**

9. **David slays Goliath.** *"And David put his hand in his bag and took out a stone, and slung it, and struck the Philistine on his forehead...and he fell on his face to the ground."* **17:49.**

10. **Eating the holy bread.** *"So the priest gave him the holy bread; for there was no bread there but the bread of the Presence."* **21:6.**

11. **The cave of Adullam.** *"David...escaped to the cave of Adullam...and every one who was in distress, and every one who was in debt, and every one who was discontented, gathered to him; and he became captain over them."* **22:1,2.**

12. **Saul consults medium.** *"So Saul disguised himself...and came to the woman by night...and he said, 'Bring up Samuel for me.'"* **28:8,11.**

13. **Saul's suicide.** *"Saul took his own sword, and fell upon it."* **31:4.**

## 2 SAMUEL

14. **David anointed.** *"And the men of Judah came, and there they anointed David king over the house of Judah."* **2:4.**

15. **David made king over Israel.** *"So all the elders of Israel came to the king at Hebron...and they anointed David king over Israel."* **5:3.**

16. **The ark comes to Jerusalem.** *"And they brought in the ark of the Lord, and set it in its place, inside the tent which David had pitched for it."* **6:17.**

17. **You are the man.** *"Nathan said to David, 'You are the man..."You have smitten Uriah the Hittite with the sword, and have taken his wife."'"* **12:7,9.**

18. **Absalom's death.** *"He took three darts in his hand, and thrust them into the heart of Absalom, while he was still alive in the oak."* **18:14.**

19. **David and the census.** *"The anger of the Lord was kindled against Israel, and he incited David against them, saying, 'Go, number Israel and Judah.'"* **24:1.**

FIRST AND SECOND
# KINGS

## 1 KINGS

## 2 KINGS

## II. OUTLINE—COMPLETE

# III. AUTHORSHIP

1. In olden times First arid Second Kings were one book.

2. The original book was a combination of **J** and **E**.

3. During and just after the glamour of the days of Josiah, there was a thorough revision by Deuteronomic editors.

4. And during the exile the **P** editors added their contributions.

5. Remember that it was Hilkiah who found Deuteronomy in the temple and so started the Josiah reforms.

6. Kings yields 51 Deuteronomic phrases—characteristic.

7. There were two definite Deuteronomic editors—the earlier and the later.

# IV. SOURCES

1. Old oral traditions.

2. The Acts of Solomon. This is the lost biography of Solomon.

3. Another lost book—the Book of the Chronicles of the Kings of Israel.

4. Also lost—the Book of the Chronicles of the Kings of Judah.

5. It was probably written around 620 B.C.

6. Kings is a compilation from at least five different sources.

# V. METHOD AND PURPOSE

1. The original author had a plan to deal with the northern and southern kingdoms contemporaneously.

2. The later editors held up Josiah as the ideal of a king of Davidic dynasty.

3. Monotheism is the theme song of Kings. *"You shall have no other gods before me—I am a jealous God."*

4. Israel's later troubles came because Solomon built shrines for the gods of his many wives:

    A. The Zidonian Astarte.
    B. Ammonite Melek. (Molech)
    C. Moabite Chemosh.

5. The same old concept is upheld: obey God and prosper; disobey and suffer —meet with disaster.

6. This book concentrates all worship at Jerusalem.

7. Jehu was condemned because he tolerated sacrifices and worship at Bethel.

8. Ahab was a "bad king" because he tolerated idols; Hezekiah was a "good king" because he made a clean sweep of idols and shrines; he even threw out of the temple the bronze serpent of Mosea.

9. Manasseh was the really "bad king"—he made his sons pass through the fire, practiced augury, used enchantments, fraternized with "familiar spirits" and with wizards.

10. The plan of Kings is:

    A. Date of kings' accession, capital.
    B. Age of king. Length of reign.
    C. Name of queen mother.
    D. King's attitude toward Deuteronomy.
    E. Death and burial.

11. Only two kings won full approval: Hezekiah and Josiah.

12. The other kings "did what was evil in the sight of the Lord."

13. The Elijah stories were not a part of the original book.

14. The wholesale condemnation of Israel's and Judah's kings was the work of the second or later Deuteronomic editor.

## VI. THE DEUTERONOMIC EDITORS

1. The first Deuteronomic editor finished his work soon after the death of Josiah (600 B.C.). There was another Deuteronomic revision about 550 B.C.

2. This second revision also included everything from Genesis to Kings.

3. The Deuteronomic editor explained Josiah's troubles upon the basis of suffering punishment for Manasseh's sins.

4. The second Deuteronomic editor knew about Cyrus and his activities. He may have also been influenced by the Second Isaiah.

5. These are also the times of Jeremiah and Ezekiel.

6. The second Deuteronomic editor was less hostile toward the kings of the northern kingdom.

7. The period covered by Kings is a little over four hundred years.

## VII. TALES OF THE NORTH

1. The outstanding figures of the northern kingdom were Elijah, Elisha, and Ahab.

2. These stories had their origin in the north, because:

    A. Nothing is said against the calf worship of Bethel.
    B. No objection to sacrifice and worship at northern "high places."

    C.   Elijah repairs the altar on Mt. Carmel.

    D.   Elijah's work devoted to the overthrow of the altars of the Tyrian Baal—introduced by Ahab's Tyrian wife Jezebel.

3.    The author of the Elijah stories was a skillful writer—as literature his work is the equal of any Old Testament writer.

4.    The Elisha stories were written by a much less competent author—they are deficient in dramatic power.

5.    The Elijah and Elisha stories show what a "wonder worker" age this was— the widow's food, the resurrected boy, the famine, the boys who ridiculed the prophet's baldness, and the bears.

6.    The Ahab narratives had a different author.

7.    The second Deuteronomic editor put all these stories together—tried to effect a conflation.

## VIII. TALES OF THE SOUTH

1.    Sennacherib's attack on Judah and unexplained withdrawal (even though Hezekiah paid tribute).

2.    Story of the miraculous destruction of the Assyrian army.

3.    Hezekiah's sickness.

4.    Insertion of stories like the embassy of Merodach-baladan, which seems to be drawn from Isaiah.

## IX. MODERN SIGNIFICANCE

1.    The folly of thinking God dwells in only *one* place.

2.    The last Deuteronomic editor taught that God is ever willing to pardon and forgive.

3.    All sin sets in motion a tragic train of consequences.

4.    Out of the sorrows of exile, there may dawn the joy of new hopes.

5.    Reading of the book of Kings should be followed by the comfort and promises of the Second Isaiah.

## X. SELECTED TEXTS
### 1 KINGS

1.    **Solomon asks for wisdom.** *"Give thy servant therefore an understanding mind to govern thy people, that I may discern between good and evil."* **3:9.**

2. **Two mothers and one child.** *"And the king said, 'Bring me a sword.' ...And the king said, 'Divide the living child in two, and give half to the one, and half to the other.'"* **3:24,25.**

3. **The gift of wisdom.** *"And God gave Solomon wisdom and understanding beyond measure, and largeness of mind like the sand on the seashore, so that Solomon's wisdom surpassed the wisdom of all the people of the east."***4:29,30.**

4. **King Hiram helps.** *"And Hiram sent to Solomon, saying...'I am ready to do all you desire in the matter of cedar and cypress timber.'"***5:8.**

5. **Solomon builds the temple.** *"So Solomon built the house, and finished it."***6:14.**

6. **Hiram the architect.** *"And King Solomon sent and brought Hiram from Tyre."***7:13.**

7. **Magnitude of God.** *"'But will God indeed dwell on the earth? Behold, heaven and the highest heaven cannot contain thee; how much less this house which I have built.'"* **8:27.**

8. **Hiram gets 20 cities.** *"And Hiram king of Tyre had supplied Solomon with cedar and cypress timber and gold, as much as he desired, King Solomon gave to Hiram twenty cities in the land of Galilee."***9:11.**

9. **The queen of Sheba.** *"And she said to the king, 'The report was true which I heard in my own land of your affairs and of your wisdom.'"* **10:6.**

10. **Solomon's wives.** *"Now King Solomon loved many foreign women: the daughter of Pharaoh, and Moabite, Ammonite, Edomite, Sidonian, and Hittite women... He had seven hundred wives, princesses, and three hundred concubines; and his wives turned away his heart."* **11:1,3.**

11. **Elijah and the rain.** *"Elijah...said to Ahab ... 'there shall be neither dew nor rain these years, except by my word.'"* **17:1.**

12. **The landlady's son.** *"Then he stretched himself upon the child three times, and cried to the Lord... 'let this child's soul come into him again.'"* **17:21.**

13. **Elijah and Ahab.** *"When Ahab saw Elijah, Ahab said to him, 'Is it you, you troubler of Israel?' And he answered, 'I have not troubled Israel, but you have...because you have forsaken the commandments of the Lord and followed the Baals.'"* **18:17,18.**

14. **Elijah and prophets of Baal.** *"And at noon Elijah mocked them, saying, 'Cry aloud, for he is a god; either he is musing, or he has gone aside, or he is on a journey, or perhaps he is asleep and must be awakened.' And they cried aloud and cut themselves...they raved on...but there was no voice; no one answered."* **18:27-29.**

15. **The still small voice.** *"And after the earthquake a fire, but the Lord was not in the fire, and after the fire a still small voice."* **19:12.16.**

16. **Jegebel's forgery.** *"So she wrote letters in Ahab's name...and let them... take him (Naboth) out, and stone him to death."* **21:8-10.**

## 2 KINGS

17. **Elijah parts the Jordan.** *"Then Elijah took his mantle...and struck the water, and the water was parted...till the two of them could go over on dry ground."* **2:8.**

18. **Elijah is translated.** *"A chariot of fire and horses of fire separated the two of them. And Elijah went up by a whirlwind into heaven."* **2:11.**

19. **The boys and the bears.** *"Some small boys came out of the city and jeered at him, saying, 'Go up, you baldhead'...He cursed them in the name of the Lord. And two she-bears came out of the woods and tore forty-two of the boys."* **2:23,24.**

20. **Elisha and the dead child.** *"When Elisha came into the house, he saw the child lying dead on the bed...Then he went in...and prayed...and lay upon the child...and as he stretched himself upon him, the flesh of the child became warm."* **4:32,34.**

21. **Naaman's leprosy.** *"And Elisha sent a messenger to him, saying, 'Go and wash in the Jordan seven times, and your flesh shall be restored.'...So he went down and dipped himself seven times in the Jordan...and his flesh was restored."* **5:10,14.**

22. **The Assyrian slaughter.** *"And that night the angel of the Lord went forth, and slew a hundred and eighty-five thousand in the camp of the Assyrians."* **19:35.**

23. **Josiah's reforms.** *"Moreover Josiah put away the mediums and the wizards and the teraphim and the idols and all the abominations that were seen in the land of Judah."* **23:24.**

24. **The fall of Jerusalem.** *"And Zedekiah rebelled against the king of Babylon... Nebuchadnezzar king of Babylon came with all his army against Jerusalem."* **25:1.**

FIRST AND SECOND

# CHRONICLES

## I. OUTLINE—BRIEF

## II. OUTLINE—COMPLETE 1
## *CHRONICLES*

## 2 CHRONICLES

## III. AUTHORSHIP

1. The Chronicler belonged to the "priestly cult." He composed First and Second Chronicles *after* the exile.

2. This is the first Old Testament book we have encountered which has no **J, E,** or **D** contributions.

3. But, after the Chronicler wrote the original book, there were many slight additions and editorial changes.

4. The book carries vast quotations from, both Samuel and Kings.

5. The unique feature of Chronicles is that it is the only book of the Old Testament giving a Hebrew philosophy of history.

6. The book was written by the same person who also authored Ezra and Nehemiah—probably Ezra.

7. It was written from 300 to 250 B.C.

## IV. CHARACTERISTICS

1. Chronicles undertakes a new interpretation of Israelite history.

2. This book is the priestly viewpoint of all things Jewish.

3. In some places the book breathes a spirit of intolerance, but on the whole it pleads for one God, one faith, one people. The Chronicler was the original "ecumenicist."

4. The book reviews all of Israelite history from Genesis to Kings, except that there are no quotations from Judges.

5. The Chronicler was hostile, almost bitter, toward everything and everybody in the northern kingdom. The later or second editor was more friendly toward the north.

6. The Chronicler dearly loved fantastically big numbers. David was made king by 339,000 warriors. His donations to the temple rival the riches of Croesus.

7. He regarded Yahweh as a God of ritual, ceremony, and sacrifice. Worship was the center of all religion.

8. The Chronicler wrote pictorial drama. The perfection of David, the splendor of Solomon, and the glory of the temple—these were the mission of this author.

9. Things were good in the southern kingdom, bad in the northern kingdom.

10. Chronicles is a call to living. *"'Believe in the Lord your God, and you shall be established; believe his prophets, and you will succeed.'"* **2 Chron. 20:20**.

11. Critics have offered several objections to Chronicles:

    A. *Unnecessary*. Endless lists of names, and so much quoted verbatim from Samuel and Kings.

    B. *Uninteresting*. True, certain parts were superior, but so much was of little present and practical value.

    C. *Defective*. It was such a lopsided history of Judah, so unfair to the northern kingdom, David is always so perfect.

    D. *Incredible*. Unreal history of the Levites. Exaggeration of numbers. Jehoshaphat had an army of 1,160,000 soldiers. Members engaged in victories and defeats—beyond all reason. On one day, in a clash with the Israelites, Ahaz lost 120,000. In another case, 200,000 men, women, and children were taken captive.

12. But Chronicles is not history. It is a drama based on history. Some of Jesus' parables may not have been factual, but they served to illustrate the *truth* he was inculcating.

13. Jesus intended to portray ideas and ideals—to tell us how best to live and worship.

14. The Chronicler wanted to translate ideals into actuality.

15. From history, he wanted to draw principles to help man deal wisely with life's vicissitudes.

16. Remember the circumstances of the author's day:

    A. The kingdom of Israel had fallen. The Assyrians had deported 30,000 Israelites.

    B. Judah fell—the Babylonians had taken captive the flower and brains of the land.

    C. Cyrus allowed some of the Jews to return to Jerusalem. They were anxious to have the genuine priests take over the temple services.

    D. The 520 B.C. substitute temple was a poor excuse for Solomon's temple.

    E. For 150 years nothing special happened. Then came Nehemiah from Babylon to rebuild the walls of Jerusalem.

    F. Shortly a caravan of 1,800 Hebrews came up from Babylon led by Ezra.

17. The Chronicler is true to Hebrew philosophy: obey God and prosper; disobey and reap disaster.

18. Kings says Asa did not abolish the "high places"; Chronicles says he did. (**2 Chron. 14:5**)

## V. SOURCES

1. The author alludes to "lost sources," but he does not quote from them as he does from both Samuel and Kings.

2. Chronicles tells a somewhat different story about the reigns of both Hezekiah and Josiah, as compared with the record in Kings.

3.   The Chronicler may not have been a poet in words, but he did have the soul of a poet.

4.   We will never really know whether or not the Chronicler had access to records which have since been lost.

## VI. SELECTED TEXTS
### *1 CHRONICLES*

1.   **The end of Saul.** *"The battle pressed hard upon Saul, and the archers found him; and he was wounded by the archers. Then Saul said to his armor-bearer, 'Draw your sword, and thrust me through with it, lest these uncircumcised come and make sport of me.' But his armor-hearer would not. …Saul took his own sword, and fell upon it."* **10:3,4.**

   *"So Saul died for his unfaithfulness…And also consulted a medium."* **10:13.**

2.   **David anointed king.** *"So all the elders of Israel came to…Hebron…and they anointed David king over Israel."* **11:3.**

3.   **Moving the ark.** *"Then let us bring again the ark of our God to us…Uzza put out his hand to hold the ark, for the oxen stumbled…and he died there before God."* **13:3,9,10.**

4.   **A tent for the ark.** *"David…prepared a place for the ark of God, and pitched a tent for it."* **15:1.**

5.   **Welfare methods.** *"When David had finished offering the burnt offerings… he…distributed to all Israel, both men and women, to each a loaf of bread, a portion of meat, and a cake of raisins."* **16:2,3.**

6.   **Solomon.** *"He shall build a house for me, and I will establish his throne forever."* **17:12.**

7.   **Taking the census.** *"Satan stood up against Israel, and incited David to number Israel."* **21:1.**

   *"So the Lord sent a pestilence upon Israel; and there fell seventy thousand men."* **21:14.**

8.   **David prepares for the temple.** *"David said, 'Solomon my son is young and inexperienced, and the house that is to be built for the Lord must be exceedingly magnificent…I will therefore make preparation for it.'"* **22:5.**

9.   **David's admonition.** *"Then David said to Solomon… 'Be strong and of good courage…for the Lord God…is with you. He will not fail you or forsake you, until all the work for the service of the house of the Lord is finished.'"* **28:20.**

## *2 CHRONICLES*

10. **Solomon's prayer**. *"'Give me now wisdom and knowledge to go out and come in before this people.'"* **1:10**.

11. **Solomon builds**. *"Then Solomon began to build the house of the Lord in Jerusalem...at the place that David had appointed."* 3:1.

12. **Temple dedication**. *"When Solomon had ended his prayer, fire came down from heaven and consumed the burnt offering...And the glory of the Lord filled the temple."* **7:1**.

# EZRA AND NEHEMIAH

## I. OUTLINE—BRIEF

## II. OUTLINE—COMPLETE
### EZRA

## NEHEMIAH

# III. AUTHORSHIP

1. The Chronicler, the author of First and Second Chronicles, is also the author of Ezra and Nehemiah.

2. We are not certain as to who this author was, but it was probably Ezra— the scribe-priest.

3. It is also probable that he wrote the Esdras books of the Apocrypha. These books cover the same events as depicted in Ezra and Nehemiah.

4. The literary style of Chronicles is identical with the style of Ezra and Nehemiah.

5. He is over-concerned with the temple and the cults. Some have thought the author was a musician—that he belonged to the guild of Asaph.

6. The Talmud says that Ezra was the author of Ezra and Nehemiah.

7. These were written during the reconstruction period following the exile.

8. The author may have had some records at his disposal which have since been lost (Book of Genealogy, Temple Records).

9. The author was a person of great imagination, inventive skill, and profound convictions.

# IV. SOME CONSIDERATIONS

1. Ezra and Nehemiah were possibly co-workers. Ezra was the managing priest while Nehemiah was the Governor—a layman.

2. Ezra was greatly concerned with the dissolution of foreign marriages.

3. It is interesting to note that neither Ezra nor Nehemiah are quoted in the New Testament.

4. Ezra was devoted to the rebuilding of Israel's worship. Nehemiah was concerned with rebuilding the walls of the city.

5. Ezra brought 1496 persons with him from Babylon—a four-month journey.

6. Ezra is probably the father of the Hebrew Sanhedrin.

7. Ezra was primarily a reformer and propagandist.

8. Nehemiah was an engineer. He was an organizer and administrator.

9. Zerubbabel was one-time Governor of Judea, with Joshua as high priest. He had so much to do with rebuilding that the temple was known as "Zerubbabel's temple."

10. The memoirs of Nehemiah were once a separate book—before being incorporated into Ezra and Nehemiah.

11. Even if Ezra wrote those books, a later editor did a great deal of work on the narrative.

12. It may be mentioned that Josephus, the Hebrew historian, makes more use of the Esdras books than of Ezra and Nehemiah for the history of this period.

13. Throughout all of this story, it should be remembered that Nehemiah was a eunuch.

## V. PRIORITY OF NEHEMIAH

1. While it is possible that Ezra and Nehemiah may have been contemporaries for a season, there is much evidence that Nehemiah was in Jerusalem long before Ezra arrived.

2. The facts which point to the priority of Nehemiah are:

   A. It is not likely that the same king would send two men to Jerusalem with the same authority to do a job at the same time.

   B. In original records, Ezra and Nehemiah seem to ignore each other.

   C. In preparing for a census Nehemiah alludes to Zerubbabel, but does not mention Ezra.

   D. Nehemiah comes to an empty city; Ezra is working in a busy city.

   E. Nehemiah finds the defenses of the city destroyed; Ezra talks about the "restored walls."

   F. Nehemiah was contemporary with the high priest Eliashib; Ezra, with the high priest Jehohanan.

   G. Nehemiah found children speaking the language of their foreign mothers. This would hardly have been so, if Ezra had already broken up these mixed marriages.

3. So it would appear that Nehemiah preceded Ezra in the return from Babylon.

## VI. HISTORICITY

1. Biblical critics, while disposed to accept Nehemiah's history as valid, have raised many questions about Ezra as a historian.

2. So little is known about the history of Israel during the "Persian period," it is difficult to check Ezra's historicity.

3. When all is said and done, most of what Ezra writes seems to ring true— it is at least plausible.

4. It is a fact that the peculiar style of the Chronicler does persist throughout Chronicles, Ezra, and Nehemiah.

## VII. THEOLOGICAL SIGNIFICANCE

1. Ezra was almost a fanatic regarding the origin and development of the temple cultus with all of its ceremonies, sacrifices, laws, and holy days.

2. Ezra was the builder of the exclusive and self-conscious post-exilic Judaism.

3. It was this same type of rigid Judaism that Paul had to contend with when he carried the gospel to the gentiles.

4. In Ezra and Nehemiah, for the first time, Aramaic sources are brought to light.

5. Ezra was anxious to point out how much trouble he and Nehemiah had with their neighbors, especially in Samaria.

6. Both of them were staunch believers in Providence—always alluding to the "hand of the Lord."

7. Ezra does not show any of the solemn grandeur of the olden prophets, but he does show diligence and skill in trying to carry into effect their admonitions.

8. They lost much "culture" by throwing out the "foreigners," but they did save the "cult."

9. Moderns look down on Ezra as a fanatical legalist, but he did, at least in his way, have an answer to the question, "What must I do to be saved?"

## VIII. SELECTED TEXTS
### EZRA

1. **Cyrus ends the exile.** *"In the first year of Cyrus king of Persia...he made a proclamation... 'Whoever is among you...let him go up to Jerusalem...and rebuild the house of the Lord.'"* **1:1-3**.

2. **The reactionaries.** *"Then the people of the land discouraged the people of Judah, and made them afraid to build, and hired counselors against them to frustrate their purpose."* **4:4,5**.

3. **Stopping the work.** *"Then the work on the house of God... stopped... until the second year... of Darius."* **4:24**.

4. **Ezra arrives.** *"Ezra went up from Babylonia. He was a scribe skilled in the law of Moses...and the king granted him all that he asked."* **7:6**.

## *NEHEMIAH*

5. **Nehemiah resumes work.** *"Let us build the wall of Jerusalem, that we may no longer suffer disgrace...Let us rise up and build.'"* **2:17,18.**

6. **The priests go to work.** *"Above the Horse Gate the priests repaired, each one opposite his own house."* **3:28.**

7. **A mind to work.** *"So we built the wall; and all the wall was joined together to half its height. For the people had a mind to work."* **4:6.**

8. **How they worked.** *"Each with one hand labored on the work and with the other held his weapon."* **4:17.**

9. **A long day.** *"So we labored at the work, and half of them held the spears from the break of dawn till the stars came out."* **4:21.**

10. **Refusal to be diverted.** *"'I am doing a great work and I cannot come down.'"* **6:3.**

11. **Ezra reads the law.** *"And Ezra the priest brought the law before the assembly...And he read from it...from early morning until mid-day."* **8:2,3.**

12. **The dedication.** *"And at the dedication of the wall of Jerusalem they sought the Levites...to bring them...to celebrate the dedication with gladness."* **12:27.**

# ESTHER

## I. OUTLINE—BRIEF

## II. OUTLINE—COMPLETE

## III. AUTHORSHIP

1. The author of this piece of Semitic historical fiction is unknown.

2. The book was written to justify the two-day feast of Purim, which had long been celebrated by the Jews.

3. There are implications that the author was a Persian Jew.

4. The author seems to have had a cynical attitude toward religion. He depended on political intrigue.

5. The author was a skillful literary artist. Esther is regarded as a masterpiece of literature.

6. Perhaps written during the third century B.C. or possibly as late as 125 B.C.

## IV. PURPOSE

1. Purim had no basis in the law. As a holiday it was probably picked up from another nation, much as modern Jews, in a secular way, celebrate Christmas.

2. The book of Esther supplies the reason for the continued celebration of the Purim festival.

3. Purim was a convivial and secular celebration and it needed some sort of racial or religious background for its justification. It was the only worldly holiday in the Jewish calendar.

4. To sum up: the book was to propagandize and justify Purim.

## V. HISTORICITY

1. Herodotus, the Greek historian, makes no mention of Xerxes having either Vashti or Esther as queen.

2. Most scholars regard the book as romance fiction—designed to tickle Jewish fancy and exalt the national ego.

3. In other words, Esther should be classed as a historical novel.

4. There were objections to the book's being received into the sacred canon, there being no mention of God, prayer, or any other religious practice.

5. The ethics and morals of the book are in every way contrary to the teachings of the Old Testament prophets and the teachings of Christianity.

## VI. SOME GENERAL CONSIDERATIONS

1. The little book is shot through with exaggerations: high gallows, six months' feast, year's beauty treatment for court maidens, 10,000 talents ($18,000,000) for financing the pogrom.

2. The book exhibits gross Jewish intolerance—75,510 gentiles were slaughtered in a single day.

3. Part of the original Book of Esther was so distasteful that it was removed and put in the Apocrypha.

4. Neither Jesus nor any New Testament writer ever quotes from or refers to the book of Esther.

5. The heroine of the book violates Jewish prohibition of marriage with the uncircumcised gentiles.

6. Esther was not accepted into the Old Testament canon until A.D. 397 at the Council of Carthage.

7. The Book of Esther may have something to do with creating and perpetuating the historic cleavage between historic Judaism and prophetic Christianity.

8. Esther is certainly contrary to the teaching of both the Second Isaiah and Jesus of Nazareth.

9. Esther became popular among the Jews because Purim was always a popular and festive holiday.

## VII. SELECTED TEXTS

1. **Beauty treatment.** *"Now when the turn came for each maiden to go in to King Ahasuerus, after being twelve months under the regulations for the women, since this was the regular period of their beautifying, six months with oil of myrrh and six months with spices and ointments."* **2:12.**

2. **Esther becomes queen.** *"The king loved Esther more than all the women...so that he set the royal crown on her head and made her queen."* **2:17.**

3. **Haman seeks destruction of Jews.** *"When Haman saw that Mordecai did not bow down...to him...Haman sought to destroy all the Jews."* **3:5,6.**

4. **Edict for destruction of Jews.** *"Letters were sent...to destroy...all Jews."* **3:13.**

5. **For such a time.** *"'And who knows whether you have not come to the kingdom for such a time as this?'"* **4:14.**

6. **The gallows.** *"'Let a gallows...be made...tell the king to have Mordecai hanged upon it.'"* **5:14.**

7. **Mordecai's kindness.** *"And it was found written how Mordecai had told about...two of the king's eunuchs...who had sought to lay hands upon King Ahasuerus."* **6:2.**

8. **Mordecai honored**. *"Then the king said to Haman, 'Make haste, take the robes and the horse, as you have said, and do so to Mordecai the Jew.'"* **6:10**.

9. **The king hangs Haman**. *"Then Queen Esther answered... 'Let my life be given me...and my people. For we are...to be destroyed'...Then King Ahasuerus answered... 'Who is he...that would presume to do this?' And Esther said... 'This wicked Haman.'"* 7:3-6.

   *"Then said...one of the eunuchs... 'the gallows which Haman has prepared for Mordecai...is standing...' And the king said, 'Hang him...' So they hanged Haman on the gallows which he had prepared for Mordecai."* **7:9,10**.

10. **The Jews saved**. *"'And you may write as you please with regard to the Jews, in the name of the king.'"* **8:8**.

11. **Origin of Purim**. *"Therefore they called these days Purim, after the term Pur."* **9:26**.

# JOB

## I. OUTLINE—BRIEF

## II. OUTLINE—COMPLETE

## III. AUTHORSHIP

1. The author or authors are unknown. Probably more than one—not to mention numerous subsequent editors.

2. The author may have been a Jew or an Edomite.

3. The author was a scholar of great learning—had a vast vocabulary. He was an original theological thinker.

4. The author of Job is the only Biblical writer who has been compared to Shakespeare.

5. The book is based on an ancient legend—the folk tale of Job.

6. Ezekiel knew about the story of Job in the sixth century—possibly before the present book was written. He refers to Job, along with Noah and Daniel (**Eze. 14:14**).

## IV. AN OVER-ALL LOOK AT JOB

1. We often hear about *"the patience of Job."* (**Jas. 5:11** King James Version) But few people know very much about the book of Job.

2. Job is a poem dealing with the meaning of life—relation of suffering to religion.

3. Job belongs to the so-called wisdom type of Hebrew literature.

4. In *The Urantia Book*, Jesus presents an instructive discussion of Job on p. 1662.

5. Jesus calls Job a *"masterpiece of Semitic literature."*

6. There are many earmarks of Edomite influence in Job. The original folk tale may have located Job in Edom.

7. There are folk stories similar to Job in India, Egypt, Babylon, and the Near East.

8. There are also numerous cases of "betting" between God and Satan.

9. Job is a revolt against the doctrine that there is only one cause of human suffering.

10. Job is the story of a just soul who suffered and despaired, but battled through to peace, hope, and victory.

11. Job is a tragic drama. It is in reality a philosophical debate.

12. The author of Job was an original thinker, a philosopher, a theologian, and a practical sociologist.

13. Job indicates that the time had come when Jews no longer believed that God was responsible for everything—including evil.

14. Personal experience triumphs over pessimistic theology.

## V. COMPOSITION AND DATE

1. The prologue and epilogue are in prose; the book itself is a poem.

2. The book was put in its present form after the exile, during a time when Satan had appeared in Jewish theology, and could be held responsible for evil.

3. The psychology of Job is both profound and modern. The authors were well versed in the wisdom of Egypt and Mesopotamia.

4. The vocabulary "affinities" in Job number fifteen to twenty, but are not sufficient to prove connection with any other Biblical books.

5. The Job story is as old as the eighth or even tenth century B.C. But the present book was written about the third or fourth century B.C.

6. The hymn of wisdom (**Chap. 28**) is an interruption of the narrative and may have separate authorship.

7. There are many passages in Job that suggest familiarity with the writings of Jeremiah.

8. There are also a few verses that suggest passages in the Second Isaiah.

9. The introduction to the discourse by Elihu is both ponderous and redundant —vastly different from the rest of Job.

10. The discourses of Yahweh seem to be directed toward raising the controversy from the finite level of man to the infinite level of God.

11. In the vocabulary of Job there are many expressions not found anywhere else in the whole Bible.

12. The literary style of Job is unsurpassed on the Bible. The sensibility, vigor, and elegance are superior to that found in any Hebrew writings.

13. The author knows astronomy. He talks about Orion, the Pleiades, and the Southern Cross.

## VI. THEOLOGICAL SIGNIFICANCE

1. There are a number of serious problems presented in Job:
   A. Why do the righteous suffer?
   B. Job's friends present a sixth century view of pain and affliction; the latter part of Job tends toward the third century attitude.
   C. The meaning of living faith.
   D. The wisdom of God vs. the wisdom of men.

2. The drama represents the revolt of individual conscience against the tyranny of orthodoxy.

3. The book attacks the problem of retributive justice.

4. It contrasts the divinity of God and the humanity of man—relations between man and God—the mission of GRACE.

5. The paradox of adversity as the reward of integrity—the mystery of the circumstances of life.

6. How the innocent can be struck with misfortune in heroic proportions.

7. Job, in facing death, begins to wonder about the future life. "If a man die, shall he live again?"

8. Job wants to prove that orthodoxy is a sort of theological sin.

9. Job craves a mediator—he wants someone to help him in dealing with the power, mystery, and perfection of God. He really foreshadows the ministry of the incarnation of Christ.

10. At last he concludes: "Even now, behold, my witness is in heaven, and he that vouches for me is on high."

11. Job asserts his faith in the resurrection, and exclaims: "I know that my Redeemer (Vindicator) lives."

12. Job says: "When he has tried me, I shall come forth as gold."

13. Belief becomes living faith. "I have heard of thee by the hearing of the ear; but now mine eye seeth thee."

14. And the final conclusion: "That righteousness is not the work of but the gift of God."

## VII. SELECTED TEXTS

1. **The sons of God.** *"Now there was a day when the sons of God came to present themselves before the Lord, and Satan also came among them."* **1:6.**

2. **The Lord gives.** *"The Lord gave, and the Lord has taken away; blessed be the name of the Lord.'"* **1:21.**

3. **Power of suggestion.** *"For the thing that I fear comes upon me, and what I dread befalls me.'"* **3:25.**

4. **Cause and effect.** *"For affliction does not come from the dust, nor does trouble sprout from the ground.'"* **5:6.**

5. **Arrows of the Almighty.** *"For the arrows of the Almighty are in me; my spirit drinks their poison; the terrors of God are arrayed against me.'"* **6:4.**

6. **God's presence.** *"Lo, he passes by me, and I see him not; he moves on, but I do not perceive him.'"* **9:11.**

7. **Tribulation.** *"'Man that is born of woman is of few days, and full of trouble.'"* **14:1.**

8. **Miserable comforters.** *"Then Job answered... 'miserable comforters are you all.'"* **16:1.**

9. **My Vindicator lives.** *"'I know that my Redeemer (Vindicator) lives.'"* **19:25.**

10. **Be at peace.** *"'Agree with God, and be at peace.'"* **22:21.**

11. **The cosmos.** *"'He stretches out the north over the void, and hangs the earth upon nothing.'"* **26:7.**

12. **Man's spirit.** *"'But it is the spirit in a man, the breath of the Almighty, that makes him understand.'"* **32:8.**

13. **The spirit of God.** *"'The spirit of God has made me, and the breath of the Almighty gives me life.'"* **33:4.**

14. **Divine acceptance.** *"'Then man prays to God, and he accepts him, he comes into his presence with joy.'"* **33:26.**

15. **Salvation.** *"'I sinned and perverted what was right, and it was not requited to me. He has redeemed my soul."* **33:27,28.**

16. **Morning stars.** *"'When the morning stars sang together, and all the sons of God shouted for joy.'"* **38:7.**

# PSALMS

## I. OUTLINE

## II. AUTHORSHIP

1. Nothing definite is known about the author of any psalm.

2. Assumed authors of Psalms are as follows:

   David—79.
   Asaph—12.
   Solomon—2. 72,27.
   Heman—1. 88.
   Jeremiah—1. 137.
   Korah—10.
   Moses—1. 90.
   Ethan—1. 89.
   Anonymous—43.

## III. GENERAL CONSIDERATIONS

1. In general, the Bible presents man talking to man, or God speaking to man, but Psalms presents man talking to God.

2. The philosophy and theology of the psalms cover a time period of almost one thousand years.

3. Each book of Psalms ends with a doxology. The last book has the last psalm as its doxology.

4. Psalms covers the whole gamut of human emotions, cheerful confidence and anxious foreboding, joyful faith and brooding despondency, loving kindness and bitter animosity, tenderness and ruthlessness.

5. The theology of Psalms ranges from the near-pagan to the high levels of the Second Isaiah.

6. The range is from praise, prayer, and thanksgiving to sublime worship.

7. Psalms is the prayer and hymn book of both Judaism and the Christian church.

8. In Books 2 and 3 the name of Deity has been changed from Yahweh to Elohim.

9. **Ps. 104:19-23** sounds like the Egyptian Hymn to Aton—by Amenophis IV (Ikhnaton).

10. There is a lot of modern psychiatry in the book of Psalms.

11. Many of the psalms were intended to be accompanied by music— wind instruments, string instruments, and percussion.

12. Psalms ranges from private prayers to all phases of public worship.

## IV. TYPES OF PSALMS

1. *Hymns*. **Ps. 8, 19, 29, 33**.

2. *Public Laments*. **Ps. 44, 74, 79**.

3. *Royal Psalms*. **Ps. 2, 18, 20**.

4. *Individual Laments*. **Ps. 3, 5, 6, 7, 13**.

5. *Songs of Thanksgiving*. **Ps. 30, 32, 34**.

6. **Sundry Groups.**

   A. *Enthronement*. **Ps. 47, 93**.

   B. *Confidence*. **Ps. 4, 11, 16, 23**.

   C. *Wisdom*. **Ps. 1, 37, 49**.

   D. *Liturgies*. **Ps. 8, 42, 43, 46**.

   E. *Prophetic*. **Ps. 12, 75**.

   F. *Mixed Poems*. **Ps. 9, 10, 40, 78**.

## V. THE PSALTER AS A COMPILATION

1. Both great variety and duplications suggest compilation.

2. Use of both Yahweh and Elohim for God shows different theologic concepts.

3. Assumption of many authors indicates compilation.

4. Wide range of doctrine shows that the individual psalms had origin over a very wide time range.

5. All but 34 psalms have some sort of superscription attached—songs for private or temple worship, Sabbath, or weddings, etc.

6. Diverse poetic structure:

   A. *Synonymous*. Second line repeats thought of the first.
   > "Hear this, all peoples!
   >    "Give ear, all inhabitants of the world." **49:1**.

B.  *Antithetic.* Second line antithetic to the first.
> "*For the Lord knows the way of the righteous,*
>> *"but the way of the wicked will perish.*"**1:6**.

C.  *Synthetic.* The second line completes the first.
> "*I cry aloud to the Lord,*
>> *"and he answers me from his holy hill.*" **3:4**.

7.  Some psalms are in stanzas, others acrostic in structure.

## VI. RELIGION OF THE PSALMISTS

1.  The Psalter does not present any systematic scheme of Jewish theology.

2.  The God concept is monotheistic, although reference is made to other "gods."

3.  God is righteous, just, merciful, and gracious. And he hears the prayers of his servants.

4.  The world is the handiwork of God. The psalmists are not nature lovers.

5.  Man lives his life and perishes "like the beasts of the field." There are but hints of survival beyond the grave.

6.  The people of God are the Hebrews, but there are references to the fact that God rules and judges all nations.

7.  But oh the whole, the psalms present a rugged Hebrew nationalism.

8.  The cultus is upheld, but there is scant attention paid to "blood" and the sacrifices. The temple is venerated, but some of its ceremonies are slighted.

9.  Certain psalms allude to the universal rule of Israel's God. They also refer to times when all men worship God.

10.  In general, the psalms refer to the "goodness of the Lord to the land of the living," but they also talk about the day of Judgment and the end of the world.

11.  Many of the psalms reflect the philosophy and religious beliefs of many ancient peoples—Egyptian, Babylonian, Assyrian, and Persian.

12.  Many psalms can hardly be called Christian. Note the following psalms of the imprecatory category—breathing vengeance: **Ps. 58, 59, 69, 109, 137,** and **149.**

## VII. PSALMS IN WORSHIP

1. The psalms were a part of the olden temple worship.

2. The psalms were associated with the annual Jewish feasts—First Fruits, Tabernacles, Pentecost, etc.

3. There is little information as to the use of the psalms in synagogue worship.

4. The psalms are still used in modern Jewish worship.

5. The Psalter has always been a part of worship in Christian churches.

6. There are 93 quotations from the Psalms in the New Testament.

7. Of all Old Testament books, the Psalter is the one book to be whole-heartedly adopted by the Christian church.

8. In contrast to the psalms of pagan hate and revenge, attention should be called to such beautiful hymns of praise, thanksgiving, and worship as Psalms **8, 29, 51, 62, 84, 105**, and **106**.

## VIII. SELECTED TEXTS

1. **The blessed man.** *"Blessed is the man who walks not in the counsel of the wicked, nor stands in the way of sinners, nor sits in the seat of scoffers; but his delight is in the law of the Lord."* **1:1,2.**

2. **The fool.** *"The fool says in his heart, 'There is no God.'"* 14:1.

3. **The goodly heritage.** *"The lines have fallen for me in pleasant places; yea, I have a goodly heritage."* 16:6.

4. **Telling the glory of God.** *"The heavens are telling the glory of God; and the firmament proclaims his handiwork."* 19:1.

5. **Godforsaken.** *"My God, my God, why hast thou forsaken me?"* 22:1.

6. **Our shepherd.** *"The Lord is my shepherd."* 23:1.

7. **Goodness and mercy.** *"Surely goodness and mercy shall follow me all the days of my life."* 23:6.

8. **Earth is the Lord's.** *"The earth is the Lord's and the fulness thereof, the world and those who dwell therein."* 24:1.

9. **Our fortress.** *"Yea, thou art my rock and my fortress; for thy name's sake lead me and guide me."* 31:3.

10. **Forgiveness.** *"Blessed is he whose transgression is forgiven, whose sin is covered."* 32:1.

11. **Making the heavens.** *"By the word of the Lord the heavens were made, and all their host by the breath of his mouth."* 33:6.

12. **Taste and see**. *"O taste and see that the Lord is good!"* **34:8**.

13. **Afflictions of the righteous.** *"Many are the afflictions of the righteous; but the Lord delivers him out of them all."* **34:19**.

14. **Care for the righteous**. *"I have been young, and now am old; yet I have not seen the righteous forsaken or his children begging bread."* **37:25**.

15. **Law in the heart**. *"I delight to do thy will, O my God; thy law is within my heart."* **40:8**.

16. **Thirst for God**. *"My soul thirsts for God, for the living God."* **42:2**.

17. **Our refuge**. *"God is our refuge and strength, a very present help in trouble."* **46:1**.

18. **Contemplation**. *"'Be still, and know that I am God.'"* **46:10**.

19. **The thousand hills**. *"For every beast of the forest is mine, the cattle on a thousand hills."* **50:10**.

20. **Purge me**. *"Purge me with hyssop, and I shall be clean; wash me, and I shall be whiter than snow."* **51:7**.

21. **A clean heart**. *"Create in me a clean heart, O God, and put a new and right spirit within me."* **51:10**.

22. **Gaining rest**. *"'O that I had wings like a dove: I would fly away and be at rest.'"* **55:6**.

23. **Cast your burden**. *"Cast your burden on the Lord, and he will sustain you."* **55:22**.

24. **The higher rock**. *"Lead thou me to the rock that is higher than I; for thou art my refuge."* **61:2,3**.

25. **The doorkeeper**. *"I would rather be a doorkeeper in the house of my God than dwell in the tents of wickedness."* **84:10**.

26. **A thousand years**. *"For a thousand years in thy sight are but as yesterday when it is past, or as a watch in the night."* **90:4**.

27. **Threescore and ten**. *"The years of our life are threescore and ten, or even by reason of strength fourscore."* **90:10**.

28. **Shadow of the Almighty**. *"He who dwells in the shelter of the Most High, who abides in the shadow of the Almighty."* **91:1**.

29. **Guardian angels**. *"For he will give his angels charge of you to guard you in all your ways."* **91:11**.

30. **We are of dust**. *"For he knows our frame; he remembers that we are dust."* **103:14**.

31. **The covering of light.** *"Who coverest thyself with light as with a garment, who hast stretched out the heavens like a tent."***104:2.**

32. **The Creative Spirit.** *"When thou sendest forth thy Spirit, they are created; and thou renewest the face of the ground."***104:30.**

33. **Wisdom.** *"The fear of the Lord is the beginning of wisdom."***111:10.**

34. **Mission of Affliction.** *"Before I was afflicted I went astray; but now I keep thy word."***119:67.**

35. **Light of the word.** *"Thy word is a lamp to my feet and a light to my path."***119:105.**

36. **Strength from the hills.** *"I lift up my eyes to the hills. From whence does my help come?"***121:1.**

37. **Kept from evil.** *"The Lord will keep you from all evil; he will keep your life."***121:7.**

38. **The divine presence.** *"Whither shall I go from thy Spirit? Or whither shall I flee from thy presence?"* **139:7.**

39. **The way everlasting.** *"Search me, O God, and know my heart I Try me and know my thoughts! And see if there be any wicked way in me, and lead me in the way everlasting."***139:23,24.**

40. **The divine kindness.** *"The Lord is just in all his ways, and kind in all his doings."***145:17.**

# PROVERBS

## I. OUTLINE—BRIEF

## II. OUTLINE—COMPLETE

# III. AUTHORSHIP

1. It is highly probable that the seven different sections of Proverbs had a different author or collector.

2. The seven sections are:

    A. Praise of Wisdom. **1:7-9:18.**
    B. Proverbs of Solomon. **10:1-22:16.**
    C. Sayings of the Wise. **22:17-24;34**
    D. More Proverbs of Solomon. **25:1-29:27.**
    E. Words of Agur. **30:1-33.**
    F. Words of Lemuel. **31:1-9.**
    G. Praise of Good Wife. **31:10-31.**

3. The majority of these proverbs are of pre-exilic origin.

4. Section I is assigned to post-exilic origin because of style, and evidence of Phoenician influence.

5. Section II is the core of the book—375 proverbs. The main characters:

    The righteous and the wicked.
    The wise and the fool.
    The rich and the poor.
    The proud and the humble.
    The thrifty and the lazy.

6. Section III shows every evidence of being derived from the Egyptian Wisdom Book—by Amenemope c. 800 B.C.

7. So-called Solomon's proverbs were collected and edited by someone associated with King Hezekiah. This is Section IV.

8. Authors of the remaining sections are uncertain, but the dates of these parts seem to be post-exilic.

9. The book in its present form dates about 400 B.C. (subject to some subsequent editing), but parts of it may extend from 800 B.C. to 250 B.C.

# IV. WISDOM LITERATURE IN GENERAL

1. Among the early wise men were:

    A. Balaam—**Num. 23, 24.**
    B. Ethan, the Ezrahite.
    C. Heman, Calcol, Darda—Edomites.

2. **Prov. 8 and 9** are of Canaanite origin.

3. **Prov. 22:17-23:14** are directly quoted from Egyptian teachings of Amenemope. (Amenemope's teachings are also found in **Ps. 1** and **Jer. 17:5-8.**)

4. Did Israel borrow from the surrounding nations, or did they borrow from Israel? Or did they both draw from an older and common source?

5. Wisdom literature denounced intemperate, dishonest, and selfish living. It advocated "common sense."

6. These olden "wise men" were the ancient humanists.

7. Tradition attributed many of these proverbs to Solomon, as so many psalms were assigned to David.

8. Two features of Proverbs ran contrary to Jewish practice:

   A. Emphasis of monogamy.
   B. Emphasis on the individual, rather than the nation.

9. Two schools of philosophy run throughout Proverbs:

   A. The secular.
   B. The religious.

10. The religious section of Proverbs presents the Deuteronomic ideals of social and spiritual living.

11. The pleasures of life which should be enjoyed in moderation are:

    A. Perfume.
    B. Wine.
    C. Honey.
    D. Friendship.
    E. Married Life.

12. Proverbs warn against:

    A. Adultery.
    B. Usury.
    C. Fraud.
    D. Theft.
    E. Ill-gotten gains.

13. Reasons for leading the "good life" are based on self-interest rather than on moral or religious grounds.

14. The wise are identical with the pious, and they are supposed to enjoy long life, security, honor, riches, and happiness.

15. The proverbs are realistic and practical. Intelligence and diligence are factors in prosperity—as well as morals and religion.

16. Throughout the book there is to be detected a strain of cynicism.

17. Wise men dealt with both proverbs and fables—parables.

## V. THE WISE MEN

1.  The Jews had three types of teachers: (**Jer. 18:18**)

    A.  Prophets.
    B.  Priests.
    C.  Wise men.

2.  About 200 B.C. the "scribes" replaced the "wise men." Scribes began to appear even in David's time. **2 Sam. 8:17**.

3.  Wise men were found in Israel before the eighth century B.C. See **Isa. 29:14; Jer. 18:18**.

4.  There were also "wise women." One such lived in Tekoa—the home of Amos. **2 Sam. 14:1-20**.

5.  Solomon's wisdom was known to *"all the kings of the earth."* **1 Kings 4:29-34**. (Possibly much of Solomon's wisdom was lost—by loss of the record.)

6.  Wise men sat at the city gate—dispensing (for a fee) both wisdom and judgment.

7.  They also gave advice in private—making "house calls."

8.  Isaiah taunts the wise men for charging fees. **Isa. 55:1**.

9.  The wise men in Israel did the work of modern psychologists and psychiatrists.

10. The wise men were naturalists—dealing with ants and other animal life.

11. Hebrew wise men often administered their wisdom in religious capsules, like "the fear of the Lord is the beginning of wisdom."

12. Many of the wise men tended to personify wisdom. (Wisdom was a member of a later Jewish and early Christian trinity.)

13. Personification of wisdom is suggested in **Job 28**. (Also **8** and **9**)

14. The New Testament concept of wisdom is suggested in **Jas. 3:17**. *"The wisdom from above is first pure, then peaceable, gentle, open to reason, full of mercy and good fruits, without uncertainty or insincerity."*

15. Like the psalms, the proverbs are formulated in three styles.

    A.  *Synonymous*. **7:1**.
    B.  *Antithetic*. **10:5**.
    C.  *Synthetic*. **18:13**.

## VI. PHILOSOPHY AND THEOLOGY

1.  The fact that Proverbs and Ecclesiastes got into the sacred canon proves that the teachings of the wise men became recognized and "respectable" in Israel.

2.  To some extent "wisdom" became equated with the law.

3.  In dealing with the practical problems of everyday life, wisdom somewhat made atonement for the grave errors of the false belief in Providence.

4.  Wisdom literature held up high standards for:

    A.  Family life—monogamy.
    B.  Respect for mother and wife.
    C.  Chastity and marital fidelity.
    Oppression of the poor was condemned, and gluttons, drunkards, sluggards, and robbers were denounced.

5.  But in spite of such high ethical standards in the proverbs, they taught that goodness was usually motivated by personal interest and success.

6.  In warning men against "strange women," the man is told to shun such a life because of its effect upon his physical and material state—nothing is said about sinfulness.

7.  Proverbs foreshadows a growing belief in the "resurrection and life after death."

8.  But in general, Proverbs teaches that all of the rewards for good ness and penalties for wickedness are fully experienced right here on earth. In neither case do they carry over into the next life.

9.  Proverbs is liberally quoted in the New Testament. In other passages the teachings of Proverbs are implied. Even Jesus quoted from Proverbs a few times.

## VII. SELECTED TEXTS

1.  **The fear of the Lord**. *"The fear of the Lord is the beginning of knowledge."* **1:7**.

2.  **The upright**. *"For the upright will inhabit the land."* **2:21**.

3.  **Trusting God**. *"Trust in the Lord with all your heart, and do not rely on your own insight."* **3:5**.

4.  **Happiness and wisdom**. *"Happy is the man who finds wisdom, and the man who gets understanding."* **3:13**.

5.  **Crooked speech**. *"Put away from you crooked speech, and put devious talk far from you."* **4:24**.

6. **Learn from the ants.** *"Go to the ant, O sluggard; consider her ways, and be wise."* **6:6.**

7. **Jealousy.** *"For jealousy makes a man furious, and he will not spare when he takes revenge."* **6:34.**

8. **Better than jewels.** *"For wisdom is better than jewels, and all that you may desire cannot compare with her."* **8:11.**

9. **Beginning of wisdom.** *"The fear of the Lord is the beginning of wisdom."* **9:10.**

10. **Stolen water.** *"'Stolen water is sweet, and bread eaten in secret is pleasant.'"* **9:17.**

11. **Hatred and love.** *"Hatred stirs up strife, but love covers all offenses."* **10:12.**

12. **Pride and disgrace.** *"When pride comes, then comes disgrace; but with the humble is wisdom."* **11:2.**

13. **Fruit of the righteous.** *"The fruit of the righteous is a tree of life."* **11:30.**

14. **Evil and the righteous.** *"No ill befalls the righteous, but the wicked are filled with trouble."* **12:21.**

15. **Hasty wealth.** *"Wealth hastily gotten will dwindle, but he who gathers little by little will increase it."* **13:11.**

16. **Sparing the rod.** *"He who spares the rod hates his son."* **13:24.**

17. **The deceptive way.** *"There is a way which seems right to a man, but its end is the way to death."* **14:12.**

18. **Tranquillity.** *"A tranquil mind gives life to the flesh, but passion makes the bones rot."* **14:30.**

19. **The soft answer.** *"A soft answer turns away wrath, but a harsh word stirs up anger."* **15:1.**

20. **The eyes of the Lord.** *"The eyes of the Lord are in every place."* **15:3.**

21. **Food and emotions.** *"Better is a dinner of herbs where love is than a fatted ox and hatred with it."* **15:17.**

22. **The hot temper.** *"A hot-tempered man stirs up strife, but he who is slow to anger quiets contention."* **15:18.**

23. **The spirit counts.** *"All the ways of a man are pure in his own eyes, but the Lord weighs the spirit."* **16:2.**

24. **The fountain of life.** *"Wisdom is a fountain of life."***16:22.**

25. **Mealtime emotions.** *"Better is a dry morsel with quiet than a house full of feasting with strife."***17:1.**

26. **Cheerfulness.** *"A cheerful heart is a good medicine."***17:22.**

27. **Virtue of silence.** *"Even a fool who keeps silent is considered wise."* **17:28.**

28. **Enduring sickness.** *"A man's spirit will endure sickness; but a broken spirit who can bear?"***18:14.**

29. **A man's gift.** *"A man's gift makes room for him and brings him before great men."***18:16.**

30. **Finding a wife.** *"He who finds a wife finds a good thing."***18:22.**

31. **Wine a mocker.** *"Wine is a mocker, strong drink a brawler."***20:1.**

32. **The spirit of man.** *"The spirit of man is the lamp of the Lord."***20:27.**

33. **Control of speech.** *"He who keeps his mouth and his tongue keeps himself out of trouble."***21:23.**

34. **A good name.** *"A good name is to be chosen rather than great riches."* **22:1.**

35. **Child training.** *"Train up a child in the way he should go, and when he is old he will not depart from it."***22:6.**

36. **Shun winebibbers.** *"Be not among winebibbers, or among gluttonous eaters of meat."***23:20.**

37. **Sparkling wine.** *"Do not look at wine when it is red, when it sparkles in the cup."***23:31.**

38. **Don't envy evildoers.** *"Fret not yourself because of evildoers, and be not envious of the wicked."***24:19.**

39. **Wise words.** *"A word fitly spoken is like apples of gold in a setting of silver."***25:11.**

40. **The fool and his folly.** *"Answer not a fool according to his folly, lest you be like him yourself."***26:4.**

41. **The tomorrow.** *"Do not boast about tomorrow, for you do not know what a day may bring forth."***27:1.**

42. **The wicked flee.** *"The wicked flee when no one pursues, but the righteous are as bold as a lion."***28:1.**

43. **Four mysteries.** *"Four (things) I do not understand:*

> *the way of an eagle in the sky,*
> *the way of a serpent on a rock,*
> *the way of a ship on the high seas,*
> *and the way of a man with a maiden."* **30:18,19.**

44. **Strong drink.** *"Give strong drink to him who is perishing, and wine to those in bitter distress."* **31:6.**

# ECCLESIASTES

## I. OUTLINE—BRIEF

## II. OUTLINE—COMPLETE

## III. AUTHORSHIP

1. The "Preacher" lived in Jerusalem or its environs, during a time of oppression.

2. He was a high-minded and realistic humanist.

3. The epilogue was added by some devout and admiring intellectual.

4. The book got in the sacred canon because it was supposed to have been written by Solomon.

5. Koheleth is a fictitious name ascribed as author by some later-day editor.

6. Date: As late as 200 B.C. It probably grew by accumulation.

## IV. GENERAL CONSIDERATIONS

1.  This was the most controversial of all books admitted into the Old Testament canon.

2.  The key to the book is: *"Vanity of vanities! All is vanity."* **1:2; 12:8.**

3.  The book possesses no form. Thirty to forty maxims are loosely held together.

4.  Ecclesiastes is a post-exilic book.

5.  Nature is presented as moving in a circle—an ever-recurring cycle. This was a widespread philosophy—Egyptian, Mesopotamian, and Greek.

6.  The book is cynical and mildly pessimistic.

7.  The book discusses wisdom, pleasure, wealth, labor, and evildoing.

8.  The plight of the oppressed, the discontented, the lonely, is presented— along with the incongruities of society.

9.  The philosophy is mildly Epicurian—*"Eat, drink, and be merry, for tomorrow we die."*

## V. CONTENTS

1.  The course of nature does not alter—the present is as the past. Nothing is new.

2.  There is but little satisfaction in great accomplishments. Better get wisdom—improve the mind. But in the end the wise man dies like the fool.

3.  The frustration of "opposites." The futile struggle of life. Weeping and laughing—what is the purpose of life?

4.  How is man better than the beast—both live and die—return to dust.

5.  It is vain to toil for riches and then leave them to others.

6.  Quietness has twice the value of toil.

7.  When you worship be humble and listen. Don't talk much.

8.  Don't make rash vows, but pay when you do make them.

9.  Don't be surprised by injustice and corruption.

10. Learn how to accept your lot—practice contentment.

11. Too much levity and mirth become fools.

12. The righteous may have misfortune, and the wicked may prosper. But the wise man will avoid extremes and fear God.

13. The author of Ecclesiastes decides that he cannot solve the *"riddle of life."*

14. As long as there is life, there is hope—but the dead know nothing.

15. Time and chance happen to all. Wisdom is the only real comfort and satisfaction.

16. Folly may plague you, but wisdom removes difficulties.

17. Take life as it is. *"Master the art of living with yourself as you are, and the world as it is."*

18. *"In the days of your youth remember your Creator."*

19. The book presents little hope for the future life. Immortality and the resurrection find no mention in Ecclesiastes.

## VI. COMPOSITION AND STRUCTURE

1. There is evidence that orthodox editors may have, here and there, added thoughts tending to correct the author's pessimism, and uphold the doctrine of God's supremacy.

2. Such an addition: *"Fear God and keep his commandments; for this is the whole duty of man. For God will bring every deed into judgment."* **12:13,14.**

3. One theory of authorship of Ecclesiastes contends that:
   A. The first author was a Greek philosopher.
   B. The next editor was a Sadducean Jew.
   C. The book was revised by an Epicurean, followed by a "wisdom" editor.
   D. The last of the redactors was a pious Hebrew who sought to introduce touches of orthodox theology.

4. Critics claim that there are thirty-seven kinds of teaching in the book.

5. Maybe the trouble in Ecclesiastes represents the conflict of an orthodox Jew's becoming a Greek humanist—complicated by the later ideas of wisdom editors.

6. When all is said and done, we still think the book was originally written by one person.

7. It has been suggested that this book was not written for the general public, but as a textbook for the wisdom schools.

8. Ecclesiastes reflects many teachings found in Greek, Egyptian, Iranian, and Babylonian literature.

## VII. THEOLOGY

1.  Ecclesiastes uses Elohim for God. The outlook is universalistic. The name Israel occurs only once.

2.  The book does not regard "nature" as a revelation of God.

3.  But the author did regard God as a Creator. But nature seemed to be a "soulless mechanism."

4.  Koheleth depersonalizes all nature. His thought is highly modern in concept.

5.  The account of opposites and contrasts is the most impressive part of the book.

6.  The book is strongly fatalistic and deterministic.

7.  The book is strongly predestination in philosophy.

8.  At death *"all go to one place—both man and beast."* There is little hope of a future life.

9.  The doctrine of Ecclesiastes is found in **2:24,25**. *"There is nothing better for a man than that he should eat and drink, and find enjoyment in his toil. This also, I saw, is from the hand of God; for apart from him who can eat or who can have enjoyment?"*

10.  On the other hand, the book declares that *"happiness is the gift of God."*

11.  The whole book, like Proverbs, exalts wisdom. Only the wise discover the "meaning of life."

12.  The whole book is marked by Hebrew skepticism, like the 28th chapter of Job.

13.  But all are warned against depending on wisdom without the recognition of God.

14.  But still the author was a conformist.

15.  The real theology of the book is to be found in the epilogue.

16.  The God of mercy and love is never mentioned. Prayer is not anywhere noted.

17.  After all, the book, taken as a whole, seems to repudiate the "humanism" which at first seems to be the keynote of the book.

18.  Koheleth was an opportunist—he was something of a modern pragmatist.

19.  But it is a far cry from these teachings to the New Testament gospel of the heavenly kingdom.

**Note: ECCLESIASTICUS**—The Wisdom of Jesus, the Son of Sirach—is one of the outstanding books of the Apocrypha, and in many respects is very much like Ecclesiastes. Some have found it difficult to understand how the one got into the sacred canon, while the other got left out.[1]

## VIII. SELECTED TEXTS

1. **Theme song.** *"Vanity of vanities! All is vanity."* **1:2.**

2. **Everpresent weariness.** *"All things are full of weariness; a man cannot utter it."* **1:8.**

3. **Fatalism.** *"'What befalls the fool will befall me also; why then have I been so very wise?'"* **2:15.**

4. **Can't take it with you.** *"I hated an my toil...seeing that I must leave it to the man who will come after me."* **2:18.**

5. **The seasons.** *"For everything there.is a season, and a time for every matter under heaven."* **3:1.**

6. **Divine stability.** *"Whatever God does endures forever; nothing can be added to it, nor anything taken from it."* **3:14.**

7. **Dust to dust.** *"All go to one place; all are from the dust, and all turn to dust again."* **3:20.**

8. **Love of money.** *"He who loves money will not be satisfied with money; nor he who loves wealth, with gains this also is vanity."* **5:10.**

9. **Sweet sleep.** *"Sweet is the sleep of a laborer, whether he eats little or much; but the surfeit of the rich will not let him sleep."* **5:12.**

10. **A good name.** *"A good name is better than precious ointment."* **7:1.**

11. **Folly of anger.** *"Be not quick to anger, for anger lodges in the bosom of fools."* **7:9.**

12. **Self-righteousness.** *"Be not righteous overmuch, and do not make yourself overwise."* **7:16.**

13. **Man's uprightness.** *"This alone I found, that God made man upright, but they have sought out many devices."* **7:29.**

14. **Delayed punishment.** *"Because sentence against an evil deed is not executed speedily, the heart of the sons of men is fully set to do evil."* **8:11.**

---

[1] *Editor's Note:* **Ecclesiasticus** *is* included in a standard, Catholic Bible. (There are seven books found in the Catholic Old Testament that are not part of the Protestant Old Testament. They are: **Tobit, Judith, First Book of Maccabees, Second Book of Maccabees, The Book of Wisdom, Ecclesiasticus, The Book of Baruch** and additional parts of **The Book of Daniel**, and additional parts of **The Book of Esther**.)

15. **Uncertain future**. *"The living know that they will die, but the dead know nothing."* **9:5**.

16. **Bread and wine.** *"Bread is made for laughter, and wine gladdens life, and money answers everything."* **10:19**.

17. **Cast your bread**. *"Cast your bread upon the waters, for you will find it after many days."* **11:11**.

18. **Remember your Creator.** *"Remember also your Creator in the days of your youth."* **12:1**.

19. **Dust to dust**. *"And the dust returns to the earth as it was, and the spirit returns to God who gave it."* 12:7.

20. **Making books**. *"Of making many books there is no end."* **12:12**.

# THE SONG OF SOLOMON

*(The Song of Songs) (Canticles)*

## I. OUTLINE

## II. AUTHORSHIP

1. There was no single author. The book is an anthology of love songs.

2. The abundant repetitions show that the book is a compilation.

3. It is folk poetry—simple and naive.

4. The collection of songs probably extended over several hundred years. The book was probably put together in the third century B.C., possibly earlier.

## III. PLACE IN THE CANON

1. It Is called "Song of Songs," as we speak of "Lord of Lords."

2. In the earlier times the book was titled "Canticles."

3. There were many objections to the inclusion of this book in the canon. It probably gained such recognition because Solomon was supposed to be the author.

4. It became Scripture notwithstanding that the name of God does not appear.

5. Its mystic and allegorical interpretations led to its acceptance into the Scripture canon.

## IV. PECULIAR FEATURES

1. It is lyric poetry—of exquisite beauty and sensuous symbols.

2. It is monologue—practically no dialogue. But it is not drama.

3.  It is shot through with repetitions.

4.  Our modern term of "love sickness" is derived from this book.

5.  It is wholly lacking in "structure."

6.  It is manifestly folk poetry.

7.  The imagery is extravagant; the metaphors are overbold and sensuous.

8.  The geography ranges from the northern kingdom through Judea and even to Trans-Jordan.

9.  The range is far wider than just the Hebrew people.

10. The Song has a vocabulary all its own—scores of words not found elsewhere in the Bible.

11. There is evidence of both Egyptian and Syrian love poetry.

12. Some features may have been derived from the earlier fertility cults.

## V. INTERPRETATIONS

1.  *Allegorical.* That the groom was Yahweh and the bride, Israel, the "chosen people," was the early concept of the book.

2.  It is the allegorical interpretation that helped Christians to accept the book—the idea that Christ is the bridegroom and the church the bride.

3.  There has been a tendency for Roman Catholics to identify the bride with the Virgin Mary.

4.  Martin Luther thought the bride was a symbol of the state.

5.  *Dramatic Interpretation.* This idea never gained much acceptance.

6.  *Wedding Ceremony.* Again this concept never gained wide belief.

7.  *Secular Love Song Interpretation.* This is the modern view of the book. Today scholars take the book for just what it appears to be.

8.  *The Liturgical Interpretation.* There may be some validity to this idea. At least this might be considered along with the fact of its being a secular collection of folk love lyrics.

## VI. SELECTED TEXTS

1.  **Flowers of love.** *"I am a rose of Sharon, a lily of the valleys."* **2:1**.

2.  **Little foxes.** *"Catch us the foxes, the little foxes, that spoil the vineyards."* **2:15**.

3. **Formidable affection**. *"'Who is this that looks forth like the dawn, fair as the moon, bright as the sun, terrible as an army with banners?'"* **6:10**.

4. **Unquenchable love**. *"Many waters cannot quench love, neither can floods drown it."* **8:7**.

# ISAIAH—THE FIRST

*Isaiah 1-39*

## I. OUTLINE—BRIEF

## II. OUTLINE—COMPLETE

## III. AUTHORSHIP

1. Isaiah the First was born about 770-760 B.C. He grew up and lived in Jerusalem and its environs.

2. He was very familiar with the temple and its services. He may have been a priest.

3. He married a "prophetess" and they had two sons.

4. Isaiah was a cultured Jew and was well educated. He associated with the elite and was a counselor of kings.

5. His forty years of public work covered the reigns of four kings:

   > Uzziah (Azariah).
   > Jotham.
   > Ahaz (Jehoahaz I).
   > Hezekiah.

6. Micah was his contemporary and Amos and Hosea were preaching in the northern kingdom.

7. Isaiah all but practiced medicine.

8. His life was divided into four major periods:

   > Early ministry. 742-734.
   > Withdrawal. 734-715.
   > Middle ministry. 715-705.
   > Later ministry. 705-701.

9. He was a statesman and a sociologist as well as a prophet.

10. Isaiah was "an aristocrat of the spirit."

11. He was probably a member of the king's supreme council.

12. He was surrounded by a group of disciples—"school of the prophets."

## IV. GENERAL CONSIDERATIONS

1. Divisions of the book:

   A. First Isaiah—Chapters 1-39.
   B. Second Isaiah—Chapters 40-55.
   C. Third Isaiah—Chapters 56-66.

2.  First Isaiah taught before the exile.
    Second Isaiah taught during the exile.
    Third Isaiah taught after the exile.

3.  The three books were put together about 180 B.C.

4.  Isaiah is the largest book in the Bible.

5.  There are possibly two reasons why the three groups of writings were
    put together:

    A.  Because they were the only major prophetic writings in
        the form of poetry—verse, meter.
    B.  Maybe the "Isaiah cult" wanted, to have a book bigger than
        Jeremiah, Ezekiel, or the minor prophets.
    (**Note:** The Psalms were all put together about 150 B.C.)

6.  Many of the minor prophets were in poetic form, but not Jeremiah or
    Ezekiel.

7.  With the exception of a few bits of historical prose, all of Isaiah is in
    verse, and it is so arranged in the Revised Standard Version.

8.  There are 17 bits of prose scattered here and there through the book.

9.  There is no such person as the Third Isaiah. This group of collected
    writings (Chapters 56-66) contains passages from both First and
    Second Isaiah.

10. There is intimation in *The Urantia Book* that the exile priests were not
    altogether friendly to the Second Isaiah. They preserved his writings
    because of their sheer grandeur and beauty. (*The Urantia Book* p. 1068).

## V. COMPONENTS AND COMPOSITION

1.  One of the major components is the oracles—reproaches, threats,
    exhortations, and promises.

2.  There are numerous memoirs—consisting of prophetic biography
    and autobiography.

3.  Other material covers history, wars, and teachings.

4.  The Isaiahs wrote most of the book, but later editors added much,
    sometimes copying from others—see **Isa. 2:2-4** and **Micah 4:1-3**.

5.  Among the Dead Sea Scrolls, the largest find was two manuscripts
    of Isaiah, dating possibly from the second century B.C.

6.  Chapters 33 and 34 bear marks of the middle of the second century
    B.C.; Chapters 24-27, after 128 B.C.

## VI. TEACHINGS OF ISAIAH THE FIRST

1. The story of the First Isaiah is also found in **2 Kings Chapters 19 and 20**.

2. Yahweh was sovereign Lord—holy, just, and good.

3. Yahweh was "the Holy One of Israel."

4. God was "weary of all the rituals" of the temple service. He wanted Israel to "cease to do evil and learn to do good."

5. He denounced "pride and self-indulgence."

6. God was an ideal and ethical aristocrat.

7. God was "universal" and would save the "remnant."

8. Isaiah had much to say about the relation of God to man and his world.

9. God was a defender as well as a judge.

10. The "Fatherhood of God"—for Israel.

11. Isaiah all but organized a "personal cult"—within Judah.

12. Righteousness and social conduct were more important than sacrifices and formal worship.

13. He thunders: "Believe the oppressed."

14. His favorite phrases:

    "Thus saith the Lord."
    "The Lord of Hosts."
    "Mighty One of Israel."
    "Let us reason together."

15. He pleads for wise leadership.

16. God will purge, but also restore.

17. Song of the vineyard, **5:1-7**, is a beautiful song and parable.

18. He denounced the rich getting richer and the poor getting poorer.

19. The story of the making of a prophet—the live coal touching his mouth.

20. In **7:14** is the passage: *"a virgin shall bear a son."* In the Revised Version—*"young woman."*

21. In **8:16** he says: *"Bind up... seal"*—the time of his withdrawal.

22. In **14:13,14** is mentioned Mount Assembly, (See *The Urantia Book* p. 489. Also **Eze. 28:14**.) Mount Assembly is the residence of the Faithful of Days on the constellation headquarters.

## VII. CONCLUDING THOUGHTS

1.  The book has been edited and rearranged many times.

2.  Four passages in the *Third* Isaiah are assigned to the *First* Isaiah in *The Urantia Book*, viz., **Isa. 60:1. 61:1. 61:10. 63:9.** (*The Urantia Book* p. 1066-7)

3.  Earmark of editor: **Isa. 7:20.** "Razor"—footnote explains that razor refers to the king of Assyria.

4.  Some quotations from Isaiah the First in *The Urantia Book*: **28:17. 14:3. 30:21. 12:2. 1:18.** (*The Urantia Book* p. 1066)

5.  There is a lot of history in Isaiah, dealing with Egypt, Assyria, and Babylon.

6.  Isaiah advocated a peace policy with Assyria; he opposed Hezekiah's alliance with Egypt.

7.  Jerusalem was saved from the army of Sennacherib by an outbreak of bubonic plague 701 B.C. But in **2 Kings** it says that Hezekiah paid a large tribute.

8.  There are two separate accounts of this siege of Jerusalem. According to history there was but one event.

## VIII. SELECTED TEXTS

1.  **Learning to do good.** *"Cease to do evil, learn to do good."* **1:16,17.**

2.  **Let us reason together.** *"Come now, let us reason together...though your sins are like scarlet, they shall be as white as snow; though they are red like crimson, they shall become like wool."* **1:18.**

3.  **Learn war no more.** *"They shall beat their swords into plowshares and their spears into pruning hooks;...neither shall they learn war any more."* **2:4.**

4.  **Alcoholism.** *"Woe to those who rise early in the morning, that they may run after strong drink, who tarry late into the evening till wine inflames them."* **5:11.**

5.  **The young woman.** *"Behold, a young woman shall conceive and bear a son, and shall call his name Immanuel."* **7:14.** (King James Version renders it *"virgin."*)

6.  **Consulting mediums.** *"When they say to you, 'Consult the mediums and the wizards who chirp and mutter,' should not a people consult their God?"* **8:19.**

7. **The seven adjutant spirits**. *"The spirit of wisdom and understanding, the spirit of counsel and might, the spirit of knowledge and the fear of the Lord."* **11:2.**

8. **The little child**. *"And a little child shall lead them."* **11:6.**

9. **Trust and not be afraid**. *"'Behold, God is my salvation; I will trust, and will not be afraid.'"* **12:2.**

10. **Downfall of Lucifer**. *"'How you are fallen from heaven, O Day Star, son of Dawn!...You said in your heart, "I will ascend to heaven; above the stars of God...I will make myself like the Most High.""'* **14:12-14.**

11. **Perfect peace**. *"'Thou dost keep him in perfect peace, whose mind is stayed on thee.'"* **26:3.**

12. **Here a little and there a little**. *"'It is precept upon precept...line upon line...here a little, there a little.'"* **28:10.**

13. **Source of our strength**. *"'In returning and rest you shall be saved; in quietness and in trust shall be your strength.'"* **30:15.**

14. **The still, small voice**. *"And your ears shall hear a word behind you, saying, 'This is the way, walk in it,' when you turn to the right or when you turn to the left."* **30:21.**

15. **The rock in a weary land**. *"Each will be like a hiding-place from the wind... like the shade of a great rock in a weary land."* **32:2.**

16. **Bread shall be sure**. *"He will dwell on the heights;...his bread will be given him, his water will be sure."* **33:16.**

17. **Joy and gladness**. *"They shall obtain joy and gladness, and sorrow and sighing shall flee away."* **35:10.**

# DEUTERO-ISAIAH

*(Isaiah 40-55—Also Third Isaiah 56-66)*

## I. OUTLINE—BRIEF

## II. OUTLINE—COMPLETE

## III. AUTHORSHIP

1. Next to nothing is known of the author—not even his name; only that he lived and preached in Babylon during the exile.

2. He is the most impersonal of all the prophets, yet he is at the top of them—comparable to Paul.

3. He is equal to any disaster, and proclaims his message with a sovereign independence.

4. He knows all the traditions of Israel and the Babylonian astrology and magic.

5. Comparison of a Cyrus cylinder with **Isa. 45:1** suggests that the author may have belonged to Cyrus's official family.

6. His anger might be great, but always his compassion triumphed.

7. He originated a "theology of world history."

8. He was the most evangelical of all the prophets.

9. He was the founder of the synagogue.

10. He was Israel's greatest poet, profoundest philosopher, and transcendent prophet.

11. He scales the heights of ecstatic praise and descends to the depths of darkest grief.

## IV. LITERARY STYLE

1. There is little in common when we compare the literary style of the First and Second Isaiahs.

2. Chapters 56-66, again, are in a different style than Chapters 40-55.

3. Careful study reveals a "wholeness" and continuity of plan in Deutero-Isaiah. The poetic form, structure, and style suggest that this book was *written*—rather than being a record of preaching.

4. It is probable that he preached his own poetry—just the reverse practice of the former prophets.

5. His oriental style may at times tend toward rhetorical excess.

6. Isaiah is much improved by being read aloud.

7. Deutero-Isaiah is the most dramatic in style of all the Old Testament writings, not excepting Job.

8. Much of this Isaiah could be the better understood by reading Jeremiah and Ezekiel.

9. The high points of his work are the four "suffering servant" songs: **42:1-4. 49:1-6. 50:1-9. 52:13-53:12.**

10. He is fond of quotations and uses them very effectively.

11. His writings are characterized by:
    A. Poetic parallelisms.
    B. Varied grammatical construction.
    C. Repetitions—a dozen types.
    D. Clever rhetorical devices.
    E. Alliterations.
    F. Even rhymes.
    G. Dramatic style.

12. His work shows Isaiah to be a master of oriental literary devices, viz.:

> Strong contrasts.
> Figurative forms.
> Question devices.
> Dialogue.
> Quotations.
> Satire (**44:9-20**).
> Historic analogue.
> Use of imperatives.
> Repetition (Comfort, comfort, **40:1**).

13. He was a master of oriental imagery. He portrayed God as:

Shepherd.

Conqueror.

Warrior.

Woman in travail.

Destroyer.

Leader of the blind.

King on his throne.

Universal judge.

Faithful husband.

Father of Israel.

Creator.

Redeemer.

Lord of nature and history.

14. There is a characteristic use of triads. See **47:4**. *"Our Redeemer—the Lord of Hosts is his name—is the Holy One of Israel."*

## V. TEACHINGS OF ISAIAH

1. Isaiah is always referring to history—Yahweh's dealings with his people.

2. The theme song: Joy in the presence of sorrow, defeat, and disaster.

3. Israel's Creator is to become a Redeemer.

4. The work is a drama of creation, history, and redemption.

5. Yahweh is the eternal—everlasting God.

6. Yahweh alone is God.

7. God reveals himself in his word.

8. Isaiah proclaimed Cyrus as God's agent of deliverance.

9. Yahweh is the Holy One of Israel.

10. Israel would be led by Yahweh.

11. Israel is chosen to become the "light of the nations."

12. Yahweh rules in the kingdom of men.

13. The teaching is dominated by promises, assurance, and exhortation.

14. There is an absence of invective and threats in contrast to the other prophets.

15. He is typically Hebrew. His poems are:

    A. Episodic—rather than rational.

    B. Dramatic—rather than expository.

    C. Lyrical—rather than prosaic.

16. A typical verse:

> "Sing, O heavens, for the Lord has done it;
>    shout, O depths of the earth;
> break forth into singing, O mountains,
>    O forest, and every tree in it!
> For the Lord has redeemed Jacob,
>    and will be glorified in Israel."

**44:23.**

17. He was fond of portraying spiritual redemption in the imagery of military victory.

18. He reiterates: Remember history and expect the new age.

19. His battle cry: "Fear not."

20. "Behold" is the theme word.

21. An earmark is: "Thus says the Lord."

22. Creation is the beginning—salvation the end.

23. The end of national gods. "I am God and there is none other."

24. Monotheism becomes of philosophic age—theologic maturity.

## VI. WORLD INFLUENCE OF THE ISAIAHS

1. In the New Testament Matthew, Mark, Luke, and John all made use of Isaiah as referring to Christ's work. There are more than 25 quotations in the New Testament.

2. Jesus many times made use of Isaiah in reference to his work.

3. The "suffering servant" is the great problem of Isaiah. Does it refer to:

    A. Some prophet?
    B. Israel?
    C. Messiah/Christ?

4. Three world religions come from Deutero-Isaiah:

    A. Judaism.
    B. Christianity.
    C. Islam.

## VII. DEUTERO-ISAIAH IN *THE URANTIA BOOK*

1. The following passages appear in Third Isaiah, but according to *The Urantia Book* (p. 1069-70) were written by Second Isaiah: **57:15. 66:1. 58:11.**

2. Quotations in *The Urantia Book*, p. 1068-70. **40:15. 55:9. 45:18. 44:6. 51:6. 41:10. 45:21. 43:1. 43:2. 49:15,16. 55:7. 40:11. 40:29-31. 57:15. 44:6. 50:2. 42:16. 43:7. 43:25. 66:1. 57:15. 58:11. 59:19.**

## VIII. THE THIRD ISAIAH

1. There was no such person as the Third Isaiah. These writings were produced by ardent members of the "Isaiah cult."

2. Chapters 56-66 were produced after the exile.

3. This third group of writings was added to Isaiah by his followers, and also because they were written in verse—poetic.

4. Jesus uses passages from Third Isaiah about his gospel message. **Luke 4:18-21. (Isa. 61:1,2)**

5. Many sayings of the first Isaiah are found in Third Isaiah. (Some examples are found on p. 1066 of *The Urantia Book*.)

6. There were several authors of Third Isaiah, as shown by inconsistencies and contradictions.

7. Third Isaiah talks about the "new age"—new heavens and the new earth.

8. Third Isaiah sounds much like the writings of Haggai and Zechariah.

9. Remember: These are the times of Ezra and Nehemiah.

10. When the passages of First and Second Isaiah are removed from Third Isaiah there is not much left of high spiritual or prophetic value.

11. There is no mention of the "servant of the Lord" in Third Isaiah.

12. Third Isaiah is more devoted to the "cult," Sabbath-keeping, fasting, temples, worship, and sacrifices.

### SUMMING IT ALL UP

If you had to put all of all three Isaiahs in one verse, it might be Isa. **41:13**:

> *"For I, the Lord your God,*
>
> > *hold your right hand;*
>
> *it is I who say to you, 'Fear not,*
>
> > *I will help you.'"*

# IX. SELECTED TEXTS

1.  **Comfort, comfort.** *"Comfort, comfort my people, says your God."* **40:1**.

2.  **The God of nature.** *"Who has measured the waters in the hollow of his hand and marked off the heavens with a span...weighed the mountains in scales and the hills in a balance."* **40:12**.

3.  **The waters of affliction.** *"When you pass through the waters I will be with you; and through the rivers, they shall not overwhelm you."* **43:2**.

4.  **Suffering with us.** *"You have burdened me with your sins, you have wearied me with your iniquities."* **43:24**.

5.  **Blotting out our sins.** *"I am He who blots out your transgressions for my own sake, and I will not remember your sins."* **43:25**.

6.  **The eternal purpose.** *"'My counsel shall stand, and I will accomplish all my purpose.'"* **46:10**.

7.  **Joy and gladness.** *"They shall obtain joy and gladness, and sorrow and sighing shall flee away."* **51:11**.

8.  **Man of sorrows.** *"He was despised and rejected by men; a man of sorrows, and acquainted with grief."* **53:3**.

9.  **Wounded for our transgressions.** *"He was wounded for our transgressions, he was bruised for our iniquities."* **53:5**.

10. **The contrite heart.** *"'I dwell...with him who is of a contrite and humble spirit.'"* **57:15**.

11. **No rest for the wicked.** *"'But the wicked are like the tossing sea; for it cannot rest, and its waters toss up mire and dirt. There is no peace, says my God, for the wicked.'"* **57:20,21**.

12. **The Lord's fast.** *"'Is not this the fast that I choose:*

    > *to loose the bonds of wickedness,*
    > *to undo the thongs of the yoke,*
    > *to let the oppressed go free,*
    > *and to break every yoke?*

    *"Then shall your light break forth like the dawn, and your healing shall spring up speedily."* **58:6,8**.

13. **Like a watered garden.** *"'And you shall be like a watered garden, like a spring of water.'"* **58:11**.

14. **Arise and shine.** *"Arise, shine; for your light has come, and the glory of the Lord has risen upon you."* **60:1**.

15. **Christ's anointing.** *"The Spirit of the Lord God is upon me, because the Lord has anointed me to bring good tidings to the afflicted."* **61:1.**

16. **Sharing our afflictions.** *"In all their affliction he was afflicted."* **63:9.**

17. **The heavenly throne.** *"Thus says the Lord: 'Heaven is my throne and the earth is my footstool."* **66:1.**

# JEREMIAH

## I. OUTLINE—BRIEF

## II. OUTLINE—COMPLETE

## III. AUTHORSHIP

1. Jeremiah and his secretary, Baruch, wrote the original book.

2. Baruch's scroll was cut up and burned by King Jehoiakim, but Jeremiah redictated it. This was in December 605 B.C.

3. The book was added to up to the times of Zedekiah.

4. Aftar the fall of Jerusalem a Deuteronomic editor revised the book

5.    The memoirs section may have been written by Baruch while in Egypt.

6.    The **D** editorship was completed about 550 B.C.

7.    All of Chapter 24 seems to be the product of the **D** editor. This is also probably true of Chapter 45.

8.    A common date of Jeremiah is 620 B.C.

## IV. JEREMIAH AND HIS MESSAGE

1.    Jeremiah was born during the reign of Josiah (640-609) and lived during the days of the downfall of empires.

2.    Josiah was killed at Megiddo in the battle with Neco of Egypt.

3.    Jehoiakim (son of Josiah) was placed on the throne by the king of Egypt, and his eleven years covered much of Jeremiah's activities.

4.    This king was pompous and proud and rejected most of the council of Jeremiah.

5.    After the battle of Carchemish he transferred his loyalty to Babylon.

6.    When Jerusalem neglected to pay tribute, the king of Babylon took the city. He put another son of Josiah on the throne—Zedekiah. He was more friendly to Jeremiah.

7.    Finally, the Babylonians captured Jerusalem and appointed Gedaliah governor. (August 587 B.C.)

8.    In five years the governor was assassinated and Jeremiah with others fled to Egypt.

9.    Jeremiah was born and grew up in a village two miles northeast of Jerusalem—Anathoth.

10.    Jeremiah was influenced by Hosea—and quotes from him.

11.    When Jeremiah prophesied trouble from the "north," the Jews thought he referred to the Scythians, but later decided that it was the Babylonians.

12.    Jeremiah was never in full favor with the kings. Even Josiah consulted Huldah, the prophetess. (**2 Kings 22:14-20**)

13.    Jeremiah was not an advocate of Josiah's Deuteronomic reforms— in fact, opposed some of them.

14.    Jeremiah always counseled submission to the Babylonians.

15.    Jeremiah was always opposed to sacrifices.

16.    When Jeremiah advised surrendering to the Babylonians, they cast him into a prison, where he sank in the mire up to his armpits.

17. To show his faith in the ultimate return from captivity, Jeremiah purchased a field in his native village.

18. The Babylonian governor took Jeremiah out of prison and gave him his liberty.

19. He was taken to Egypt against his will.

20. There is a legend that Jeremiah was stoned to death in Egypt by his exasperated fellow countrymen.

21. Jeremiah was not a mystic. He had a strong personality. We know more about the "inner life" of Jeremiah than of any other prophet.

22. It is possible that he was forbidden to marry. **(16:1-13)**

23. He suffered many seasons of bitterness and despair. But he was no "weeping prophet."

24. The idea of his being a "weeping prophet" comes from ascribing authorship of the book of Lamentations to him.

25. At one time he did pray for vengeance on his enemies—even on their wives and children.

26. Jeremiah was comforted by a very loyal African servant.

27. Jeremiah came from a wealthy priestly family.

28. The kings and princes regarded Jeremiah as a traitor.

29. He proclaimed a "new covenant" to be "written upon men's hearts."

30. And this is the beginning of individual religion, as contrasted with nationalistic religion.

## V. JEREMIAH'S THEOLOGY

1. Jeremiah was not a theologian, but his writings were theologically sound.

2. He did not adore God with awe like Isaiah and Ezekiel; he wrestled with God like Jacob.

3. He believed in the sovereignty of God—God as the Creator of the natural order.

4. Yahweh was the controller and director of history.

5. He was "a God at hand and a God afar off"—both immanent and transcendent.

6. A God of love—justice, mercy, and power.

7. The Father of Israel.

8. *"I have loved you with an everlasting love."*

9. God wants not sacrifice and ritual, but repentance and obedience.

10. Jeremiah was a real monotheist.

11. He taught religion for the individual—rather than for the nation.

12. He taught a new covenant for the heart of each individual.

13. Yahweh deals with man's heart—seat of both mind and the emotions.

14. Jeremiah was the prophet of personal religious experience.

15. You will find God if you "seek him with a whole heart."

16. He taught the religion of sin, repentance, and salvation.

17. Human nature is fickle. *"The heart is deceitful above all things, and desperately corrupt."* **17:9.**

18. He regarded man as being innately stubborn.

19. Repentance means "conscious turning away from all evil."

20. Jeremiah is author of the proverb about the Ethiopian changing his skin or the leopard his spots.

21. Motivation becomes a big part of religious experience.

## VI. SUMMARY OF JEREMIAH'S LIFE

Jeremiah lived 100 years after Isaiah, during the capture and destruction of Jerusalem. His life (640-587 B.C.) brought him in contact with events in the reigns of the last of the Judean kings:

1. Manasseh *(687-642)* .................. **2 Chron. 33. Jer. 15:4.**

2. Amon *(642-640)*................................ **2 Kings 21:18-2**
   **2 Chron. 33:21-24. Jer. 1:2**

3. Josiah *(640-609)* ................. **2 Kings 21:24-26; 23:29,30**
   **Jer. 25:3**

4. Jehoahaz II *(609 - 3 mos.)* ................... **2 Kings 23:31-34**
   **Jer. 22:11**

5. Jehoiakim *(609-598)* ...................... **2 Kings 23:36-24:6**
   **Jer. 22:18**

6. Jehoiachin *(598 - 3 mos.)* ................... **2 Kings 24:6-15**
   **Jer. 52:31-34**

7. Zedekiah *(598-587)* ......................... **2 Kings 24:17-20**
   **Jer. 2:1-7; 34:1-11; 52:1-11**

## VII. SELECTED TEXTS

1.  **The start of Jeremiah's work**. *"Before I formed you in the womb I knew you, and before you were born I consecrated you; I appointed you a prophet to the nations."* **1:5**.

   (**Note:** This text recalls teachings of *The Urantia Book*, respecting Thought Adjusters getting advance projections regarding their prospective human subjects, as found on pages 1185-6.)

2.  **Broken cisterns**. *"My people have committed two evils: they have forsaken me, the fountain of living waters, and hewed out cisterns for themselves, broken cisterns, that can hold no water."* **2:13**.

3.  **What was wrong**. *"From the least to the greatest of them, every one is greedy for unjust gain; and from prophet to priest, every one deals falsely. They have healed the wound of my people lightly, saying, "Peace, peace," when there is no peace."* **6:13,14**.

4.  **No peace**. *"We looked for peace, but no good came, for a time of healing, but behold, terror."* **8:15**.

5.  **No balm in Gilead**. *"Is there no balm in Gilead? Is there no physician there? Why then has the health of the daughter of my people not been restored?"* **8:22**.

6.  **We glory in the Lord**. *"But let him who glories glory in this, that he understands and knows me, that I am the Lord who practice kindness, justice, and righteousness in the earth; for in these things I delight."* **9:24**.

7.  **The deceitful heart**. *"The heart is deceitful above all things, and desperately corrupt; who can understand it?"* **17:9**.

8.  **Jeremiah in stocks**. *"Then Pashhur beat Jeremiah the prophet, and put him in the stocks that were in the upper Benjamin Gate of the house of the Lord."* **20:2**.

9.  **Pashhur's fate**. *"And you, Pashhur...shall go into captivity...and there you shall die...you and all your friends, to whom you have prophesied falsely."* **20:6**.

10. **A God at hand**. *"Am I a God at hand...and not a God afar off?...Do I not fill heaven and earth?"* **23:23,24**.

11. **Jeremiah surrenders**. *"Only know for certain that if you put me to death, you will bring innocent blood upon yourselves."* **26:15**.

12. **Finding God**. *"You will seek me and find me; when you seek me with all your heart."* **29:13**.

13. **Joy for mourning**. *"I will turn their mourning into joy, I will comfort them, and give them gladness for sorrow."* **31:13**.

14. **Eating sour grapes**. *"In those days they shall no longer say:"The fathers have eaten sour grapes, and the children's teeth are set on edge." ...Each man who eats sour grapes, his teeth shall be set on edge."* **31:29,30**.

15. **Jeremiah's scroll**. *"Then Jeremiah took another scroll and gave it to Baruch ...who wrote on it at the dictation of Jeremiah all the words...which Jehoiakim king of Judah had burned in the fire."* **36:32**.

16. **Jeremiah in the pit**. *"They took Jeremiah and cast him into the cistern... And there was no water in the cistern, but only mire, and Jeremiah sank in the mire."* **38:6**.

17. **The fate of Zedekiah**. *"He put out the eyes of Zedekiah, and bound him in fetters...The Chaldeans burned the king's house...and broke down the walls of Jerusalem."* **39:7,8**.

18. **Jeremiah goes to Mizpah**. *"Then Jeremiah went to...Mizpah, and dwelt... among the people who were left in the land."* **40:6**.

19. **Go to Egypt against Jeremiah**. *"And they came into the land of Egypt, for they did not obey the voice of the Lord."* **43:7**.

# LAMENTATIONS

## I. OUTLINE

## II. AUTHORSHIP

1. Jeremiah was not the author of Lamentations. The book was ascribed to him probably because of **2 Chron. 35:25**.

2. The five poems were by different authors.

3. The nature of the book differs from Jeremiah in that there is:

   A. Higher regard for kings, princes, and priests than Jeremiah had.
   B. More concern for the cultus than Jeremiah had.
   C. Expectation of help from Egypt, which is contrary to the counsel of Jeremiah. **(Lam. 4:17. Jer. 42:13-17)**

4. Date: Probably 586-500 B.C.

## III. FORM AND STRUCTURE

1. These dirges originated as a funeral spell to keep the dead in place and thus protect the living.

2. These dirges were composed by women professionals.

3. Lamentations has to do with sorrow over the fall and destruction of Jerusalem.

4. The first four poems are arranged as an alphabetic acrostic of twenty-two lines—one for each letter in the Hebrew alphabet.

5. The book is a good illustration of perfect metrical structure.

6. These poems are really elegies.

- - - - - -

It is the intent of this book to memorialize the tragic destruction of Jerusalem—to teach the lesson of the penalty for sin and, afford hope for the future.

## IV. SELECTED TEXTS

1.  **Wormwood and gall.** *"Remember my affliction and my bitterness, the wormwood and the gall!"* **3:19.**

2.  **Waiting for salvation.** *"It is good that one should wait quietly for the salvation of the Lord."* **3:26.**

3.  **Source of affliction.** *"For he does not willingly afflict or grieve the sons of men."* **3:33.**

# EZEKIEL

## I. OUTLINE—BRIEF

## II. OUTLINE—COMPLETE

## III. AUTHORSHIP

1.   Ezekiel was author of the original book. But the book was subjected to a thorough job of rewriting by a later editor.

2.   The editorial work was so extensive as to almost make this editor a coauthor.

3.   The editor greatly amplified the reasons for the captivity: idolatry, lewdness, false prophets, Sabbath-breaking, immorality, social sins, etc.

4.   The editor may have also been a priest.

5.   The editor made use of more than fifty characteristic words or phrases in his work. The phrase "Then they will know that I am the Lord" he uses 56 times.

6.   Date: Generally accepted—593-571 B.C.

## IV. EZEKIEL HIMSELF

1.   The author was familiar with the temple and had heard the preaching of Jeremiah.

2.   His book covers 22 years of his life.

3.   He was taken to Babylon along with King Jehoiachin.

4.   He lived in a colony of exiles at Tel Abib on the Chebar, a canal of the Euphrates irrigation system.

5.   He was married and had a house of his own. His great tragedy was the loss of his wife.

6.   In trying to solve his problems, Ezekiel failed to make adjustment to reality; he retreated into a dream world of his own fantasy.

7. It would seem that he finally resolved his conflicts on the higher level of religious adjustment and became a prophet.

8. He had visions and was addicted to allegories.

9. He contributed much to the doctrine of angelology among the Hebrews.

10. It is strange that neither Jeremiah nor Ezekiel ever mentions the other. The same is true of Amos and Hosea.

11. From **3:25,26, 4:4, 24:27,** and **33:22** we may conclude that his ailment was catatonic schizophrenia.

12. You recall that King Saul was afflicted with manic-depressive psychosis. Now we have Ezekiel with schizophrenia.

## V. CHAPTERS 40-48

1. It is doubtful if Ezekiel wrote these chapters. The concept of a "new age" belongs to the editor rather than Ezekiel.

2. The new Jerusalem and new ideas about inner religious experience also belong to the editor.

3. Ezekiel was more pessimistic than the editor.

4. The Book of Ezekiel is replete with new ideas and concepts. And this all suggests that numerous writers and editors contributed to the book as we now have it.

## VI. EZEKIEL'S MESSAGE

1. Like Isaiah, he protested against foreign alliances.

2. He is the outstanding prophet teaching about angels.

3. Yahweh had as wives two sisters; one consorted with the Assyrians and was punished; the other with the Egyptians and was likewise destroyed.

4. He was the prophet of allegories—winds, fire, wheels within wheels, etc.

5. He introduced the idea of God as a shepherd, which Jesus used so effectively.

6. He talked about *"individual religious experience"—"God's law written on the tablets of the heart."*

7. Individual responsibility for sin—*"Whoso sinneth, he shall die."* He denounced concept of fathers' eating sour grapes and the children's teeth being set on edge.

8.  Ezekiel tried to reform the Jewish ritual. Not so much against ceremonies as was Jeremiah.

9.  He uttered curses against Ammon, Moab, Edom, Philistia, Sidon, and Egypt.

10. He presented a universal God, but not a universal religion—Yahweh and Israel belonged together.

11. It would seem that the allegories of Ezekiel had considerable influence on the author of Revelation—the river of life, foursquare city, etc.

## VII. SELECTED TEXTS

1.  **Seraphic velocity.** *"And the living creatures darted to and fro, like a flash of lightning."* **1:14.**

2.  **Called "Son of man."** *"And he said to me, 'Son of man, eat what is offered to you; eat this scroll, and go, speak to the house of Israel.'"* **3:1.**

3.  **Divine wrath and anger.** *"Thus shall my anger spend itself, and I will vent my fury upon them and satisfy myself; and they shall know that I, the Lord, have spoken in my jealousy.'"* **5:13.**

4.  **Cause and effect.** *"And you shall know that I have not done without cause all that I have done in it, says the Lord God.'"* **14:23.**

5.  **Like mother, like daughter.** *"Behold, every one...will use this proverb about you, 'Like mother, like daughter.'"'"* **16:44.**

6.  **Eating sour grapes.** *"What do you mean..."The fathers have eaten sour grapes, and the children's teeth are set on edge'? As I live, says the Lord God, this proverb shall no more be used by you in Israel.'"* **18:2,3.**

7.  **No pleasure in death of the wicked.** *"Have I any pleasure in the death of the wicked, says the Lord God.'"* **18:23.**

8.  **References to Lucifer.** *"You were blameless in your ways from the day you were created, till iniquity was found in you...Your heart was proud because of your beauty; you corrupted your wisdom for the sake of your splendor.'"* **28:15,17.**

9.  **His aphonia cured.** *"So my mouth was opened, and I was no longer dumb."* **33:22.**

10. **Showers of blessing.** *"And I will send down the showers in their season; they shall be showers of blessing.'"* **34:26.**

11. **Being unafraid.** *"They shall dwell securely, and none shall make them afraid.'"* **34:28.**

12. **A new heart**. *"A new heart I will give you, and a new spirit I will put within you."* **36:26**.

13. **The valley of dry bones**. *"There was a noise, and behold, a rattling; and the bones came together, bone to its bone."* **37:7**.

14. **Gog and Magog**. *"I will summon every kind of terror against Gog."* **38:21**. *"You shall fall...for I have spoken, says the Lord God."* **39:5**.

(**Note**: For a hundred years prophetic students have referred this prophecy about Gog and Magog to Russia.)

# DANIEL

## I. OUTLINE

## II. AUTHORSHIP

1.    Book was written during the Maccabean wars.

2.    It was written during the reign of Antiochus IV (Epiphanes).

3.    The writer knew about Jeremiah.

4.    Daniel is mentioned as a prophet in **Matt. 24:15**.

5.    The book was not written during the captivity.

6.    It was not written by Daniel, though he was probably a real person.

7.    The book is the work of one author.

8.    Copies of Daniel were found among the Dead Sea scrolls.

9.    It was written about 165 B.C.

## III. HISTORICAL BACKGROUND

1.    Greek culture is spreading and a Greek Bible is produced.

2.    In 175 B.C. Antiochus IV (Epiphanes) becomes ruler of the Seleucid empire.

3.    Antiochus determines to stamp out the Jewish religion. He plunders the temple, kills Jews, and razes the walls of Jerusalem.

4. In 168 B.C. he sets up an altar in the temple (Jupiter), profanes the Sabbath, and forbids circumcision.

5. All this brings on the Maccabean revolt. The temple was cleansed and rededicated.

6. The book of Daniel was written to help the Jews withstand the persecutions of Antiochus.

7. Antiochus died in his campaign against the Parthians in 163 B.C.

## IV. COMPOSITION OF THE BOOK

1. Daniel interprets Nebuchadnezzar's dream—the golden idol, and the fiery furnace.

2. Then comes the feast of Belshazzar and the lions' den.

3. Then the vision of the four beasts and the little horn.

4. Interpretation of the little horn:

    A. Protestants, in general, have referred it to Antiochus Epiphanes.
    B. Seventh Day Adventists and other sects refer it to the Papacy.
    C. Others have referred it to Hitler, Stalin, etc.

5. Other visions have to do with empire history, Alexander the Great, and Roman history.

6. Daniel becomes "head of the wise men" of Babylon.

## V. TEACHINGS OF DANIEL

1. Daniel is the first of the apocalyptic books—the doctrine of the end of the age.

2. The kingdom is literal—the Messiah sits on David's throne. It is an "everlasting kingdom."

3. Daniel presents an advanced theology regarding angels, survival, the resurrection, and many other features.

4. He presents the concept of "the Son of Man," along with Enoch, and may have had some part in Jesus' deciding to adopt such a title.

5. The theology is that God foreknows all things and determines everything.

6. In theology Daniel is midway between the doctrines of the olden prophets and the times of Jesus.

7. Daniel gives angels a new and enlarged personal dignity.

8. The book of Daniel is the prime textbook of all the Adventist denominations.

## VI. SELECTED TEXTS

1.  **A dietetic test.** *"'Test your servants for ten days; let us be given vegetables to eat and water to drink. Then let our appearance...be observed by you, and according to what you see deal with your servants.' At the end of ten days it was seen that they were better in appearance and fatter in flesh than all the youths who ate the king's rich food."* **1:12,13,15.**

2.  **Wise men and the king's dream.** *"Because of this the king was angry and very furious, and commanded that all the wise men of Babylon be destroyed."* **2:12.**

    *"Daniel answered the king, 'No wise men, enchanters, magicians, or astrologers can show to the king the mystery which the king has asked, but there is a God in heaven who reveals mysteries.'"* **2:27,28.**

3.  **Daniel honored.** *"Then the king gave Daniel high honors and many great gifts."* **2:48.**

4.  **Three worthies in the fiery furnace.** *"He answered, 'But I see four men loose, walking in the midst of the fire, and they are not hurt; and the appearance of the fourth is like a son of the gods.'"* **3:25.**

5.  **Rule of the Most Highs.** *"'To the end that the living may know that the Most High rules in the kingdom of men.'"* **4:17.**

6.  **Handwriting on the wall.** *"The fingers of a man's hand appeared and wrote on the plaster of the wall of the king's palace."* **5:5.**

    *"'This is the interpretation of the matter...God has numbered the days of your kingdom...You have been weighed in the balances and found wanting... your kingdom is divided and given to the Medes and Persians.'"* **5:26-28.**

7.  **Daniel in the lions' den.** *"And Daniel was...cast into the den of lions... Then Daniel said to the king...'My God sent his angel and shut the lions' mouths, and they have not hurt me.'"* **6:16,21,22.**

8.  **Vision of the four beasts.** *"'And four great beasts came up out of the sea, different from one another...I considered the horns, and behold, there came up among them another horn, a little one, before which three of the first horns were plucked...As I looked, thrones were placed and one that was ancient of days took his seat.'"* **7:3,8,9.**

9.  **Alexander the Great.** *"Behold, a he-goat came from the west...without touching the ground; and the goat had a conspicuous horn between his eyes."* **8:5.**

10. **The 2,300 days.** *"'For two thousand and three hundred evenings and mornings; then the sanctuary shall be restored to its rightful state.'"* **8:14.**

11. **The abomination of desolation.** *"And they shall set up the abomination that makes desolate."* **11:31**.

12. **Mention of Michael.** *"'At that time shall arise Michael, the great prince who has charge of your people.'"* **12:1**.

13. **A special resurrection.** *"'And many of those who sleep in the dust of the earth shall awake, some to everlasting life, and some to shame and everlasting contempt.'"* **12:2**.

# HOSEA

## I. OUTLINE

## II. AUTHORSHIP

1. Hosea, prophet to the northern kingdom, wrote the book, probably about 750 B.C.

2. He wrote during the reign of Jeroboam, shortly before Isaiah the First.

3. Soon after the writing a Judaic editor made slight changes and additions.

## III. SERMONS AND ADDRESSES

1. He denounced the fertility cults, the calf of Samaria.

2. He preached against political intrigue—foreign alliances.

3. He held up the "covenant of love" and asked Israel to return to its "first love."

4. Much of Hosea's preaching was done at the autumn festival.

6. He preached a coming retribution.

5. He made a new presentation of Yahweh as:

    A. Almighty Power.
    B. Judge.
    C. Savior.
    D. Giver of Victory.
    E. Giver of Rain.

7. We have every reason to believe that they had written laws at this time.

## IV. THE PROPHET AND HIS HOME

1. Hosea had a home in the country, and was a man of the country.

2. He says the Lord instructed him to marry a harlot. Probably a temple prostitute.

3. Accordingly, he married Gomer and they had three children.

4. Gomer left him, returned to harlotry, and ended up in the slave market, where Hosea found her and took her back.

5. Hosea used this experience with Gomer as an illustration of how Israel had gone after other gods, and how Yahweh had forgiven and taken Israel back.

6. He made an allegory of his marriage and applied it to Israel and its relationship to Yahweh.

## V. THE BOOK

1. Hosea is a small but very influential book among Old Testament writings. More than 30 direct and indirect quotations from it are contained in the New Testament.

2. Hosea was among the early prophets to teach personal relations with God.

3. His religion sounds like the Second Isaiah and the later New Testament Gospels.

4. Jeremiah knew about Hosea and made use of his writings.

5. Hosea taught that God was righteous in all his acts.

6. His message was: *"Come, let us return to the Lord."* (**6:1**)

## VI. SELECTED TEXTS

1.  **Sons of God.** *"It shall be said to them, 'Sons of the living God."* **1:10.**

2.  **Hosea marries a harlot.** *"For their mother has played the harlot.'"* **2:5.**

3.  **Value of knowledge.** *"My people are destroyed for lack of knowledge."* **4:6.**

4.  **Returning to God.** *"'Come, let us return to the Lord;...he has stricken, and he will bind us up.'"* **6:1.**

5.  **Love, not sacrifice.** *"For I desire steadfast love and not sacrifice."* **6:6.**

# JOEL

## I. OUTLINE

## II. AUTHORSHIP

1.  Joel was the author and he lived in or near Jerusalem.

2.  He has been called the "temple prophet."

3.  The book was written about 350 B.C.; certainly later than 400.

4.  Joel was a great borrower. He quotes, without credit, from Isaiah, Ezekiel, Obadiah, Zephaniah, Psalms, Nehemiah, Exodus, Jonah, Zechariah, Amos, and Micah.

5.  His quoting from so many prophets makes him one of the later prophets.

## III. LOOK AT THE BOOK

1.  It is a rhythmic book—even when not in poetic form.

2.  Joel is clever in using contrasts, repetitions, metaphors, and alliterations.

3.  The real locust plague he describes is attributed to Yahweh, because of wrongdoing; the curse is removed upon repentance. (Joel did not know about the 17-year locusts.)

4.  The exponents of the "social gospel" point to Joel to prove that man's spiritual capacity is improved by satisfaction of physical needs.

5.  It was Joel's prediction of the pouring out of the Spirit upon all flesh that Peter quoted on the Day of Pentecost. (**Acts 2:16-21. Joel 2:28-32**)

6.  But for the time being, God's spirit dwelt only with Israel.

7.  Cried Joel: *"Rend your hearts and not your garments."* **2:13**.

8.  Joel pronounced judgment upon all nations who had sold Jews into slavery.

## IV. LEADING IDEAS

1.  Blessings and judgments through nature (the locusts).

2.  Necessity for heartfelt repentance.

3.  Salvation by grace through faith.

4.  Importance of formal worship.

5.  Israel as the "chosen people."

6.  God in history.

7.  The "Day of the Lord."

8.  Outpouring of the Spirit.

9.  Final judgment of the nations.

10.  Final blessings of Israel.

11.  The little book of Joel had considerable influence upon many writers of the New Testament.

## V. SELECTED TEXTS

1.  **Rend your hearts**. *"'Rend your hearts and not your garments.' Return to the Lord, your God, for he is gracious and merciful, slow to anger, and abounding in steadfast love, and repents of evil."* **2:13**.

2.  **Pouring out the spirit**. *"'And it shall come to pass afterward, that I will pour out my spirit on all flesh.'"* **2:28**.

3.  **Darkened sun and moon**. *"'The sun shall be turned to darkness, and the moon to blood, before the great and terrible day of the Lord comes.'"* **2:31**.

4.  **Plowshares into swords**. *"Beat your plowshares into swords, and your pruning hooks into spears; let the weak say 'I am a warrior.'"* **3:10**.

5.  **The valley of decision**. *"Multitudes, multitides, in the valley of decision!"* **3:14**.

# Amos

## I. OUTLINE

## II. AUTHORSHIP

1. Amos was the first of the prophets who left us a record of his message.

2. Amos came from Tekoa—six miles south of Jerusalem. Now a cluster of ruins on a hill.

3. Amos was a shepherd and a dresser of sycamores—wild fig trees. He was not an untutored rustic—he was an educated man.

4. While he came from the south, he preached in the northern kingdom.

5. He taught during the reign of Jeroboam II, 786-746 B.C.

6. Amos was a great student and observer of nature.

7. He was not a prophet by profession—he did not belong to the "school of the prophets."

8. Amos did not write the book as we have it, but he supplied the material. From writings and tradition his disciples compiled the book.

9. A later optimist was bold to add three passages of hope—**4:13, 5:8,9, and 9:5,6.**

10. Date: Around 750 B.C.

## III. THE MESSAGE OF AMOS

1. Amos denounced the neglect of the poor and the sensuality of the rich.

2. He was a "prophet of doom." He proclaimed the downfall of the kingdom.

3. The Israelites thought that they were the "chosen people"—that Yahweh belonged to them.

4. Yahweh was "Lord of nature" as well as "Ruler of nations."

5. Yahweh is a "God of righteousness."

6. He proclaimed a doom that was final and complete.

7. The "ivory embellishments" denounced by Amos have recently been excavated and are to be found in the Palestine museum.

8. Amos said: The ritual cannot take the place of righteousness.

9. Amos extended the moral jurisdiction of Yahweh over all nations.

10. He planted the roots of universal monotheism as it pervaded Judaism, Christianity, and Islam.

11. Amos was the Martin Luther of the Jewish religion.

12. His reforms were so radical that Amaziah accused him of sedition.

13. Amos proclaimed the new and unlimited sovereignty of God.

14. His originality was complete.

## IV. SELECTED TEXTS

1. **Revealing his secrets.** *"Surely the Lord God does nothing, without revealing his secret to his servants the prophets.'"* **3:7.**

2. **The God of nature.** *"He who made the Pleiades and Orion, and turns deep darkness into the morning, and darkens the day into night, who calls for the waters of the sea, and pours them out upon the surface of the earth."* **5:8.**

3. **Seeking the good.** *"Seek good, and not evil, that you may live."* **5:14.**

4. **Hating evil.** *"Hate evil, and love good, and establish justice in the gate."* **5:15.**

5. **Justice and righteousness.** *"Let justice roll down like waters, and righteousness like an overflowing stream."* **5:24**.

6. **Ease and security.** *"'Woe to those who are at ease in Zion, and to those who feel secure on the mountain of Samaria.'"* **6:1**.

7. **Again the dark sun and moon.** *"'I will make the sun go down at noon, and darken the earth in broad daylight.'"* **8:9.**

# OBADIAH

## I. OUTLINE

## II. AUTHORSHIP

1. The author is unknown. Some think there were two authors.

2. The book was written after the exile.

3. Date: Sometime during the 5th century B.C.

## III. LOOK AT THE BOOK

1. The book deals with the traditional enemies of Israel. The Edomites refused to let the Israelites pass through their land when entering Canaan.

2. Israel and Edom are supposed to be descendants of twin brothers—Jacob and Esau.

3. Edomites were very cruel to Jews during the destruction of Jerusalem, aided their enemies, and persecuted refugees.

4. Some passages are found in Jeremiah and Joel. **(Jer. 49:7-22. Joel 3:19. Obad. v. 1-4.)** Perhaps all quoted from an earlier oracle.

5. The first half deals with the expulsion of the Edomites; the second half with the coming of the kingdom of God.

6. **Joel 2:32** quotes Obadiah, so this book was written before Joel. **(Obad. v.17)**

## IV. LEADING IDEAS

1. God's judgment of the nations through history.

2. Obadiah was somewhat of a narrow nationalist.

3.    His doctrine does not sound much like the teachings of the Second Isaiah.

4.    The soul-sleepers rely much on the doctrine of **verse 16.**

5.    The last half of the book is among the strongest pictures of the "everlasting kingdom"—comparable with Daniel and Revelation.

## V. SELECTED TEXTS

1.    **State of the dead.** *"They shall drink and stagger, and shall be as though they had not been."* **v. 16.**

# JONAH

## I. OUTLINE

## II. AUTHORSHIP

1. Author is unknown. The book was post-exilic. Date: Somewhere between 400 and 300 B.C.

2. It could not have been written by the prophet Jonah mentioned in **2 Kings 14:25** (eighth century).

3. It is a skillful piece of literature. While it is unique among all Old Testament writings, it deserves a place among the Scriptures.

4. Jonah is the noblest missionary evangelistic tract in the Bible.

## III. JONAH IN *THE URANTIA BOOK*

1. On page 1423 Jesus used the story of Jonah to teach a valuable lesson to the young man at Joppa. He did not inform his pupil as to whether the story was history or parable.

2. On page 1767 Jesus discussed Jonah with Nathaniel. He as much as said Jonah was an evangelistic parable or allegory.

3. The references in **Matt. 12:39-41** and **Luke 11:29-32**, where Jesus refers to Jonah in connection with his own death, do not appear in *The Urantia Book*.

4. Even if Jesus did make use of the Jonah story, it does not follow that such use of the story means that Jesus is validating the Jonah narrative as history. If a modern preacher refers to Shakespeare's Macbeth, it does not mean that he regards Macbeth as a historical person.

5. Jesus, in referring to the prodigal son, in the parable of that name, does not mean that this prodigal son was a historical character.

## IV. HISTORY OR PARABLE?

1. In the Old Testament we have psalms, proverbs, histories, sermons, letters, and parables. It is important that any book should be placed in its proper category.

2. In the case of the real prophets, little or nothing is said about the prophet—all attention is paid to his message. In the case of Jonah, all attention is paid to the so-called prophet, while his message is granted but eight words.

3. Would a real prophet turn his back upon God's call and run away in the opposite direction, taking a ship for Spain?

4. And when he did reluctantly return to his mission, would he stupidly mourn over the success of his work?

5. A storm is created to plague Jonah's boat, and a calm ensues when he is thrown overboard.

6. Three days in the fish's belly—and then coming up alive—is just too much to accept.

7. History recognizes no "king of Nineveh." The size of the city as shown by its ruins is not the preposterous size given in Jonah.

8. Could a gourd grow into the size of a shade tree overnight?

9. Could Jonah warn and convert a whole city in one month?

10. This parable is a protest against the bitterness of the Jews toward gentiles—especially against the edict directing all Jews to give up their gentile wives and children.

11. The book does present a powerful spiritual message—one of tolerance, divine mercy, and love.

## V. LOOK AT THE BOOK

1. Regarded as a parable or an allegory, the story is well done—it is really a masterpiece.

2. The name for God is both Yahweh and Elohim. This would not occur in a serious religious narrative.

3. In olden times Jonah was spoken of as being three days in "the belly of hell." They did not regard the book as factual.

4. The psalm introduced in Chapter 2 is much like those found elsewhere in the Old Testament. In almost a dozen psalms there are passages remindful of Jonah.

## VI. SELECTED TEXTS

1. **Jonah's commission.** *"'Arise, go to Nineveh...and cry out against it.'... But Jonah rose to flee to Tarshish...He went down to Joppa and found a ship...so he paid the fare, and went on board."* **1:2,3.**

2.  **Jonah thrown overboard.** *"So they took up Jonah and threw him into the sea."* **1:15.**

3.  **The big fish.** *"And the Lord appointed a great fish to swallow up Jonah; and Jonah was in the belly of the fish three days and three nights."* **1:17.**

4.  **Jonah prays.** *"Then Jonah prayed to the Lord his God from the belly of the fish."* **2:1.**

5.  **God speaks to the fish.** *"And the Lord spoke to the fish, and it vomited out Jonah upon the dry land."* **2:10.**

6.  **Jonah's disappointment.** *"But it displeased Jonah exceedingly, and he was angry...And he...said... 'It is better for me to die."* **4:1-3.**

7.  **And God creates a plant.** *"God appointed a plant...that it might be a shade over his head...So Jonah was exceedingly glad because of the plant. But... God appointed a worm which attacked the plant...and the sun beat upon Jonah's head so that he was faint."* **4:6-8.**

8.  **Mercy for mankind.** *"'You pity the plant... should not I pity Nineveh, that great city?'"* **4:10,11.**

# MICAH

## I. OUTLINE

## II. AUTHORSHIP

1.  The book was the work of Micah.

2.  Micah lived at Moresheth, which survives today as Morissa, in southwestern Palestine.

3.  He was a contemporary of Isaiah.

4.  He lived only twenty miles from Amos.

5.  His work was of more importance than was generally recognized.

6.  He was a "proletarian" prophet. He was but little influenced by Isaiah.

7.  Most of his work was done in the days of Hezekiah—715-686 B.C.

8.  Micah was a poet—he wrote in verse.

## III. MICAH AND HIS TIMES

1.  Micah does not talk much about either idolatry or immortality. His message is: "Do justly, love kindness, and walk humbly with your God."

2.  The three parts of the book deal with:

    A.  Judgment.
    B.  Comfort.
    C.  Salvation.

3.  Micah longed for a universal religion.

4.  Almost a hundred years later, Jeremiah remembered Micah. (**Jer. 26:18,19**)

5.  He exposed the dishonest and corrupt officials.

6.  Micah was not in the literary class of Deutero-Isaiah and Amos, but he was far superior to Ezekiel.

7.  Micah is one of the best unified books in the Old Testament. It has received but little editorial tampering.

8.  Micah started the campaign of "social reform" that was taken up by Zephaniah, the psalmists, John the Baptist, Jesus, Francis of Assisi, and John Wesley.

## IV. SELECTED TEXTS

1.  **Futility of prayer.** *"Then they will cry to the Lord, but he will not answer them; he will hide his face from them at that time, because they have made their deeds evil."* **3:4**.

2.  **Conversion of the nations.** *"And many nations shall come, and say: 'Come, let us go up to the mountain of the Lord, to the house of the God of Jacob.'"* **4:2**.

3.  **Swords into plowshares.** *"And they shall beat their swords into plowshares, and their spears into pruning hooks...neither shall they learn war any more."* **4:3**.

4.  **Individual character.** *"They shall sit every man under his vine and under his fig tree, and none shall make them afraid."* **4:4**.

5.  **Worthless sacrifices.** *"'Will the Lord be pleased with thousands of rams, with ten thousands of rivers of oil? Shall I give my first-born for my transgression, the fruit of my body for the sin of my soul?'"* **6:7**.

6. **What the Lord requires.** *"He has showed you, O man, what is good; and what does the Lord require of you but to do justice, and love kindness, and to walk humbly with your God?'"* **6:8.**

7. **Attributes of God.** *"Who is a God like thee, pardoning iniquity and passing over transgression for the remnant of his inheritance? He does not retain his anger forever because he delights in steadfast love."* **7:18.**

# NAHUM

## I. OUTLINE

## II. AUTHORSHIP

1.  The main poem is by Nahum.

2.  Nahum lived in Elkosh—an unknown location.

3.  The introductory or short poem may have been supplied by a later editor.

4.  Date: Nineveh fell in August 612. The book was probably written sometime between 614 and 612 B.C.

## III. COMPOSITION

1.  There is none of the spirit of Amos, Hosea, Micah, or Isaiah in Nahum.

2.  Nahum gloats over the fall of Nineveh—the Assyrian capital.

3.  Despite its spiritual deficiencies, Nahum is one of the outstanding literary masterpieces of the Bible.

4.  It is an oracle of vengeance. For vigor and fervor, it holds a place all its own.

5.  In **2:4** it reads: *"The chariots rage in the streets, they rush to and fro through the squares."* This verse has been construed as a prophecy—foretelling railroads and automobiles.

6.  It is a poem of revenge—a masterpiece of vindictive literature.

7.  To the Jews, Assyria was a symbol of the incarnation of evil—a bloodthirsty militarism.

8.  Nahum was a contemporary of Zephaniah, Habakkuk, and Jeremiah.

9.   It is supposed to portray the moral indignation of a righteous God, who is international in his jurisdiction.

10.   Tyrants become corrupt, dissolute, drunken, and effeminate, and then they are doomed.

## IV. SELECTED TEXTS

1.   **The divine stronghold.** *"The Lord is good, a stronghold in the day of trouble."* **1:7**.

2.   **Peace messengers.** *"Behold, on the mountains the feet of him who brings good tidings, who proclaims peace!"* **1:15**.

3.   **Railroads and automobiles.** *"The chariots rage in the streets, they rush to and fro through the squares; they gleam like torches, they dart like lightening."* **2:4**.

# HABAKKUK

## I. OUTLINE

## II. AUTHORSHIP

1. In 1948 a commentary scroll was discovered in a cave near the Dead Sea.

2. Habakkuk was a Levitical temple musician.

3. Habakkuk, with the help of one or two editors, wrote the book.

4. Date: From about 615 to 605, perhaps about the date of the battle of Carchemish.

## III. TEACHING OF HABAKKUK

1. Habakkuk was a philosophical prophet. He wrestled with the problem: "Why should a righteous God allow the wicked to prosper and to triumph over the saints?"

2. The outstanding text: *"The righteous shall live by his faith."* **2:4**. Twice quoted by Paul—**Rom. 1:17, Gal. 3:11**. Also noted in **Heb. 10:38**.

3. While Habakkuk does not fully answer the question of why the forces of violence and oppression are allowed to swallow up the righteous, he does present one of the higher flights of poetry to be found in all of the Old Testament.

4. There are four divisions of the book:

   A. Why does the God of right permit the rule of wrong?
   B. The oracle—why is a foreign nation allowed to plunder the people of God?
   C. Woes on the robbers—"greedy as hell, insatiable as death"—selfish plunderers, oppressors, insulting idolaters.
   D. A psalm of deliverance.

5. Habakkuk quotes from Isaiah, Jeremiah, and Hosea.

6. A favorite verse: *"The Lord is in his holy temple; let all the earth keep silence before him."* **2:20.**

7. This old problem of evil is dealt with in Job and in many of the psalms—note: **Ps. 73.**

8. Habakkuk seems to conclude: "Evil carries in it the seeds of its own destruction."

9. The fellowship with God is the greatest of all riches.

## IV. SELECTED TEXTS

1. **Living by faith.** *"But the righteous shall live by his faith."* **2:4.**

2. **Earth filled with the glory of the Lord.** *"For the earth will be filled with the knowledge of the glory of the Lord, as the waters cover the sea."* **2:14.**

# ZEPHANIAH

## I. OUTLINE

## II. AUTHORSHIP

1.  Zephaniah was an aristocratic citizen of Jerusalem. He has little or nothing to say about the poor.

2.  He was a contemporary of Jeremiah and borrowed from both Amos and Isaiah.

3.  He was the fourth generation descendant of King Hezekiah and a second cousin once removed of Josiah, the king.

4.  Most of the passages of comfort and promise are regarded as the work of later editors.

## III. TEACHINGS OF THE BOOK

1. His loud cry: *"The day of the Lord—a day of wrath, trouble, distress, and darkness."*

2. His pronouncements were made with a vast and rapidly changing international background.

3. Perhaps Zephaniah was the first Old Testament prophet to change the "day of the Lord" from the "Messianic age" to the coming of Yahweh himself—"the end of the world."

4. This book is a good illustration of how the editors did not hesitate to append their notes with God speaking in the first person.

5. Some of the additions sound more like Deutero-Isaiah than like Zephaniah.

6. In Zephaniah God has a conscience. He cannot allow the sins of even his "chosen people" to go unpunished.

7. There is a hint in this book that during the "new age" all peoples will be converted to Yahweh.

8. One of the major conclusions of the book is: "The Lord resists the proud and rewards the humble."

*The book is devoid of outstanding and significant passages.*

# HAGGAI

## I. OUTLINE

## II. AUTHORSHIP

1.  Haggai was a post-exilic prophet, but he did not write the book.

2.  Some interested party, from notes supplied by Haggai, wrote the book. All of his work is referred to in the third person.

3.  Haggai was probably of a priestly family.

4.  He was born in Babylon, and later lived in Jerusalem.

5.  He was a contemporary and co-worker of Zechariah.

6.  In its present form, the book presents evidence of later editors making changes.

7.  Date: About 520 B.C.

## III. LOOK AT THE BOOK

1.  Notwithstanding what has been said about rebuilding the temple—it was really Haggai who got the job going and finished in four years.

2.  Times were bad—there was a shortage of food. There was also inflation. "Wages" were compared to a "bag with holes in it."

3.  The best known verse is **2:7** referring to the Messiah as *"the desire of all nations."* (King James Version)

4.  This book is unlike any other in the Old Testament in that it is not a prophet's message first-handed, but rather an account of a prophet's teaching and the results.

5.  Haggai was indeed a "minor" prophet. Spiritually regarded, he could be regarded even as a second or third class prophet.

6.  But he did arouse the people to rebuild the temple.

7.  When Zerubbabel, of David's line, was appointed governor of Palestine, Haggai thought it was evidence that the line of David was to rule the country. But he never became king.

8.  Both Haggai and Zechariah were great enemies of the Samaritans. This was the start of the long-lasting bad feelings between the Jews and the Samaritans.

9.  In Chapter 1, verse 6, there is a strong suggestion of inflation. *"And he who earns wages earns wages to put them into a bag with holes."*

*There are no outstanding passages.*

# ZECHARIAH

## I. OUTLINE

## II. AUTHORSHIP

1.  Zechariah was a contemporary of Haggai. Haggai was an old man; Zechariah a young man.

2.  Zechariah taught from 520 to 518 B.C. He began to teach during the last month of Haggai's ministry.

3.  He was a priest as well as a prophet.

4.  Zechariah was author of the first eight chapters, though they were later subjected to some editing.

5.  The Second Zechariah, of unknown identity, formulated Chapters 9 to 14.

6. The First Zechariah wrote during the Persian period; the Second Zechariah during the later Greek period (in the third century).

7. He continued the work of Haggai as regarded the urge to rebuild the temple and exclude the Samaritans.

## III. THE BOOK

1. The three main sections of the first part:
   A. The call to repentance.
   B. The eight visions.
   C. Coming of the Messianic age.
2. The eight visions:
   A. The four horsemen.
   B. Four horns and four smiths.
   C. Angel with measuring line.
   D. Acquittal of Joshua.
   E. Seven-branched lamp stand and the two olive trees.
   F. The flying scroll.
   G. Woman and the measure.
   H. The four chariots.
3. Zechariah fully believed that the Messianic age was about to dawn. He regarded Zerubbabel as being of the "seed of David" and as about to occupy the "throne of David."

4. But the secret police of Darius, getting wind of such things, soon hurried Zerubbabel off the stage of action.

5. The last half of the book seems to pertain to the times of Alexander the Great.

6. Yahweh is getting farther and farther away from the prophets. Formerly they talked directly to Yahweh. Now God only speaks in visions, which are interpreted by angels.

7. The book of Zechariah introduces two almost new concepts:
   A. *Angelology*. Angels attain new heights of importance.
   B. *Satan*. He first appears as a personality.
8. The interpretation of the eight visions had, in general, to do with the coming of the Messianic kingdom.

9. Zechariah is quoted often in the New Testament. The episodes associated with Zechariah are:
   A. Triumphant entry into Jerusalem. **Zech. 9:9. Matt. 21:5. John 12:15.**

B.  Betrayal for 30 pieces of silver. **Zech. 11:12,13. Matt. 27:9,10.** (This is incorrectly ascribed to Jeremiah.)
C.  The pierced hands. **Zech. 12:10. John 19:37.**
D.  The smitten shepherd. **Zech. 13:7. Matt. 26:31. Mark 14:27.**

## IV. ZECHARIAH AND OLD TESTAMENT RELIGION

1.  Along with Haggai, he was foremost in the rebuilding of the temple.

2.  He was also a strong influence in keeping up enmity against the Samaritans.

3.  He was the first prophet actually to proclaim the Messianic age, which takes definite form as a future hope of the Jews.

4.  He proclaimed that he had had a direct revelation from Yahweh—a new experience for post-exilic prophets.

5.  He established the technique of "visions" as a new and more common method for Yahweh to reveal himself to prophets.

6.  Angelology, introduced by Ezekiel, is now an established feature in Hebrew theology.

7.  Satan finds his place in all later-day Jewish religion.

8.  The gentiles are to share in the glory of the rule of the Messiah over all the world.

9.  But Israel must be cleansed from all sin and iniquity.

10. And it was in fulfillment of these conditions that John the Baptist came preaching repentance, baptism, and the kingdom of heaven.

## V. SELECTED TEXTS

1.  **The apple of his eye.** *"He who touches you touches the apple of his eye."* **2:8.**

2.  **The brand plucked from the burning.** *"Then he showed me Joshua the high priest standing before the angel of the Lord, and Satan standing at his right hand to accuse him. And the Lord said to Satan, 'The Lord rebuke you, O Satan!...Is not this a brand plucked from the fire?'"* **3:1,2.**

3.  **Not by might or power.** *"Then he said to me... 'Not by might, nor by power, but by my Spirit,' says the Lord of hosts."* **4:6.**

4.  **His people.** *"'And they shall be my people and I will be their God, in faithfulness and in righteousness.'"* **8:8.**

5. **Promoting peace.** *"'Speak truth to one another, render...judgments that are true and make for peace, do not devise evil in your hearts against one another, and love no false oath, for all these things I hate, says the Lord.'"* **8:16,17.**

6. **The king riding on a colt.** *"Lo, your king comes to you; triumphant and victorious is he, humble and riding on an ass, on a colt.'"* **9:9.**

7. **Man's spirit.** *"Thus says the Lord, who stretched out the heavens and founded the earth and formed the spirit of man within him."* **12:1.**

8. **Him whom they pierced.** *"'So that, when they look on him whom they have pierced, they shall mourn for him.'"* **12:10.**

9. **Wounded in house of a friend.** *"What are these wounds on your back?" He will say, "The wounds I received in the house of my friends."* **13:6.**

10. **God and his angels.** *"The Lord your God will come, and all the holy ones with him."* **14:5.**

# MALACHI

## I. OUTLINE

## II. AUTHORSHIP

1. Nothing is known of Malachi except what is disclosed in the book.

2. The Jews were under a Persian governor, so it is dated about 460 to 450 B.C.

3. There is a unity of thought and mannerism which suggests that the book was written by one person.

## III. THE TIME

1. Malachi says the priests are slovenly about their duties and the people neglect to pay tithes and offerings.

2. This suggests sometime before Nehemiah began his reforms.

3. This time is also suggested by the conquest of the Edomites by the Nabataean Arabs.

4. The people are discouraged. *"Where is the God of justice?"* **2:17**. *"What evidence that God loves us?"* **1:2**.

5. Malachi might be subtitled "A message for an age of discouragement."

## IV. THE MESSAGE

1. Malachi offers three answers to the wailing of the people—where is the God of justice?

   A. The hard times caused by the disloyalty of the people.
   B. The punishment of their old adversaries—the Edomites.
   C. The justice of the final judgment.

2. This book presents the first real denunciation of divorce by a Hebrew prophet.

3. Malachi presents the first actual mention of the *"Fatherhood of God and the brotherhood of man."* **2:10.**

4. The book is dominated by a passion for God associated with profound sympathy for man.

5. Malachi vies with all the other Old Testament prophets in exalting the universal nature of God.

6. Malachi is directly or indirectly quoted in the New Testament: **Mark 1:2 (Mal. 3:1); Mark 9:11 and Luke 1:17 (Mal. 4:5); Rom. 9:13 (Mal. 1:2,3).**

## V. SELECTED TEXTS

1. **God hates divorce.** *"For I hate divorce, says the Lord God of Israel."* **2:16.**

2. **God's changelessness.** *"For I the Lord do not change."* **3:6.**

3. **Robbing God.** *"You are robbing me…in your tithes and offerings."* **3:8.**

4. **The book of remembrance.** *"Those who feared the Lord spoke with one another; …and a book of remembrance was written before him of those who feared the Lord and thought on his name."* **3:16.**

5. **The sun of righteousness.** *"But for you who fear my name the sun of righteousness shall rise, with healing in its wings."* **4:2.**

6. **The sending of Elijah.** *"Behold, I will send you Elijah the prophet before the great and terrible day of the Lord comes."* **4:5.**

# PART TWO

## BOOKS OF THE NEW TESTAMENT

# MATTHEW

## I. OUTLINE—BRIEF

## II. OUTLINE—COMPLETE

## III. AUTHORSHIP

1. Matthew was written by Isador, a disciple of Matthew.

2. Isador wrote in Greek, but he had an Aramaic record of the "sayings of Jesus" compiled by Matthew.

3. Isador wrote Matthew in A.D. 71 at Pella. He had Matthew's notes which had been revised in A.D. 40.

4. Isador also had four-fifths of Mark's record.

5. The last copy of Matthew's notes was destroyed in the burning of a Syrian monastery in A.D. 416.

   (The above facts regarding authorship of Matthew are from *The Urantia Book*, p. 1341-2.)

6. Scholars have doubted that Matthew wrote this Gospel because it does not seem that the author was an eyewitness. They believe it was written about A.D. 75 to 80.

7. It is the Jewish viewpoint of Christ's life and work.

## IV. CHARACTER

1. In the early times, Matthew was the "best seller" among Christian documents.

2. For several centuries it was the most quoted of the four Gospels.

3. The Roman Catholics like Matthew because it exalts Peter. They have called it the "most important book in the world."

4. Constantly Jesus' work is presented as the fulfillment of Old Testament prophecy—"*that it might be fulfilled,*" as spoken by the prophet.

5. Matthew is a complete and well organized version of Jesus' life and teaching.

6. Isador took the Sermon on the Mount—Jesus' ordination charge to the twelve—and made it into a "new law and gospel" for the Christian church.

7. Matthew presents the law of the church—deals with divorce and other church regulations.

8.   This is the only Gospel that uses the term "church"—two times.

9.   It provides for church government and lays down the rules for excommunication of disorderly members.

10.  Isador was especially interested in prayer, fasting, and almsgiving.

11.  Isador goes out of his way to prove that Jesus was truly the Messiah.

12.  Isador was at great pains to safeguard the doctrine of Jesus' divinity.

13.  Jesus is no longer just a carpenter—but the "son of a carpenter."

14.  Isador pays special attention to the genealogy of Jesus—to prove that he was a descendant of David.

15.  Isador equates the "church" with the "kingdom of heaven."

16.  This Gospel pays little attention to chronology. Many talks of Jesus are brought together as one long sermon.

## V. FRAMEWORK

1.   Matthew is a literary reorganization of Mark's chronological narrative.

2.   Isador frequently expands Mark's editorial comments.

3.   Matthew is an artistic combination of the topical and the chronological arrangement.

4.   Matthew reproduces 90 per cent of Mark's material.

5.   Most of the 55 verses of Mark which Matthew omitted were left out for doctrinal reasons.

6.   The Matthew gospel is a great literary improvement upon the rather rough style of Mark.

7.   In Matthew Jesus pays special attention to the Jews and always is respectful of the "Law of Moses."

8.   Some features of Matthew are original—not found in Mark or elsewhere in earlier records:

> Story of Jesus' birth.
> Peter walking on the water.
> The temple tax.
> Fate of Judas.
> Dream of Pilate's wife.
> Pilate's washing of his hands.
> Earthquake at Jesus' death.
> Sealing of the tomb.
> Appearance to women, etc.

9. Isador puts all of Jesus' teachings into five master discourses.

10. The five great discourses might be captioned as follows:

   A. Sermon on the Mount.
   B. The Great Evangelistic Charge.
   C. Parables of the Kingdom.
   D. Humility and Forgiveness.
   E. The End of the Age.

11. Matthew tends to group all his work into threes, fives, and sevens.

## VI. SELECTED TEXTS

1. **The virgin birth.** *"'Behold, a virgin shall conceive and bear a son, and his name shall be called Enmanuel.'"* **1:23. (Isa. 7:14)**

2. **The star of Bethlehem.** *"The star which they had seen in the East went before them, till it came to rest over the place where the child was."* **2:9.**

3. **John's preaching.** *"In those days came John the Baptist, preaching... 'Repent, for the kingdom of heaven is at hand.'"* **3:1,2.**

4. **Jesus' baptism.** *"And when Jesus was baptized...he saw the Spirit of God descending like a dove...and lo, a voice from heaven, saying, 'This is my beloved Son, with whom I am well pleased.'"* **3:16.**

5. **Ministry of angels.** *"Then the devil left him, and behold, angels came and ministered to him."* **4:11.**

6. **Fishers of men.** *"And he said to them, 'Follow me, and I will make you fishers of men.'"* **4:19.**

7. **The Beatitudes.** *"'Blessed are the poor in spirit, for theirs is the kingdom of heaven.'"* **5:3.**

8. **Light of the world.** *"'You are the light of the world.'"* **5:14.**

9. **The perfection mandate.** *"'You, therefore, must be perfect, as your heavenly Father is perfect.'"* **5:48.**

10. **Secret charity.** *"'When you give alms, do not let your left hand know what your right hand is doing, so that your alms may be in secret.'"* **6:3,4.**

11. **Verbose praying.** *"'And in praying do not heap up empty phrases as the Gentiles do, for they think they will be heard for their many words.'"* **6:7.**

12. **The Lord's Prayer. 6:9-13.**

13. **Two masters.** *"'No one can serve two masters.'"* **6:24.**

14. **Seek first the kingdom.** *"'Seek first his kingdom...and all these things shall be yours as well.'"* **6:33.**

15. **Judge not.** *"'Judge not, that you be not judged.'"* **7:1**.

16. **Pearls before swine.** *"Do not throw your pearls before swine.'"* **7:6**.

17. **Nowhere to lay his head.** *"Foxes have holes, and birds of the air have nests; but the Son of man has nowhere to lay his head.'"* **8:20**.

18. **Authority to forgive.** *"But that you may know that the Son of man has authority on earth to forgive sins—he then said to the paralytic— 'Rise, take up your bed and go home.'"* **9:6**.

19. **Calling sinners.** *"'I came not to call the righteous, but sinners.'"* **9:13**.

20. **Wisdom of the serpent.** *"Be wise as serpents and innocent as doves.'"* **10:16**.

21. **Becoming like a child.** *"'Unless you turn and become like children, you will never enter the kingdom of heaven.'"* **18:3**.

22. **Paying taxes.** *"'Render therefore to Caeser the things that are Cassar's, and to God the things that are God's.'"* **22:21**.

23. **Being consistent.** *"'You blind guides, straining out a gnat and swallowing a camel.'"* **23:24**.

24. **The second advent.** *"'But of that day and hour no one knows, not even the angels of heaven, nor the Son, but the Father only.'"* **24:36**.

25. **Stewardship.** *"'But from him who has not, even what he has will be taken away.'"* **25:29**.

26. **To one of the least.** *"'As you did it to one of the least of these my brethren, you did it to me.'"* **25:40**.

27. **Passing of the cup.** *"He fell on his face and prayed, 'My father, if it be possible, let this cup pass from me; nevertheless, not as I will, but as thou wilt.'"* **26:39**.

28. **Twelve legions of angels.** *"'Do you think that I cannot appeal to my Father, and he will at once send me more than twelve legions of angels?'"* **26:53**.

29. **Supreme sovereignty.** *"And Jesus...said to them, 'All authority in heaven and on earth has been given to me.'"* **28:18**.

30. **Always with us.** *"'And lo, I am with you always, to the close of the age.'"* **28:20**.

# MARK

## I. OUTLINE—BRIEF

## II. OUTLINE—COMPLETE

## III. AUTHORSHIP

1. The book was written by John Mark. It is the earliest record of Jesus' life—except for the notes of Andrew.

2. It is really the Gospel according to the teachings of Peter and the oral traditions of the church at Rome.

3. It was completed soon after Peter's death—near the end of A.D. 68.

4. The record has been considerably changed. The latter one-fifth of the original Gospel was lost before the first manuscript was ever copied.

   (The above facts come from *The Urantia Book*, p. 1341.)

5. Scholars believe the book was written by Mark sometime between A.D. 64 and 85, perhaps around A.D. 75.

**QUESTION**: How is it that so little of Mark's personal experiences got into this record?

**ANSWER**:

1. Peter had probably prepared some written notes which Mark used.

2. The oral traditions were carefully committed to memory—just like a creed or prayer would be.

3. Since Mark was writing at the request of the church at Rome, he felt under obligation to prepare a statement that would represent Peter's way of telling the story of Jesus and his teachings.

4. He was not writing either a history of Jesus' life or his own biography.

## IV. JOHN MARK IN *THE URANTIA BOOK*

1. He first appeared as the "boy of all chores" assigned to the twelve apostles. *The Urantia Book*, p. 1700.

2. Mark was only partially convinced about Peter's story about walking on the water, so he left part of it out of his record. p. 1703.

3. John Mark spent a whole day alone with Jesus in the hills. p. 1920.

4. John kept a watchful eye on Jesus and the twelve. p. 1963.

5. John watched over Jesus at the olive press, just before his arrest. p. 1971.

6. John lost his coat to the soldier when he escaped. p. 1975.

7. John followed the apostles into Galilee after the resurrection. p. 2045.

8. John recognized Jesus on the shores of Lake Galilee. p. 2046.

9. John served breakfast to the apostles. p. 2047.

10. John returned home upon the sudden death of his father, Elijah Mark. p. 2051.

11. John went forth to call the apostles and leading disciples to gather at his mother's home for the Pentecost meeting. p. 2057.

## V. MARK'S BIOGRAPHY IN THE NEW TESTAMENT

1. John was the son of Mary Mark—a well-to-do Jerusalemite. **Acts 12:12-17.**

2. He was a kinsman of Barnabas. **Col. 4:10.**

3. He accompanied Barnabas and Paul to Antioch. **Acts 12:25. 13:1.**

4. He was an attendant on the first missionary journey. **Acts 13:5.**

5. He deserted the party at Perga. **Acts 13:13.**

6. Accordingly, Paul declined to take John on the second trip. **Acts 15:38.**

7. This caused trouble between Paul and Barnabas. **Acts 15:36-41.**

8. Barnabas took John with him to Cyprus. **Acts 15:39.**

9. Later on, Mark seemed to be on good terms with Paul. **Col. 4:10. Phmon. v. 24.**

10. Mark made good on a visit to the Colossian church, and Paul wanted him to come to Rome. **Acts 13:5.**

11. Peter referred to Mark as his son. **1 Peter 5:13.**

12. The anonymous "young man" (**Mark 14:51**) undoubtedly refers to John Mark.

13. Several early church fathers refer to John as interpreter for Peter.

14. Tradition claims that John Mark was the founder of the church at Alexandria.

15. There was a supposed transfer of Mark's body from Egypt to Venice A.D. 832. His bones are supposed to rest beneath the altar in St. Mark's Church in Venice.

## VI. ANTECEDENTS

1. These Gospels are not histories or biographies. They are didactic and apologetic—evangelical writings. They describe a "way of life."

2. Mark seems to have been written for believers—people who were already Christians.

3. Mark sometimes telescoped his stories—one being inserted within the frame-work of another—as in **2:1-12; 5:21-43**.

4. From a literary standpoint, Mark is the most inferior of all New Testament books. It is poorly organized and unpolished in rhetoric.

## VII. MARK'S THEOLOGY

1. Mark's theology tends to be Hellenistic—in contrast with Matthew's Jewish theology.

2. Mark's theology is hardly his own—more a blend of Petrine and church of Rome theology.

3. Paul seems to have had little or no influence on Mark's theology. Mark talks about Jesus' "mighty work"—and Paul never once mentions Jesus' miracles.

4. Mark represents an era in which the theology of Christianity is in process of reinterpretation from the Jewish to the gentile.

5. In Mark, Jesus never fully, unequivocally, and unambiguously claimed to be the Messiah.

6. Paul's atonement doctrine "ransom" does appear here and there in Mark.

7. Mark clings to the "mystery" concept of Christian theology—the esotoric idea that the "inner circle" knew special things of which the rank and file of believers were wholly ignorant.

8. All Near East religions had this "mystery" idea—in fact, were known as "mystery cults."

9. The blindness and obtuseness of the Jewish people were not stupidity, but some sort of divine judgment which had overtaken them—like God hardening Pharaoh's heart.

10. There was an early trace of anti-Semitism—or rather, anti-Judaism in Mark's Gospel.

11. When all is said and done, you can't help feeling that Mark really Knows that Jesus was the Messiah—not the Jewish, but the Christian.

12. Mark is one of the most "precious" books ever written, but it does not give us a full account of Jesus' life.

## VIII. SELECTED TEXTS

1. **John the Baptist appears**. *"John the Baptizer appeared in the wilderness, preaching a baptism of repentance for the forgiveness of sin."* **1:4**.

2. **Baptism of the Holy Spirit**. *"'I have baptized you with water; but he will baptize you with the Holy Spirit.'"* **1:8**.

3. **Fishers of men**. *"'Follow me and I will make you fishers of men.'"* **1:17**.

4. **The sundown healing**. *"That evening, at sundown, they brought to him all who were sick or possessed with demons...And he healed many who were sick with various diseases, and cast out many demons."* **1:32,34**.

5. **Forgiving sins**. *"'Which is easier, to say to the paralytic, "Your sins are forgiven," or to say "Rise, take up your pallet and walk." But that you may know that the Son of man has authority on earth to forgive sins'—he said to the paralytic— 'I say to you, rise, take up your pallet and go home.'"* **2:9-11**.

6. **Calling sinners**. *"'I came not to call the righteous, but sinners.'"* **2:17**.

7. **Sabbath made for man**. *"And he said to them, 'The sabbath was made for man, not man for the sabbath; so the Son of man is lord even of the sabbath.'"* **2:27,28**.

8. **Speaking in parables**. *"He did not speak to them without a parable, but privately to his own disciples he explained everything."* **4:34**.

9. **Stills the waves**. *"And he...rebuked the wind, and said to the sea, 'Peace! Be still' And the wind ceased, and there was a great calm."* **4-39**.

10. **Peculiar type of healing**. *"And Jesus, perceiving in himself that power had gone forth from him, immediately turned about in the crowd, and said, 'Who touched my garments?'"* **5:30**.

11. **Prophet and honor**. *"And Jesus said to them, 'A prophet is not without honor, except in his own country.'"* **6:4**.

12. **Feeding five thousand**. *"And those who ate the loaves were five thousand men,"* **6:44**.

13. **Dogs eat the crumbs**. *"But she answered him, 'Yes, Lord; yet even the dogs under the table eat the children's crumbs.'"* **7:28**.

14. **You are the Christ**. *"And he asked them, 'But who do you say that I am?' Peter answered him, 'You are the Christ.'"* **8:29**.

15. **Gaining the whole world.** *"What does it profit a man, to gain the whole world and forfeit his life?'"* **8:36.**

16. **Help my unbelief.** *"The father of the child...said, 'I believe; help my unbelief.'"* **9:24.**

17. **The little children.** *"'Let the children come to me, do not hinder them; for to such belongs the kingdom of God.'"* **10:14.**

18. **Cursing the fig tree.** *"And seeing in the distance a fig tree in leaf, he went to see if he could find anything on it. When he came to it, he found nothing but leaves, for it was not the season for figs. And he said to it, 'May no man ever eat fruit from you again.'...As they passed by in the morning, they saw the fig tree withered away to its roots."* **11:13,14,20.**

19. **Taxation problems.** *"Jesus said to them, 'Render to Caesar the things that are Caesar's, and to God the things that are God's.'"* **12:17.**

20. **Marriage in heaven.** *"For when they rise from the dead, they neither marry nor are given in marriage, but are like angels in heaven.'"* **12:25.**

21. **The widow's mite.** *"Truly, I say to you, this poor widow has put in more than all those who are contributing to the treasury...she out of her poverty has put in everything she had.'"* **12:43,44.**

22. **Anointing his feet.** *"'This ointment might have been sold...and given to the poor.'...But Jesus said, 'Let her alone; why do you trouble her? She has done a beautiful thing to me.'"* **14:5,6.**

23. **Watch and pray.** *"'Watch and pray that you may not enter into temptation; the spirit indeed is willing but the flesh is weak.'"* **14:38.**

24. **John Mark's escape.** *"And a young man followed him, with nothing but a linen cloth about his body; and they seized him, but he left the linen cloth and ran away naked."* **14:51,52.**

25. **The empty tomb.** *"'He has risen, he is not here; see the place where they laid him.'"* **16:6.**

26. **Deadly poisons.** In a forged appendix appears the passage about snakes and drinking deadly poisons.

# LUKE

## I. OUTLINE—BRIEF

## II. OUTLINE—COMPLETE

## III. AUTHORSHIP

1.   Luke wrote more than one quarter of the whole New Testament—the Book of Luke and the Acts.

2.   Luke was an educated man, a physician, and a sometime companion of Paul.

3.   He was with Paul on parts of both the second and third missionary tours.

4. He was undoubtedly Paul's private physician—as Paul suffered from several physical ailments. Paul called him the *"beloved physician."* **Col. 4:14.**

5. Luke was a good reporter and a fairly good historian. He talked with many eyewitnesses of Jesus' lifework.

6. As might be expected, Luke pays special attention to things of interest to a physician:

The great fever.
Jairus's daughter's eating meat.
The good Samaritan.
First aid.
Prayer miracles.

7. Luke had Matthew (Isador), Mark, and **Q** (Andrew's notes). About one-third comes from Mark. Along with Matthew he derives much from **Q** (252 verses), but almost half of Luke is original. He also had Paul's story and a brief record made in A.D. 78 at Antioch by one Cedes. See *The Urantia Book*, p. 1342.

8. Apparently Luke got many verses from the Cedes manuscript; this document paid special attention to women.

9. The Cedes book was rich in parables: notably, good Samaritan, rich fool, rich man and Lazarus, and the Pharisee and tax collector.

10. Some things in Mark which Luke disregards:

Execution of John the Baptist.
Request of Zebedee sons.
Cursing of the fig tree.
Secretly growing seed.
Saying about greatness.
Question about great commandment.
Anointing at Bethany.
Jesus walking on the sea.
The Syrophoenician woman.
Healings by spittle.
Feeding of 4,000.

11. The original features of Luke are:

Birth narratives ........................................... 1:5–2:52
Parable of the friend at midnight ......................... 11:5–8
Parables of lost coin and lost son .............. 15:8–10, 11–32
Dives and Lazarus ...................................... 16:19–31
Conversion of Zacchaeus ............................... 19:1–10

Thief on the cross ...................................... **23:40-43**
The walk to Emmaus .................................. **24:13-35**
The ascension  ........................................ **24:50-53**
(And many other minor features.)

12.   Luke is the best organized book in the New Testament.

13.   While Luke was not a classicist—writing in the international style of Greek—he did write the best literary work of the New Testament, except for the book of Hebrews.

14.   Luke's literary skill is best shown in the way he polished up many of Mark's rather crude passages, for example:

> **Mark**: *"And at evening, when the sun did set."* **Mark 1:32.** (King James Version)
> **Luke**: *"Now when the sun was setting."* **Luke 4:40.** (King James Version)

15.   It was never intended that the book of Acts should be separated from Luke.

16.   Luke wrote in A.D. 82 at Achaia. He planned to write three books on Christianity, but he died in A.D. 90 just before finishing Acts. *The Urantia Book*, p. 1342.

17.   In a general way, Luke may be said to be the Gospel according to Paul.

## IV. HISTORY AND TRADITION IN LUKE

1.   Jesus spoke in Aramaic, but his followers wrote in Koine Greek.

2.   In the times of Jesus, all Jews were bilingual.

3.   Peter's Pentecost sermon seems to have set a pattern for all subsequent types of preaching.

4.   Paul bases his belief in the resurrection on Jesus' post-resurrection appearances, Mark on the empty tomb, and Matthew on both.

5.   Jesus' miracles made a great appeal to the populace.

6.   The early spread of the gospel was by "lay preachers."

7.   An early church father called Luke "the most beautiful book ever written."

8.   The outstanding literary features of Luke are:

A.   The Last Supper ......................................... 22:15-17
B.   Discourse of true greatness  .......................... 22:25-27
C.   Future judges ............................................. 22:28-30
D.   Prediction of desertion ................................. 22:31,32

9.  *The Marcion defection.* Marcion was born A.D. 85 in Roman Pontus on the Black Sea. He visited most Christian churches and went to Rome about A.D. 139. He gave $30,000 to the Rome church (later returned) and made a big "stir." He rejected all of the Old Testament. Luke was his gospel —with some writings of his own. He also used some of Paul's letters. Later on, he rewrote Luke. He had Jesus come full-fledgedly from heaven with divine authority on earth. It was Marcion's new testament that forced the "fathers" to get busy with a *real* New Testament.

10. Luke's special motives:

    A.  To make a good literary production.
    B.  To make a universal appeal.
    C.  To be humanitarian (emphasis on the poor).
    D.  To put emphasis on prayer.
    E.  To magnify the Holy Spirit.
    F.  To make clear that Christianity was in no way a subversive religion— get it out of trouble with the Roman authorities.
    G.  To tell the story with little or no theology. There are few quotations from the Old Testament.

## V. SELECTED TEXTS

1.  **The angel and Mary.** *"And the angel said to her. 'Do not be afraid, Mary, for you have found favor with God.'"* **1:30.**

2.  **Jesus' birth.** *"And she gave birth to her first-born son and wrapped him in swaddling cloths, and laid him in a manger, because there was no place for them in the inn."* **2:7.**

3.  **Peace on earth and good will.** *"And suddenly there was with the angel a multitude of the heavenly host praising God and saying, 'Glory to God in the highest, and on earth peace among men with whom he is pleased!'"* **2:13,14.**

4.  **About the Father's business.** *"And he said to them, 'How is it that you sought me? Did you not know that I must be in my Father's house?'"* **2:49.**

5.  **Jesus grows up.** *"And Jesus increased in wisdom and in stature, and in favor with God and man."* **2:52.**

6. **The Holy Spirit and fire.** *"'I baptise you with water;...he will baptize you with the Holy Spirit and with fire.'"* **3:16.**

7. **Jesus' baptism.** *"And a voice came from heaven, 'Thou art my beloved Son; with thee I am well pleased.'"* **3:22.**

8. **The forty days.** *"And Jesus, full of the Holy Spirit, returned from the Jordan, and was led by the Spirit for forty days in the wilderness, tempted by the devil."* **4:1,2.9.**

9. **The sundown healing.** *"Now when the sun was setting, all those who had any that were sick with various diseases brought them to him; and he laid his hands on every one of them and healed them."* **4:40.**

10. **Catching men.** *"And Jesus said to Simon, 'Do not be afraid; henceforth you will be catching men.'"* **5:10.**

11. **Authority to forgive sins.** *"'But that you nay know that the Son of man has authority on earth to forgive sins.'"* **5:24.**

12. **To call sinners.** *"'I have not come to call the righteous, but sinners to repentance.'"* **5:32.**

13. **Lord of the sabbath.** *"And he said to them, 'The Son of man is lord of the sabbath.'"* **6:5.**

14. **His prayer life.** *"In these days he went out into the hills to pray; and all night he continued in prayer to God."* 6:12.

15. **Turn the other cheek.** *"'To him who strikes you on the cheek, offer the other also.'"* **6:29.**

16. **Show mercy.** *"'Be merciful, even as your Father is merciful.'"* **6:36.**

17. **The log in your own eye.** *"'Why do you see the speck that is in your brother's eye, but do not notice the log that is in your own eye?'"* **6:41.**

18. **The widow's son.** *"And he said, 'Young man, I say to you, arise.' And the dead man sat up, and began to speak."* **7:14,15.**

19. **Someone touched me.** *"But Jesus said, 'Some one touched me; for I perceive that power has gone forth from me.'"* **8:46.**

20. **Net dead, but sleeping.** *"But he said, 'Do not weep; for she is not dead but sleeping.'"* **8:52.**

21. **Peter's confession.** *"'But who do you say that I am?' And Peter answered, 'The Christ of God.'"* **9:20.**

22. **Looking back.** *"'No one who puts his hand to the plow and looks back is fit for the kingdom of God.'"* **9:62.**

23. **The good Samaritan**. *"'Which of these three, do you think, proved neighbor to the man who fell among the robbers?' He said, 'The one who showed mercy on him.' And Jesus said to him, 'Go and do likewise.'"* **10:36,37.**

24. **Troubled about trifles**. *"'Martha, Martha, you are anxious and troubled about many things; one thing is needful. Mary has chosen the good portion, which shall not be taken away from her.'"* **10:41,42.**

25. **He who seeks finds**. *"'For everyone who asks receives, and he who seeks finds, and to him who knocks it will be opened.'"* **11:10.**

26. **Neglecting weighty matters**. *"'But woe to you Pharisees! for you tithe mint and rue and every herb, and neglect justice and the love of God.'"* **11:42.**

27. **Hairs of your head**. *"'Even the hairs of your head are all numbered. Fear not; you are of more value than many sparrows.'"* **12:7.**

28. **Needless anxiety**. *"'Do not be anxious about your life, what you shall eat, nor about your body, what you shall put on.'"* **12:22.**

   *"'Consider the lilies, how they grow; they neither toil nor spin; yet I tell you, even Solomon in all his glory was not arrayed like one of these.'"* **12:27.**

29. **Gaining the kingdom**. *"'Fear not, little flock, for it is your father's good pleasure to give you the kingdom.'"* **12:32.**

30. **Good salt**. *"'Salt is good; but if salt has lost its taste, how shall its saltiness be restored?'"* **14:34.**

31. **Joy in heaven**. *"'There will be more joy in heaven over one sinner who repents than over ninety-nine righteous persons who need no repentance.'"* **15:7.**

32. **One leper in ten**. *"Then said Jesus, 'Were not ten cleansed? Where are the nine? Was no one found to return and give praise to God except this foreigner?'"* **17:17,18.**

33. **Ought always to pray**. *"That they ought always to pray and not lose heart."* **18:1.**

34. **The tax collector**. *"But the tax collector, standing far off, would not even lift up his eyes to heaven, but beat his breast, saying, 'God, be merciful to me a sinner!'"* **18:13.**

35. **Sojourn with Zacchaeus**. *"Jesus...looked up and said to him, 'Zacchaeus, make haste and come down; for I must stay at your house today.'"* **19:5.**

36. **The faithful servant**. *"'Well done, good servant ! Because you have been faithful in a very little, you shall have authority over ten cities.'"***19:17**.

37. **Paying taxes**. *"He said to them, 'Then render to Caesar the things that are Caesar's, and to God the things that are God's.'"* **20:25**.

38. **Watchful waiting**. *"'But take heed to yourselves lest your hearts be weighed down with dissipation and drunkenness and cares of this life, and that day come upon you suddenly like a snare.'"***21:34**.

39. **The terrible cup**. *"'Father, if thou art willing, remove this cup from me; nevertheless not my will, but thine, be done.'"* **22:42**.

40. **Following at a distance**. *"Then they...led him...into the high priest's house. Peter followed at a distance."* **22:54**.

41. **Thief on the cross**. *"'Jesus, remember me when you come in your kingly power.' And he said to him, 'Truly, I say to you, today you will be with me in Paradise.'"***23:42,43**.

42. **Jesus' spirit**. *"Then Jesus, crying with a loud voice, said, 'Father, into thy hands I commit my spirit.'"***23:46**.

43. **Power from on high**. *"'But stay in the city, until you are clothed with power from on high.'"***24:49**.

44. **The ascension**. *"Then he led them out as far as Bethany, and lifting up his hands he blessed them.While he blessed them, he parted from them."* **24:50,51**.

# JOHN

## I. OUTLINE—BRIEF

## II. OUTLINE—COMPLETE

## III. AUTHORSHIP

1.  John was written in A.D. 101 by Nathan, a Greek Jew from Caesarea, under the direction of John. The book of **1 John** was written by John himself as a covering letter. *The Urantia Book*, p. 1342.

2.  The fact that Nathan wrote the Gospel enabled John the more gracefully to refer to himself as "the disciple whom Jesus loved."

3.  Nathan was probably a mild-mannered man, which would explain how the ambitious young "son of thunder" could have become the "apostle of love"— even in his old age.

4. It is difficult to regard the Gospel of John and Revelation as being written by the same person.

5. John's purpose:
   A. To supply what the Gospels of Matthew, Mark, and Luke had left out.
   B. To bring Christian theology up to date.
   C. To control the growing cult of John the Baptist. Some even taught that John was the real Messiah.
   D. To withstand Gnosticism, especially the Docetist cult—which denied the incarnation.

6. It is interesting to note what John omits:
   A. Account of the baptism.
   B. The transfiguration.
   C. Agony in Gethsemane.
   D. All reference to casting out demons.
   E. All parables.
   F. Miracles are not acts of compassion, but revelations of divine power.

7. In this book the statement that Jesus was sent by God is made 26 times directly, 18 indirectly. Jesus himself refers to "Him who sent me."

8. John was little influenced by the Old Testament, but greatly influenced by Paul and the Book of Hebrews.

9. The appendix does not claim that John was the author.

10. There is some indication that John's manuscript got mixed up before our present-day versions were finally copied.

## IV. CHIEF CONSIDERATIONS

1. John is the "crown of the New Testament." It is the most simple and yet the most profound of all the New Testament books.

2. It is the philosophical and theological Gospel—the story is subordinated to doctrine.

3. John recognizes the "humanity" of Jesus, but his divine traits largely overshadow his humanity.

4. In the Synoptics, Jesus gradually arrives at a comprehension of his divine mission. In John, he always knew of the divinity of his bestowal.

5. John plays down the work of John the Baptist and plays up his endorsement of Jesus.

6. John spreads Jesus' ministry over about three years. Mark appears to limit it to about one year.

7. John puts the Last Supper on the evening before the Passover.

8. As regards the chronology of the Last Supper, Paul agrees with John.

9. *The Urantia Book* agrees with John where he differs from the others on the times of the Last Supper and other events.

10. The Godhead is the center of the theology of John—then the Son (Logos) and the Spirit.

11. John is clearly trinitarian.

12. The high point— *"I am the way, and the truth, and the life."* **14:6.**

13. John makes the only attempt in the Gospels to define God:

    God is spirit.
    God is light.
    God is love.

14. John smacks of determinism. There is much leaning toward predestination.

15. John talks like Paul about the new birth.

16. John does not say much about the "age to come." He seems to think that the "new age" is already here.

17. The author of John is something of a sacramental mystic. He recognizes a church and its ministry.

18. In a way, John is a drama—a conflict between light and darkness, something like the Persian philosophy.

## V. CONTEMPORARY RELATIONSHIPS

1. The living Word is the whole concern of the fourth Gospel.

2. The Logos idea was, in part, borrowed from the Stoics.

3. The Logos concept shows Hellenistic influence in general, and Philo in particular.

4. Philo uses Logos to express the personified activity of God.

5. The Logos is "light and life"—even life eternal.

6. Forty years before John, Paul was fighting Gnosticism at Colossae.

7. John is silent about Simon's bearing the cross. One of the Gnostic beliefs was that it was Simon who went to death in the place of Jesus.

8. John was also combatting the "Hermes" cult. This cult produced a work on the "Shepherd of Men," but it was tainted with "speculative Egyptian mysticism." Wisdom is the womb of the "new birth."

9. Some of the Hermes literature was written long after John, but the ideas were early in circulation.

10. John also had in mind the mystery religions which were already in vogue at the time of the writing of his Gospel.

11. *Mandaeism.* Forty years ago there was discovered in the lower Euphrates a sect of John the Baptist's followers known as the Mandeaans. They are hostile to both Jews and Christians. Christ is alluded to as the "liar" and false Messiah.

12. They claim the true Messiah instigated the crucifixion of Jesus.

13. At the time of John's writing the "cult of the Virgin Mary" had not become widespread—accordingly John ignores the question.

## VI. SELECTED TEXTS

1. **The Word was God**. *"In the beginning was the Word, and the Word was with God, and the Word was God."* **1:1**.

2. **The light of men**. *"In him was life, and the life was the light of men."* **1:4.**

3. **The true light**. *"The true light that enlightens every man was coming into the world."* **1:9**.

4. **Becoming children of God**. *"But to all…who believed in his name, he gave power to become children of God."* **1:12**.

5. **Word becomes flesh**. *"And the Word became flesh and dwelt among us."* **1:14.**

6. **John and Jesus**. *"He saw Jesus coming toward him, and said, 'Behold, the Lamb of God, who takes away the sin of the world'"* **1:29**.

7. **Nathaniel and Nazareth**. *"Nathaniel said to him, 'Can anything good come out of Nazareth?.'"* **1:46**.

8. **Cleansing the temple**. *"And making a whip of cords, he drove them all, with the sheep and oxen, out of the temple."* **2:15**.

9. **His body temple**. *"Jesus answered them, 'Destroy this temple, and in three days I will raise it up'."* **2:19**.

10. **The new birth**. *"'I say to you, unless one is born anew, he cannot see the kingdom of God.'"* **3:3**.

11. **God so loved the world**. *"For God so loved the world that he gave his only Son, that whoever believes in him should not perish but have eternal life."* **3:16**.

12. **Jesus and baptism.** *"Jesus himself did not baptize, but only his disciples."* **4:2.**

13. **The water of life.** *"Whoever drinks of the water that I shall give him will never thirst; the water...will become in him a spring of water welling up to eternal life."* **4:14.**

14. **Spirit.** *"God is spirit."* **4:24.**

15. **Confesses his divinity.** *"Jesus said to her, 'I who speak to you am he.'"* **4:26.**

16. **Gather up the fragments.** *"He told his disciples, 'Gather up the fragments left over, that nothing may be lost.'"* **6:12.**

17. **The king episode.** *"Perceiving then that they were about to come and take him by force to make him king, Jesus withdrew."* **6:15.**

18. **The bread of life.** *"'I am the bread of life; he who comes to me shall not hunger, and he who believes in me shall never thirst.'"* **6:35.**

19. **Eternal life.** *"'He who believes has eternal life.'"* **6:47.**

20. **Come and drink.** *"Jesus stood up and proclaimed, 'If any one thirst, let him come to me and drink.'"* **7:37.**

21. **Light of the world.** *"Jesus spoke to them, saying, 'I am the light of the world; he who follows me will not walk in darkness, but will have the light of life.'"* **8:12.**

22. **Real freedom.** *"'If the Son makes you free, you will be free indeed.'"* **8:36.**

23. **Never see death.** *"'If any one keeps my word, he will never see death.'"* **8:51.**

24. **The blind man.** *"'One thing I know, that though I was blind, now I see.'"* **9:25.**

25. **Abundant life.** *"'I came that you may have life, and have it abundantly.'"* **10:10.**

26. **Eternal security.** *"'I give them eternal life, and they shall never perish, and no one shall snatch them out of my hand.'"* **10:28.**

27. **Thomas's courage.** *"Thomas...said to his fellow disciples, 'Let us also go, that we may die with him.'"* **11:16.**

28. **I am the resurrection.** *"Jesus said to her, 'I am the resurrection and the life.'"* **11:25.**

29. **Jesus wept.** *"Jesus wept."* **11:35.**

30. **Ever-present poverty.** *"'The poor you always have with you, but you do not always have me.'"* **12:8.**

31. **Triumphal entry.** *"So they took branches of palm trees and went out to meet him, crying, 'Hosanna! Blessed be he who comes in the name of the Lord.'"* **12:13.**

32. **Parable of humility.** *"Then he...began to wash the disciples' feet, and to wipe them with the towel with which he was girded."* **13:5.**

33. **Disciple whom Jesus loved.** *"One of his disciples, whom Jesus loved, was lying close to the breast of Jesus."* **13:23.**

34. **The new commandment.** *"'A new commandment I give to you, that you love one another; even as I have loved you.'"* **13:34.**

35. **Freedom from fear.** *"'Let not your hearts be troubled; believe in God, believe also in me.'"* **14:1.**

36. **The many mansions.** *"'In my Father's house are many rooms.'"* **14:2.**

37. **Perfect peace.** *"'Peace I leave with you; my peace I give to you.'"* **14:27.**

38. **Light and guilt.** *"'If I had not come...they would not have sin; but now they have no excuse for their sin.'"* **15:22.**

39. **Receptivity for truth.** *"'I have yet many things to say to you, but you cannot bear them now.'"* **16:12.**

40. **Spirit of truth.** *"'When the Spirit of truth comes, he will guide you into all the truth.'"* **16:13.**

41. **Worldly tribulation.** *"'In the world you have tribulation; but be of good cheer, I have overcome the world,'"* **16:33.**

42. **Creator glory.** *"'Father, glorify thou me in thy own presence with the glory which I had with thee before the world was made.'"* **17:5.**

43. **Sanctity of truth.** *"'Sanctify them in the truth; thy word is truth.'"* **17:17.**

44. **What is truth?** *"Pilate said to him, 'What is truth?'"* **18:38.**

45. **Bears his cross.** *"So they took Jesus...bearing his own cross."* **19:17.**

46 **Jesus and John.** *"When Jesus saw his mother, and the disciple whom he loved standing near...he said to the disciple, 'Behold your mother!' And from that hour the disciple took her to his own home."* **19:26,27.**

47. **The end.** *"'It is finished'; and he bowed his head and gave up his spirit."* **19:30.**

48. **The empty tomb.** *"Then the other disciple, who reached the tomb first, also went in, and he saw and believed."* **20:8.**

49. **The morontia Jesus.** *"Jesus said to her, 'Do not hold me, for I have not yet ascended to the Father.'"* **20:17.**

50. **Jesus visits the apostles.** *"Jesus came and stood among them and said to them, 'Peace be with you.'"* **20:19.**

51. **Breakfast with Jesus.** *"Jesus said to them, 'Come and have breakfast.' ...Jesus...took the bread and gave it to them, and so with the fish."* **21:12,13.**

# ACTS

## I. OUTLINE—BRIEF

## II. OUTLINE—COMPLETE

## III. AUTHORSHIP

1.  Luke wrote the book of Acts, probably at Rome, about A.D. 90. He died just before finishing Acts. (See *The Urantia Book* p. 1342.)

2.  Luke was from Antioch of Pisidia.

3.  He was a companion of Paul for several years—his private physician.

4.  Paul refers to Luke as one of his fellow workers. **Phmon. v. 24.**

5.  The latter portion of Acts—the "we" sections—was based on Luke's diary.

6. The abrupt ending of Acts is explained by the author's death. Just how much is missing from what was planned, we will never know.

7. We have no knowledge as to when and by whose influence Luke became a Christian.

## IV. LOOKING AT ACTS

1. Like the Gospel of Luke, Acts is a superb literary production.

2. Without Acts, we would know very little concerning the early days of Christianity.

3. Luke's book of Acts helps us to understand the real difference between the religion *of* Jesus and the religion *about* Jesus.

4. Like Luke, Acts shows sympathy for the poor and antipathy for the rich, along with the sanctity of "stewardship."

5. Luke is greatly interested in women's part in gospel work.

6. The fullest account of the ascension of Jesus is found in Acts.

7. As in Luke, so in Acts the author always shows special interest in all things having a health or medical aspect.

8. Luke shows great interest in Paul—as a person—but neither Luke nor Acts reflects any interest in Paul's epistles.

9. Luke was a physician and Christian historian—not a theologian.

## V. SELECTED TEXTS

1. **Jesus' ascension.** *"As they were looking on he was lifted up, and a cloud took him out of their sight...behold, two men stood by them...and said, 'Men of Galilee, why do you stand looking into heaven? This Jesus, who was taken up from you into heaven, will come in the same way as you saw him go into heaven.'"* **1:9-11.**

2. **Coming of the Comforter.** *"When the day of Pentecost had come, they were all together in one place...And they were all filled with the Holy Spirit."* **2:1,4.**

3. **Speaking with tongues.** *"And they were amazed and wondered, saying, 'Are not all these who are speaking Galileans? And how is it that we hear, each of us in his own native language?'"* **2:7,8.**

4. **Gift of the Spirit.** *"'Having received from the lather the promise of the Holy Spirit, he has poured out this which you see and hear.'"* **2:33.**

5. **Three thousand baptized.** *"Those who received his ward were baptized, and there were added that day about three thousand souls."* **2:41.**

6.  **The message.** *"'Repent, therefore, and turn again, that your sins may be blotted out, that times of refreshing may come from the presence of the lord.'"* **3:19.**

7.  **Another harvest of souls.** *"Many of those who heard the word believed; and the number of the men came to about five thousand."* **4:4.**

8.  **The saving name.** *"'And there is salvation in no one else, for there is no other name under heaven given among men by which we must be saved.'"* **4:12.**

9.  **All things in common.** *"The company of those who believed were of one heart and soul, and no one said that any of the things which he possessed was his own, but they had everything in common."* **4:32.**

10. **Falsehood of Ananias.** *"When Ananias heard these words, he fell down and died. And great fear came upon all who heard of it."* **5:5.**

11. **Peter's healing shadow.** *"They even carried out the sick into the streets, and laid them on beds and pallets, that as Peter came by at least his shadow might fall on some of them."* **5:15.**

12. **Angel opens the prison.** *"An angel of the Lord opened the prison doors and brought them out."* **5:19.**

13. **Gamaliel's advice.** *"'I tell you, keep away from these men and let them alone; for if this plan...is of men, it will fail; but if it is of God, you will not be able to overthrow them. You might even be found opposing God!'"* **5:38,39.**

14. **Stoning Stephen.** *"As they were stoning Stephen, he prayed, 'Lord Jesus, receive my spirit.'"* **7:59.**

15. **Saul consents.** *"And Saul was consenting to his death."* **8:1.**

16. **Philip and the eunuch.** *"They both went down into the water...and he baptized him...the Spirit of the Lord caught up Philip; and the eunuch saw him no more."* **8:38,39.**

17. **Saul's conversion.** *"And he...heard a voice saying to him, 'Saul, Saul, why do you persecute me?' And he said, 'Who are you, Lord?' And he said, I am Jesus, whom you are persecuting.'"* **9:4,5.**

18. **Saul begins his work.** *"But Saul increased all the more in strength, and confounded the Jews who lived in Damascus by proving that Jesus was the Christ."* **9:22.**

19. **Barnabas fellowships Paul.** *"When he had come to Jerusalem...they were all afraid of him...But Barnabas...brought him to the apostles."* **9:26,27.**

20. **Peter raises Dorcas.** *"But Peter...knelt down and prayed; then turning to the body he said, '...rise.' And she opened her eyes."* **9:40.**

21. **The keynote.** *"'How God anointed Jesus of Nazareth with the Holy Spirit and with power; how he went about doing good and healing all who were oppressed by the devil, for God was with him.'"* **10:38.**

22. **First called Christians.** *"In Antioch the disciples were for the first time called Christians."* **11:26.**

23. **Herod's persecutions.** *"Herod the king laid violent hands upon some who belonged to the church. He killed James the brother of John with the sword."* **12:1,2.**

24. **Angel liberates Peter.** *"An angel of the lord...woke him, saying, 'Get up quickly.' And the chains fell off his hands."* **12:7.**

25. **Ordination of Paul and Barnabas.** *"The Holy Spirit said, 'Set apart for me Barnabas and Saul for the work to which I have called them.'"* **13:2.**

26. **Healing the cripple.** *"There was a man...who had never walked...And Paul... said... 'Stand upright on your feet.' And he sprang up and walked. And when the crowds saw what Paul had done, they lifted up their voices, saying... 'The gods have come down to us in the likeness of men!'"* **14:8-11.**

27. **Paul stoned.** *"They stoned Paul and dragged him out of the city, supposing that he was dead."* **14:19.**

28. **James frees the Gentiles.** *"'My judgment is that we should not trouble those of the Gentiles who turn to God.'"* **15:19.**

29. **The Macedonian call.** *"A vision appeared to Paul...a man..saying, 'Come over to Macedonia and help us.'"* **16:9.**

30. **The jail opens.** *"About midnight Paul and Silas were praying...and suddenly there was a great earthquake, so that the prison...doors were opened and every one's fetters were unfastened."* **16;25,26.**

31. **Turning the world upside down.** *"'These men who have turned the world upside down have come here also.'"* **17:6.**

32. **Aquila and Friscilla.** *"He stayed with them, and they worked, for by trade they were tentmakers,"* **18:3.**

33. **The magic "hankies."** *"God did extraordinary miracles by the hands of Paul, so that handkerchiefs or aprons were carried away from his body to the sick, and diseases left them, and the evil spirits came out of them."* **19:11,12.**

34. **Converted magicians**. *"Those who practiced magic arts brought their books together and burned them in the sight of all; and they counted the value of them and found it came to fifty thousand pieces of silver."* **19:19**.

35. **Breaking bread**. *"On the first day of the week, when we were gathered together to break bread, Paul talked with them."* **20:70**.

36. **Paul appeals to Caesar**. *"I appeal to Caesar."* **25:11**.

37. **Festus calls Paul mad**. *"Festus said… 'Paul, you are mad; your great learning is turning you mad.'"* **26:24**.

38. **Agrippa and Paul**. *"Agrippa said to Paul, 'In a short time you think to make me a Christian!'"* **26:28**.

39. **Paul and the viper**. *"When a viper came out because of the heat and fastened on his hand…He, however, shook off the creature into the fire and suffered no harm."* **28:3,5**.

40. **Some freedom at Rome**. *"When we came to Rome, Paul was allowed to stay by himself, with the soldier that guarded him."* **28:16**.

41. **Two years at Rome**. *"And he lived there two whole years at his own expense, and welcomed all who came to him."* **28:30**.

# ROMANS

## I. OUTLINE—BRIEF

## II. OUTLINE—COMPLETE

## III. AUTHORSHIP

1.  Paul wrote Romans. It is his longest and weightiest letter to the churches.

2.  Some think Paul did not write the last two chapters.

3.  Romans was written during Paul's longest period of rest and lei-
    sure— probably at Corinth in A.D. 58 during his third and last visit.

4.  Romans may have been a general letter to all the churches. The last
    two chapters might have been added to the Rome copy.

5.  The heretic Marcion made the first collection of Paul's letters.

6.  Purpose of the letter was to pave the way for his visit to Rome on the
    way to Spain.

7.  Paul was not too sure of being well received at Rome. Jerusalem was
    the seat of conservative and Jewish Christianity. Rome was the center
    of the radical and gentile branch of Christendom.

8.  We really do not know who founded the church at Rome. Peter has
    been credited, but we cannot be sure.

9.  If Peter had been founder of the Rome church, Paul would undoubt-
    edly have mentioned him.

## IV. PAUL'S MESSAGE

1.  Paul was not so much a theologian as a preacher and evangelist. But
    he was the leading theologian of all Christendom.

2.  Romans is the most important theological book ever written. It is the
    only systematic statement of Paul's theology.

3.  He preached the doctrine of salvation.

4.  Paul all but personalized sin—and he believed in "original sin." As in
    Adam all died, so in Christ all are made alive.

5.  By sin, man is estranged from God; by Christ he becomes reconciled.

6.  It seems that Paul recognized three parts of man: body, soul, and spirit.

7.  Christ pays a ransom for man's sin-enslaved soul.

8.   Much of Romans has to do with LAW—how Christ takes man from being "under the law" and puts him "under grace."

9.   The Christian church is a "colony of heaven."

10.  Paul's theology is summed up in: "Justification by faith."

11.  Paul's attitude: *"I am not ashamed of the gospel: it is the power of God for salvation."* **1:16.**

12.  Romans shows that Paul is the propounder of the atonement doctrine.

**Note:** As concerns the great conflict between the flesh and the Spirit— see *The Urantia Book*, p. 382-3.

## V. SELECTED TEXTS

1.   **Paul's gospel.** *"I am not ashamed of the gospel: it is the power of God for salvation to every one who has faith."* **1:16.**

2.   **Homosexuality.** *"The men likewise gave up natural relations with women and were consumed with passion for one another, men committing shameless acts with men."* **1:27.**

3.   **God's kindness.** *"Do you not know that God's kindness is meant to lead you to repentance?"* **2:4.**

4.   **Universal sin.** *"Since all have sinned and fall short of the glory of God."* **3:23.**

5.   **Justification by faith.** *"We hold that a man is justified by faith apart from works of law."* **3:28.**

6.   **Abraham's faith.** *"'Abraham believed God, and it was reckoned to him as righteousness.'"* **4:3.**

7.   **Christ's atonement.** *"Who was put to death for our trespasses and raised for our justification."* **4:25.**

8.   **Peace of justification.** *"Since we are justified by faith, we have peace with God through our Lord Jesus Christ."* **5:1.**

9.   **Mission of suffering.** *"We rejoice in our sufferings, knowing that suffering produces endurance, and endurance produces character, and character produces hope, and hope does not disappoint us, because God's love has been poured into our hearts."* **5:3,4.**

10.  **God loves sinners.** *"God shows his love for us in that while we were yet sinners Christ died for us."* **5:8.**

11.  **Original sin.** *"For as by one man's disobedience many were made sinners, so by one man's obedience many will be made righteous."* **5:19.**

12. **Presumptuous sin.** *"Are we to continue in sin that grace may abound?"* **6:1.**

13. **Being dead to sin.** *"Let not sin therefore reign in your mortal bodies, to make you obey their passions."* **6:12.**

14. **The wages of sin.** *"The wages of sin is death, but the free gift of God is eternal life in Christ Jesus our Lord."* **6:23.**

15. **The mortal conflict.** *"I do not understand my own actions. For I do not do what I want, but I do the very thing I hate. Now if I do what I do not want, I agree that the law is good. So then it is no longer I that do it, but sin which dwells within me."* **7:15-17.**

16. **Wretched man.** *"Wretched man that I am! Who will deliver me from this body of death? Thanks be to God through Christ our Lord."* **7:24,25.**

17. **Spiritual freedom.** *"The law of the Spirit of life in Christ Jesus has set me free from the law of sin and death."* **8:2.**

18. **The sons of God.** *"For all who are led by the Spirit of God are sons of God."* **8:14.**

19. **Assurance of sonship.** *"It is the Spirit himself bearing witness with our spirit that we are the children of God."* **8:16.**

20. **Reward of suffering.** *"I consider that the sufferings of this present time are not worth comparing with the glory that is to be revealed in us."* **8:18.**

21. **Spirit help in prayer.** *"Likewise the Spirit helps us in our weakness; for we do not know how to pray as we ought, but the Spirit himself intercedes for us with sighs too deep for words."* **8:26.**

22. **All to the good.** *"We know that in everything God works for good with those who love him, who are called according to his purpose."* **8:28.**

23. **God for us.** *"If God is for us, who is against us?"* **8:31.**

24. **Security in Christ.** *"Who shall separate us from the love of Christ? Shall tribulation, or distress, or persecution, or peril, or sword?"* **8:35.**

25. **More than conquerors.** *"In all these things we are more than conquerors through him who loved us."* **8:37.**

26. **Zeal without knowledge.** *"They have a zeal for God, but it is not enlightened."* **10:2.**

27. **Salvation.** *"If you confess...that Jesus is Lord and believe in your heart that God raised him from the dead, you will be saved."* **10:9.**

28. **Call on his name.** *"Every one who calls upon the name of the Lord will be saved.'"* **10:13.**

29. **Divine infinitude.** *"O the depth of the riches and wisdom and knowledge of God! How unsearchable are his judgments and how inscrutable his ways!"* **11:33.**

30. **Mental transformation.** *"Do not be conformed to this world but be transformed by the renewal of your mind."* **12:2.**

31. **Genuine love.** *"Let love be genuine, hate what is evil, hold fast to what is good; love one another with brotherly affection."* **12:9.**

32. **Fraternity.** *"Rejoice with those who rejoice, weep with those who weep."* **12:15.**

33. **Dealing with enemies.** *"'If your enemy is hungry, feed him; if he is thirsty, give him drink; for by so doing you will heap burning coals upon his head."* **12:20.**

34. **Civil obedience.** *"Let every person be subject to the governing authorities. For there is no authority except from God, and those that exist have been instituted by God."* **13:1.**

35. **Personal opinions.** *"One believes he may eat anything, while the weak man eats only vegetables."* **14:2.** *"One man esteems one day as better than another, while another man esteems all days alike. Let every one be fully convinced in his own mind."* **14:5.**

36. **Socialization.** *"None of us lives to himself, and none of us dies to himself."* **14:7.**

37. **Meaning of the kingdom.** *"The kingdom of God does not mean food and drink but righteousness and peace and joy in the Holy Spirit."* **14:17.**

# CORINTHIANS

## I. OUTLINE

## II. AUTHORSHIP

1. Paul wrote 1 Corinthians from Ephesus in A.D. 54.

2. Paul sent four letters to the church at Corinth.

3. The first letter written from Ephesus has been lost, but a fragment (**2 Cor. 6:14-7:1**) is thought to have been preserved.

4. The second letter is our 1 Corinthians.

5. Most of the third letter (referred to in **2 Cor. 2:4** and **7:8**) is also lost. A fragment of it is believed to be **2 Cor. 10-13**. It was written from Ephesus.

6.  Paul's fourth letter is our **2 Corinthians 1-9** (except **6:14-7:1**).

7.  Paul spent eighteen months at Corinth, where he wrote Romans and the two Thessalonians.

## III. OCCASION FOR THE LETTERS

1.  Apollos, of Alexandria, did considerable work in Corinth, Priacilla and Aquila gave him advanced instruction.

2.  Peter may have visited this church, since there was a three-way division. Some said they were of Apollos, some Cephas, others Paul.

3.  Paul's letter deals with the following troubles:

    Party divisions.
    Marriage.
    Meat offered idols.
    Spiritual gifts.
    Incest.
    Legal disputes.
    Disorders at Lord's Supper.
    Denial of the resurrection.

4.  Speaking with tongues made trouble at Corinth—as well as in other churches.

5.  This is not a doctrinal letter—it deals with practical and daily living problems.

6.  Paul advocated women's wearing veils in church.

7.  A keynote in Paul's advice: *"Let all things be done decently and in order."*

8.  Always remember: In these early years, Paul was expecting the second advent of Christ any day.

9.  Paul was a bang-up evangelist and the leading theologian of his time, but he was not a profound philosopher.

## IV. SELECTED TEXTS

1.  **Church factions.** *"It has been reported to me...that there is quarreling among you...Each one of you says, 'I belong to Paul,' or 'I belong to Apollos,' or 'I belong to Cephas.'"* **1:11,12.**

2.  **Dedicated teacher.** *"I decided to know nothing among you except Jesus Christ and him crucified."* **2:2.**

3.  **Co-operation.** *"I planted, Apollos watered, but God gave the growth."* **3:6.**

4.  **We are temples.** *"You are God's temple and...God's Spirit dwells in you."* **3:16.**

5.  **Kingdom power.** *"For the kingdom of God does not consist in talk but in power."* **4:20.**

6.  **Incest.** *"There is immorality among you...a man is living with his father's wife."* **5:1.**

7.  **Paul's marriage attitude.** *"To the unmarried and the widows I say that it is well for them to remain single as I do."* **7:8.**

8.  **Marriage a compromise.** *"But if they cannot exercise self-control, they should marry."* **7:9.**

9.  **Vocational stability.** *"In whatever state each was called, there let him remain with God."* **7:24.**

10. **Avoid being a stumbling block.** *"If food is a cause of my brother's falling, I will never eat meat."* **8:13.**

11. **Adaptation.** *"I have become all things to all men, that I might by all means save some."* **9:22.**

12. **Self-control.** *"But I pommel my body and subdue it, lest after preaching to others I myself should be disqualified."* **9:27.**

13. **Over-self-confidence.** *"Let anyone who thinks that he stands take heed lest he fall."* **10:12.**

14. **Measured temptation.** *"No temptation has overtaken you that is not common to man. God is faithful, and he will not let you be tempted beyond your strength, but with the temptation will also provide the way to escape, that you may be able to endure it."* **10:13.**

15. **Women and veils.** *"That is why a woman ought to have a veil on her head, because of the angels."* **11:10.**

16. **The remembrance supper.** *"And when he had given thanks, he broke it, and said, 'This is my body which is for you. Do this in remembrance of me.'"* **11:24.**

17. **Love is paramount.** *"If I speak in the tongues of men and of angels, but have not love, I am a noisy gong or a clanging cymbal."* **13:1.**

18. **Love is supreme.** *"Love bears all things, believes all things, hopes all things, endures all things."* **13:7.**

19. **Love the greatest.** *"So faith, hope, love abide, these three. But the greatest of these is love."* **13:13.**

20. **Woman's silence.** *"The women should keep silence in the churches."* **14:34.** *"For it is shameful for a woman to speak in church."* **14:35.**

21. **Original sin.** *"For as in Adam all die, so also in Christ shall all be made alive."* **15:22.**

22. **Baptism for the dead.** *"Otherwise, what do people mean by being baptized on behalf of the dead? If the dead are not raised at all, why are people baptized on their behalf?"* **15:29.**

23. **Morontia body.** *"It is sown a physical body; it is raised a spiritual body."* **15:44.**

24. **Second advent.** *"We shall not all sleep, but we shall all be changed, in a moment, in the twinkling of an eye, at the last trumpet...The dead will be raised imperishable, and we shall be changed."* **15:51,52.**

25. **The courageous life.** *"Be watchful, stand firm in your faith, be courageous, be strong. Let all that you do be done in love."* **16:13,14.**

# CORINTHIANS
SECOND

## I. OUTLINE

## II. AUTHORSHIP

1.  Second Corinthians is Paul's fourth letter. It was written in A.D. 55 from Macedonia.

2.  This is the most personal of all of Paul's letters to the churches.

3.  This 2 Corinthians—the fourth letter—has been called the "thankful" epistle.

4.  Some have thought that 2 Cor. 6:14-7:1 is a fragment from the first letter.

5.  Paul's third letter (largely lost) was a severe rebuke—and seems to have been effective.

6.  This stern letter was probably written from Ephesus and sent by Titus.

7.  Some believe that 2 Cor. Chapters 10-13 are a fragment of the stem third letter. This is hardly an appropriate way to end a "thankful" letter to a reunited church.

## III. CENTRAL THEMES

1. We do not have a very clear picture of just what Paul's detractors were preaching. One thing certain, they were hard at work to undermine Paul's influence and status.

2. They accused Paul of being "tricky and insincere," weak in voice and appearance, having "visions," and being "mentally unbalanced."

3. Paul denounced his adversaries as being "domineering, arrogant, greedy, and brutal." He would hardly admit that they were "Christians."

4. Paul's collection for the Jerusalem church was a strategic move to promote Jewish-gentile unity.

5. **Major theme**—God and Father of the Lord Jesus Christ, the Father of mercies and the God of all comfort.

6. He did not belittle Satan—called him "God of this world."

7. He presents the Christ, who "was rich," but for our sake "became poor."

8. The new order of God, through Christ, is the gift of the Holy Spirit.

9. Paul recognizes the Old Testament as "scripture," but Christ is its fulfillment.

10. He portrays the "mission of suffering." His power is "made perfect in weakness."

11. Hope is the twin of true faith.

12. Prayer is the mainstay of religion.

13. Christian giving—charity.

14. He admits his own afflictions and his "thorn in the flesh."

15. He glories in his infirmities.

16. Paul does not hesitate to make a bold and courageous defense of himself.

17. God lives and works in man. The body is the temple of the Holy Spirit.

18. Jesus is a unique revelation of God.

## IV. SELECTED TEXTS

1. **God of all comfort**. *"Blessed be the God and Father of our Lord Jesus Christ, the Father of mercies, and God of all comfort."* **1:3.**

2. **Spirit gives life**. *"The written code kills, but the Spirit gives life."* **3:6.**

3. **Spiritual liberty.** *"Where the Spirit of the Lord is, there is freedom."* **3:17.**

4. **Earthen vessels.** *"But we have this treasure in earthen vessels."* **4:7.**

5. **The eternal reward.** *"For this slight momentary affliction is preparing us for an eternal weight of glory beyond all comparison."* **4:17.**

6. **The morontia body.** *"We know that if the earthly tent we live in is destroyed, we have a building from God, a house not made with hands, eternal in the heavens."* **5:1.**

7. **The new creature.** *"Therefore, if any one is in Christ, he is a new creation; the old has passed away, behold, the new has come."* **5:17.**

8. **Divine reconciliation.** *"God was in Christ reconciling the world to himself."* **5:19.**

9. **Unbeliever marriages.** *"Do not be mismated with unbelievers."* **6:14.**

10. **Temples of God.** *"For we are the temple of the living God."* **6:16.**

11. **Clean living.** *"Let us cleanse ourselves from every defilement of body and spirit, and make holiness perfect in the fear of God."* **7:1.**

12. **According to ability.** *"If the readiness is there, it is acceptable according to what a man has, not according to what he has not."* **8:12.**

13. **Satanic disguise.** *"And no wonder, for even Satan disguises himself as an angel of light."* **11:14.**

14. **Paul's revelation.** *"This man was caught up into Paradise...and he heard things that cannot be told."* **12:3.4.**

15. **The thorn in the flesh.** *"And to keep me from being too elated by the abundance of revelations, a thorn was given me in the flesh, a messenger of Satan, to harass me, to keep me from being too elated."* **12:7.**

16. **Power of grace.** *"'My grace is sufficient for you, for my power is made perfect in weakness.'"* **12:9.**

17. **Spiritual strength.** *"When I am weak, then am I strong."* **12:10.**

18. **Self-examination.** *"Examine yourselves, to see whether you are holding to your faith. Test yourselves."* **13:5.**

# GALATIANS

## I. OUTLINE

## II. AUTHORSHIP

1.  Galatians was not written to a single church. It was sent to all the churches in Galatia—Antioch in Pisidia, Iconium, Lystra, and Derbe.

2.  Galatians, written by Paul, is probably our oldest Christian document.

3.  We cannot be sure as to whether it was written at Ephesus or at Antioch in Syria.

4.  The date of Galatians is uncertain.

    A.  If Galatians is Paul's first letter, it was probably written at Antioch in A.D. 49.

    B.  If it is his third letter and written at Ephesus, the date is probably A.D. 52.

5.  Galatians was Luther's favorite epistle.

## III. THE PURPOSE

1.  Galatians is Paul's declaration of religious independence.

2.  In some respects, Galatians is the most important theological document ever written.

3.  Of all Paul's writings, Galatians is the shortest, most rigorous and forthright statement of his theology.

4.  Galatians is the Magna Charta of the Christian faith.

5.  In Galatians "LAW" means the "whole scheme of living"—social, ceremonial, moral, and theologic—the religion of works.

6.  Paul makes clear that liberty is not *license*.

7.  The "Judaizers" attacked Paul's credentials as well as his Gospel.

8.  There were two groups of mischief makers:

    A.  Judaizers—those who said you must become a Jew—be circumcised, etc. —before you could become a Christian.
    B.  Those who went Paul one better, saying, since Christians were free from the law, they could indulge in all sorts of immorality.

9.  Justification by faith was Paul's basic concept of the Gospel.

10. Christ is the sole sufficiency of salvation—no intermediaries.

11. Paul had trouble defending his apostleship—already "apostolic succession" had sprung up.

12. Paul shifted validity of his credentials from religious tradition to personal religious experience. (This is the teaching of *The Urantia Book*.)

13. But the new Gospel was not an easy way—instead of license it involved great responsibility.

14. Paul taught over-all Christian UNITY—no struggle for power, honor, or influence.

15. He said the Lord's Supper forbade divisions and separatists.

16. But he demanded a "church" for growth, worship, and "missions."

17. Paul was a master organizer and fair administrator.

## IV. PAULINE CHARACTERISTICS

1.  Paul was "dead to the world"; he had "risen with Christ." He was living in the "new age."

2.  It was revolutionary to teach that salvation could be had without "merit"—that faith alone could save.

3.   Paul claimed that Christ's death had redeemed all men.

4.   Faith delivers mortal man from guilt and sin. Salvation is God's free gift.

5.   Paul acknowledges his infirmities, but glories in his weakness—that the strength of "grace" may be made manifest.

## V. SELECTED TEXTS

1.   **Prenatal aspects.** *"But when he who had set me apart before I was born, and had called me through his grace."* **1:15**. (Here again is the idea of Thought Adjusters' having forecasts of human beings.)

2.   **Justified by faith.** *"We have believed in Christ Jesus, in order to be justified by faith."* **2:16**.

3.   **The new life.** *"I have been crucified with Christ; it is no longer I who live, but Christ who lives in me; and the life I now live in the flesh I live by faith in the Son of God."* **2:20**.

4.   **The atonement.** *"Christ redeemed us from the curse of the law, having become a curse for us."* **3:13**.

5.   **Sonship.** *"In Jesus Christ you are all Sons of God, through faith."* **3:26**.

6.   **Spirit of sonship.** *"And because you are sons, God has sent the Spirit of his Son into our hearts."* **4:6**.

7.   **Paul's eye trouble.** *"If possible, you would have plucked out your eyes and given them to me."* **4:15**.

8.   **Freedom in Christ.** *"For freedom Christ has set us free; stand fast therefore, and do not submit again to a yoke of slavery."* **5:1**.

9.   **Our hope.** *"Through the Spirit, by faith, we wait for the hope of righteousness."* **5:5**.

10.  **Misuse of freedom.** *"You were called to freedom, brethren; only do not use your freedom as an opportunity for the flesh, but through love be servants of one another."* **5:13**.

11.  **Love your neighbor.** *"The whole law is fulfilled in one word, 'You shall love your neighbor as yourself.'"* **5:14**.

12.  **The Spirit life.** *"Walk by the Spirit, and do not gratify the desires of the flesh."* **5:16**.

13.  **Fruits of the Spirit.** *"The fruit of the Spirit is love, joy, peace, patience, kindness, goodness, faithfulness, gentleness, self-control; against such there is no law,"* **5:22,23**.

14. **Burden bearing**. *"Bear one another's burdens, and so fulfil the law of Christ."* **6:2**.

15. **Sowing and reaping**. *"Do not be deceived; God is not mocked, for whatever a man sows, that he will also reap."* **6:7**.

# EPHESIANS

## I. OUTLINE

## II. AUTHORSHIP

1.  Paul wrote Ephesians. The doctrinal half is Paul's theology; the philosophical half is Paul's teaching.

2.  But the polished literary style throughout is *not* Paul's. After Paul wrote the epistle, some well qualified Christian editor rewrote the letter —making it one of the most polished pieces of literature to be found in either the Old or the New Testament.

3.  The letter was not written just to the church at Ephesus. It was a general epistle addressed to all the churches. (The Revised Standard Version leaves off "Ephesus" in the introduction.)

4.  There are 82 words in Ephesians not to be found in any of Paul's other letters.

5.  The chief topics of this letter conform to Paul's teaching, but there are at least four secondary ideas that seem foreign to Paul's thinking.

    A.  **Paul's mission**. He did not claim to be the only missionary to the genetiles. There were earlier teachers—see **Acts 11:20**.

B. **Spiritual Gifts.** Ephesians suggests they are imparted, not by the Spirit, but by Christ.

C. **The idea of descending into Hades.** This concept is not found in Paul's other writings.

D. **Apostolic authority.** Ephesians imparts more authority to apostles and prophets than do the other epistles.

6. Paul wrote this letter from prison in Rome—A.D. 59-62.

7. The editor of Ephesians probably was with Paul during his Rome imprisonment.

8. The editor of Ephesians probably was familiar with Paul's letter to the Colossians. He was undoubtedly a Jew.

## III. PURPOSE OF EPHESIANS

1. Ephesians is free from all controversy. That is unique for Paul's writings.

2. This letter represents Paul's teachings divested of the tinge of disputes and argument.

3. Ephesians is a sort of anthology of Paulinism.

4. The editor of Ephesians is attempting to formulate a "philosophy of religion" out of the doctrinal and often highly controversial writings of Paul.

5. Ephesians is an attempt to systematize Paul's hurried and energetic letters to the churches.

6. Colossians had little to say about Judaism. It dealt more with paganism—Gnosticism—something the Church would have to face for several generations.

7. The purpose is to present to the Church *"the unsearchable riches of Christ … and the manifold wisdom of God."* **3:8-10.**

## IV. THEOLOGY OF EPHESIANS

1. It cannot be denied that this book is strongly "tainted" with predestination.

2. The brotherhood concept gains its chief support from Ephesians.

3. Ephesians is up to date. Its battle cry—"Unite or perish."

4. The goal is *unity*—"in the fullness of time."

5. The theme—all creation moving toward ultimate unity in Christ.

6. All the time Ephesians preaches unity—"till we all come into the unity of the faith."

7. It presents a picture of a sort of "Christian imperialism," all mankind united in the service of Christ.

8. The Fatherhood of God is a chief thought. He is a universal Father— "one God and Father of all."

9. The "mystery of God" is openly revealed "in Christ."

10. In Ephesians the church has fully displaced the "kingdom."

11. The letter fully upholds all of Paul's preaching about "Christ and him crucified."

12. The Jewish Messiah is displaced by a transcendental and cosmic Messiah of infinite attributes.

13. The letter is true to Paul's doctrine of the atonement.

14. The theology of Ephesians is interspersed with prayers that border on grandeur and beauty.

**Note**: Predestination is the Christian analogue of the "chosen people" doctrine of the Jews.

## V. SELECTED TEXTS

1. **Foreordination**. *"Even as he chose us in him before the foundation of the world, that we should be holy and blameless before him."* **1:4**.

2. **The eternal plan**. *"According to his purpose which he set forth in Christ as a plan for the fulness of time, to unite all things in him, things in heaven and things on earth."* **1:9,10**.

3. **The supremacy of Christ**. *"And he has put all things under his feet and has made him the head over all things for the church, which is his body, the fulness of him who fills all in all."* **1:22,23**.

4. **Free salvation**. *"For by grace you have been saved through faith, and this is not your own doing, it is the gift of God."* **2:8**.

5. **Christ our peace**. *"For he is our peace, who has made us both one, and has broken down the dividing wall of hostility."* **2:14**.

6. **Fellowship with the saints**. *"So then you are no longer strangers and sojourners, but you are fellow citizens with the saints and members of the household of God."* **2:19**.

7. **The eternal purpose**. *"This was according to the eternal purpose which he has realized in Christ Jesus our Lord."* **3:11**.

8. **Spiritual strength**. *"That according to the riches of his glory he may grant you to be strengthened with might through his Spirit in the inner man."* **3:16**.

9. **The fullness of God.** *"And to know the love of Christ which surpasses knowledge, that you may be filled with all the fulness of God."* **3:19.**

10. **The divine omnipresence.** *"One God and Father of us all, who is above all and through all and in all."* **4:6.**

11. **The new nature.** *"And be renewed in the spirit of your minds, and put on the new nature, created after the likeness of God in true righteousness and holiness."* **4:23,24.**

12. **Marriage relationships.** *"Be subject to one another out of reverence for Christ. Wives, be subject to your husbands, as to the Lord."* **5:21,22.**

13. **Marriage love.** *"Husbands, love your wives, as Christ loved the church and gave himself up for her."* **5:25.**

14. **Parental obedience.** *"Children, obey your parents in the Lord, for this is right."* **6:1.**

15. **Subjection of slaves.** *"Slaves, be obedient to those who are your earthly masters, with fear and trembling, in singleness of heart, as to Christ,"* **6:5.**

16. **Spiritual strength.** *"Finally, be strong in the Lord and in the strength of his might. Put on the whole armor of God, that you may be able to stand against the wiles of the devil."* **6:10,11.**

17. **Effective armor.** *"And take the helmet of salvation, and the sword of the Spirit, which is the word of God."* **6:17.**

# PHILIPPIANS

## I. OUTLINE

## II. PURPOSE AND OCCASION

1. The church at Philippi had sent a gift of money to Paul by Epaphroditus, who was stricken with a grave illness, and on recovery brought Paul's letter back to the church at Philippi.

2. This epistle was a letter of thanks for their gift—the only one of its kind Paul ever accepted from one of his churches.

   **Note:** It is thought that Paul got an inheritance from a wealthy relative about the time of his first imprisonment.

3. Here at Philippi Paul made his first effort in Europe, and this became the first Christian church in Europe.

4. He was accompanied by Silas, Timothy, and Luke.

5. The best account of Paul's visit to Philippi is Luke's record in Acts.

6. Paul's imbroglio with the slave girl got him in prison and scourged; but his Roman citizenship got him out of trouble.

7.   A nocturnal earthquake helped to get Paul and Silas out of jail.

8.   Arguments have been presented to show that this letter came from Ephesus or Caesarea, but most authorities agree that it came from Rome.

9.   The date is from A.D. 60 to 62.

## III. A LOOK AT THE LETTER

1.   **Phil. 3:8-14** is probably the most moving and elevated passage Paul ever wrote.

2.   The rhythmical trend of **2:5-11** suggests that it may have originally been a hymn.

3.   Women were prominent in the church at Philippi, notably Lydia. Paul knew about the small cliques and petty rivalries in the church.

4.   Paul no longer expected to see the Lord come any day in "the clouds of heaven." He was becoming reconciled to the idea of death.

5.   There is little theologic argument in this letter—and it ends differently from his other epistles. The end (see **4:8**) is followed by the postscript.

6.   The cheerful tone of this letter suggests that Paul was expecting to get out of prison soon.

7.   This has been called the "joy" epistle—because the word is so frequently used.

8.   This is the most personal and touchingly beautiful of all Paul's letters.

9.   Of all Paul's writings this is more like a "letter"—just a friendly message to his flock at Philippi.

## IV. SELECTED TEXTS

1.   **Paul's wish for us.** *"And it is my prayer that your love may abound more and more, with knowledge and all discernment, so that you may approve what is excellent, and may be pure and blameless for the day of Christ."* **1:9,10**.

2.   **Paul's imprisonment.** *"And most of the brethren have been made confident of the Lord because of my imprisonment, and are much more bold to speak the word of God without fear."* **1:14**.

3.   **The sure profit.** *"For to me to live is Christ, and to die is gain."* **1:21**.

4.   **True humility.** *"Do nothing from selfishness or conceit, but in humility count others better than yourselves."* **2:3**.

5.  **The incarnation.** *"And being found in human form he humbled himself and became obedient unto death, even death on a cross."* **2:8.**

6.  **Working out salvation.** *"Work out your own salvation with fear and trembling."* **2:12.**

7.  **Sharing the Christ life.** *"That I may know him and the power of his resurrection, and may share his sufferings, becoming like him in his death."* **3:10.**

8.  **The forward look.** *"But one thing I do, forgetting what lies behind and straining forward to what lies ahead, I press on toward the goal for the prize of the upward call of God in Christ Jesus."* **3:13,14.**

9.  **Peace of God.** *"Have no anxiety about anything, but in everything by prayer and supplication with thanksgiving let your requests be made known to God. And the peace of God, which passes all understanding, will keep your hearts and your minds in Christ Jesus."* **4:6,7.**

10. **The Christ life.** *"Finally, brethren, whatever is true, whatever is honorable, whatever is just, whatever is pure, whatever is lovely, whatever is gracious, if there is any excellence, if there is anything worthy of praise, think about these things."* **4:3.**

11. **Contentment.** *"I have learned, in whatever state I am, to be content."* **4:11.**

12. **Divine strength.** *"I can do all things in him who strengthens me."* **4:13.**

13. **Supplying our needs.** *"And my God will supply every need of yours according to his riches in glory in Christ Jesus."* **4:19.**

# COLOSSIANS

## I. OUTLINE

## II. AN OVER-ALL LOOK

1. Paul writes this letter from prison—most likely from Rome, although some have thought the letter might have been written from Caesarea or Ephesus.

2. Paul was living in his own rented house at Rome. It is believed that he received an inheritance from a relative about this time.

3. Epaphras was probably one of Paul's Ephesian converts. It was he, not Paul, who founded the church at Colossae.

4. There is some evidence that the slave-philosopher, Epictetus, may have met Epaphras. Epictetus was a Stoic, but his teachings show many traces of Paul's teaching.

5. In Colossians the center of interest shifts from the work of Christ to the *person* of Christ.

6. The doctrine of "justification by faith" is presented in a new setting in this epistle.

7. There is much in this letter that sounds like Ephesians. This is one of the strongest reasons for believing that Paul was the author of the original Ephesians.

8. The date is probably A.D. 59 to 61.

## III. THE COLOSSIAN "HERESY"

1. The Colossians were being subjected to the forerunners of early Gnosticism.

2. Some of the errors of the Colossians:

   A. Heresy about angels. *"The elemental spirits of the universe."* **2:8**.
   B. A celestial hierarchy. **1:16**.
   C. Asceticism.
   D. Legalisms.
   E. Docetic restrictions.
   F. Sabbath cult. **2:16**.
   G. Taboos. **2:21**.
   H. Circumcision. **2:11**.
   I. Aspects of the mystery cults.
   J. Greek philosophy.
   K. Probably some doctrines of Plato and Philo.

   **Note:** While there may have been some truth in the concept of angels, the basic error was that they were objects of worship—displacing Christ.

3. The chief error of this teaching was the doctrine of "angelic mediators"—many features are reflected in later doctrines of the Roman Catholic church.

4. Paul sets forth Christ as the sole mediator. And he stands far above all others. **1:16,17,18, 19**.

5. Paul wants them to shun "elemental spirits" and put Christ at the head of all. **2:9**.

6. Worst of all—there was a moral laxity associated with all these claims of "advanced truth."

7. Paul's answer to all this was the doctrine of the "fullness of Christ." **2:9,10**.

8. Paul warned them against the "mystic visions" of the leaders of the new cult.

9. Colossians in some respects foreshadows the theology of the Gospel of John and Hebrews.

## V. SELECTED TEXTS

1.  **The divine strength**. *"May you be strengthened with all power, according to his glorious might, for all endurance and patience with joy."* **1:11.**

2.  **The transcendent life**. *"He has delivered us from the dominion of darkness and transferred us to the kingdom of his beloved Son, in whom we have redemption, the forgiveness of sins."* **1:13,14.**

3.  **Infinite cohesion**. *"He is before all things, and in him all things hold together."* **1:17.**

4.  **The incarnation**. *"For in him all the fulness of God was pleased to dwell."* **1:19.**

5.  **The divine mystery**. *"God chose to make known how great...are the riches of the glory of this mystery, which is Christ in you, the hope of glory."* **1:27.**

6.  **God's mystery**. *"To have all the riches of assured understanding and the knowledge of God's mystery, of Christ, in whom are hid all the treasures of wisdom and knowledge."* **2:2,3.**

7.  **Deceptive doctrines**. *"See to it that no one makes a prey of you by philosophy and empty deceit, according to human tradition, according to the elemental spirits of the universe, and not according to Christ. For in him the whole fulness of deity dwells bodily."* **2:8,9.**

8.  **Religious liberty**. *"Let no one pass judgment on you in questions of food and drink or with regard to a festival or a new moon or a sabbath."* **2:16.**

9.  **Living in Christ**. *"If then you have been raised with Christ, seek the things that are above, where Christ is, seated at the right hand of God."* **3:1.**

10. **Life hid with Christ**. *"And your life is hid with Christ in God."* **3:3.**

11. **The new nature**. *"And have put on the new nature, which is being renewed in knowledge after the image of its creator."* **3:10.**

12. **Supremacy of love**. *"And above all these put on love, which binds everything together in perfect harmony."* **3:14.**

13. **Gracious speech**. *"Let your speech always be gracious, seasoned with salt, so that you may know how you ought to answer every one."* **4:6.**

14. **Paul's fetters**. *"I, Paul, write this greeting with my own hand. Remember my fetters. Grace be with you."* **4:18.**

# THESSALONIANS

## I. OUTLINE

### 1 THESSALONIANS

### 2 THESSALONIANS

## II. GENERAL CONSIDERATIONS

1. Silas and Timothy were Paul's companions in the founding of this church.

2. Timothy had a Greek father and a Jewish mother.

3. These letters are peculiar in that Paul does not characterize himself as an apostle, etc., as in his other letters.

4. These letters were probably written from Corinth A.D. 50 or 51.

5. 1 Thessalonians is Paul's first letter to any of his churches.

6. Thessalonica (modern Salonica) was the provincial capital and was on the great travel route of East and West.

## III. THE MESSAGE

1. The first letter is warm-hearted, personal, and contains but little theology.

2. The second letter is much like the first, but is more formal, and has more theology.

3. Some have thought that there must have been two churches—1 Thessalonians written to the gentiles, 2 Thessalonians to the Jews.

4. The first letter has more to say about the *immediate* coming of Christ than any of the other Pauline epistles.

5. In the first letter Paul seems to look for the second coming "any day." In the second letter, a whole line of events is to precede the second coming.

6. Maybe Paul's first letter had led to over-expectation about the second advent and he tries to quiet them down in his second letter.

7. Thinking Christ was coming so soon, some of the church members had quit work.

8. Paul defends himself against accusations made by his enemies.

9. Expecting the early return of Christ, they had worried about some of their number who had died.

10. Paul explains that they will be resurrected to "share in his glory."

11. The message of these letters is "thanksgiving" and a plea for the Christian virtues.

12. In the case of the gentiles, there was always some trouble in these early churches regarding sex morality.

## IV. SELECTED TEXTS
## 1 THESSALONIANS

1. **Their faith well known.** *"Your faith in God has gone forth everywhere, so that we need not say anything."* **1:8.**

2. **Their conversion.** *"And how you turned to God from idols, to serve the living and true God."* **1:9.**

3. **Mutual affection.** *"Being affectionately desirous of you, we were ready to share with you not only the gospel of God, but also our own selves, because you had become very dear to us."* **2:6.**

4. **The divine call.** *"To lead a life worthy of God» who calls you into his own kingdom and glory."* **2:12.**

5. **Abounding in love.** *"May the Lord make you increase and abound in love to one another and to all men, as we do to you."* **3:12.**

6. **True marriage.** *"For this is the will of God, your sanctification: that you abstain from immorality; that each one of you know how to take a wife for himself in holiness and honor."* **4:3,4.**

7. **Ideal living.** *"To aspire to live quietly, to mind your own affairs, and to work with your hands, as we charged you; so that you may command the respect of outsiders, and be dependent on nobody."* **4:11,12.**

8. **Resurrection of believers.** *"We would not have you ignorant, brethren, concerning those who are asleep, that you may not grieve as others do who have no hope. For since we believe that Jesus died and rose again, even so, through Jesus, God will bring with him those who have fallen asleep."* **4:13,14.**

9. **The second coming.** *"For the Lord himself will descend from heaven with a cry of command, with the archangel's call, and with the sound of the trumpet of God. And the dead in Christ will rise first; then we who are alive, who are left, shall be caught up together with them in the clouds to meet the Lord in the air; and so we shall always be with the Lord."* **4:16,17.**

10. **Comes like a thief.** *"For you yourselves know well that the day of the Lord will come like a thief in the night."* **5:2.**

11. **Spiritual armor.** *"But since we belong to the day, let us be sober, and put on the breastplate of faith and love, and for a helmet the hope of salvation."* **5:8.**

12. **Christian living.** *"Admonish the idle, encourage the faint-hearted, help the weak, be patient with them all. See that none of you repays evil for evil,*

*but always seek to do good to one another and to all. Bejoice always, pray constantly, give thanks in all circumstances; for this is the will of God in Christ Jesus for you. Do not quench the Spirit."***5:14-19.**

## 2 THESSALONIANS

13. **The second advent.** *"When the Lord Jesus is revealed from heaven with his mighty angels in flaming fire, inflicting vengeance upon those who do not know God and upon those who do not obey the gospel of our Lord Jesus. They shall suffer the punishment of eternal destruction and exclusion from the presence of the Lord and from the glory of his might."***1:7-9.**

14. **The son of perdition.** *"Let no one deceive you in any way; for that day will not come, unless the rebellion comes first, and the man of lawlessness is revealed, the son of perdition, who opposes and exalts himself against every so-called god or object of worship, so that he takes his seat in the temple of God, proclaiming himself to be God."***2:3,4.**

15. **The great deception.** *"The coming of the lawless one by the activity of Satan will be with all power and with pretended signs and wonders, and with all wicked deception for those who are to perish, because they refused to love the truth and so be saved. Therefore God sends upon them a strong delusion, to make them believe what is false, so that all may be condemned who did not believe the truth but had pleasure in unrighteousness."***2:9-12.**

16. **The divine safeguard.** *"But the Lord is faithful; he will strengthen you and guard you from evil."***3:3.**

17. **Self-support.** *"We did not eat any one's bread without paying, but with toil and labor we worked night and day, that we might not burden any of you."***3:8.**

18. **Idleness penalty.** *"If any one will not work, let him not eat."***3:10.**

19. **Persist in good.** *"Brethren, do not be weary in well-doing."***3:13.**

FIRST AND SECOND
# Timothy

AND

# Titus

## I. OUTLINE
### *1 TIMOTHY*

## TITUS

## II. TIMOTHY AHD TITUS

1.    Timothy, son of a Greek father and Jewish mother, was probably converted under Paul at Lystra.

2.    Timothy carried out many missions to the churches for Paul. He joined Paul at Rome, then went to Ephesus.

3.    We know but little of the gentile Titus. Later he became Bishop of Crete.

4.    Timothy was Paul's "beloved child." 2 Tim. 1:2.

## III. BACKGROUND AND PURPOSE

1.    These letters present a picture of a highly complex ecclesiastical church organization.

2.    They are concerned with the work of church officials and all orders of church administrators.

3.    Apostles and prophets have been succeeded by bishops and archbishops.

4.    Worship must be regulated. Heresy must be resisted. Discipline must be maintained.

5.    Worship must be supervised—ministers regulated and supported.

6.    These letters deal with "proud, arrogant, and abusive men," "deceitful spirits and doctrine of demons," "imposters and deceivers."

7.    Theology is recognized—"workmen...rightly dividing the word of truth."

8. The purpose of preaching is practical—not speculative.

9. Ministers are to be *"good soldiers of Jesus Christ."*Says Paul; *"I have fought the good fight, I have finished the race, I have kept the faith."***4:7**.

10. Activities of women in the church are greatly restricted.

11. Eighteen characteristics of the false teacher. **2Tim. 3:2-5**.

12. The epistles denounce the "craving for controversy and for disputes about words,""Godless chatter."

13. The church is contending with two types of heresy:

   A. Jewish doctrines.
   B. Hellenic heresy.

14. These epistles are combating:

   A. Jewish teacning—"the circumcision party."
   B. Magic—Eastern charms and hypnotism.
   C. Asceticism—Essene errors.
   D. Hellenism and Gnostic teachings.
   E. Marcion and his heresy.
   F. Docetism—rejection of the second advent.

## IV. LANGUAGE AND STYLE

1. These epistles use hundreds of words not found in Paul's other letters; 175 not found in all of the New Testament.

2. The word "doctrine" occurs 15 times in these pastorals—6 times in all the rest of the New Testament.

3. The vocabulary of these epistles is more like that of the early Christian writers than Paul.

4. There are some passages in these letters that are undoubtedly Pauline— but on the whole the language is foreign to Paul.

5. There is much non-Pauline theology and church organization in these epistles.

6. Paul was a "mystic"—the author of the pastorals is an "ecclesiastic."

7. These pastorals are decidedly more Jewish than Paul's writings.

8. Attitude towards marriage, wine, and society is largely Jewish.

9. Paul's free "spirit" leadership has become a ritual of "laying on of hands."

10. Paul's "faith" in these pastorals becomes the "creed."

11. These are the only books of the New Testament addressed to *individuals*—ministers.

12. These letters sound like those of Ignatius and Polycarp written from A.D. 110 to 117.

## V. PLACE AND DATE

1. These letters have been dated all the way from A.D. 61 to 180, but were probably written between 110 and 140.

2. The unknown author of these epistles has Paul write from prison, and does his best to make it appear that Paul really wrote these letters to Timothy and Titus.

3. It seems likely that these three epistles were based on fragments of messages to Timothy and Titus, but fifty years later were rewritten by an admirer and follower of Paul.

## VI. SELECTED TEXTS
### *1 TIMOTHY*

1. **Sound doctrine.** *"That you may charge certain persons not to teach any different doctrine, nor to occupy themselves with myths and endless genealogies which promote speculations rather than the divine training that is in faith."* **1:3,4**.

2. **To save sinners.** *"The saying is sure...that Christ Jesus came into the world to save sinners."* **1:15**.

3. **Universal salvation.** *"Who desires all men to be saved and to come to the knowledge of the truth."* **2:4**.

4. **Christ as mediator.** *"There is one mediator between God and men, the man Christ Jesus, who gave himself as a ransom for all."* **2:5,6**.

5. **Restrictions on women.** *"I permit no woman to teach or to have authority over men; she is to keep silent."* **2:12**.

6. **Family discipline.** *"For if a man does not know how to manage his own household, how can he care for God's church."* **3:5**.

7. **Qualification for deacons.** *"Deacons likewise must be serious, not double-tongued, not addicted to much wine, not greedy for gain; they mist hold the mystery of the faith with a clear conscience."* **3:8,9**.

8. **The falling away.** *"In the latter times some will depart from the faith by giving heed to deceitful spirits and doctrines of demons."* **4:1**.

9. **Plea for maturity.** *"Have nothing to do with godless and silly myths. Train yourselves in godliness."* **4:7.**

10. **Youthful rights.** *"Let no one despise your youth, but set the believers an example in speech and conduct, in love, in faith, in purity."* **4:12.**

11. **Attend to your gift.** *"Do not neglect the gift you have."* **4:14.**

12. **Family obligations.** *"If any one does not provide for his relatives, and especially for his own family, he has disowned the faith and is worse than an unbeliever."* **5:8.**

13. **Female deportment.** *"They learn to be idlers, gadding about from house to house, and not only idlers but gossips and busybodies, saying what they should not."* **5:13.**

14. **Advice to young widows.** *"So I would have younger widows marry, bear children, rule their households, and give the enemy no occasion to revile us."* **5:14.**

15. **About wine.** *"No longer drink only water, but use a little wine for the sake of your stomach and your frequent ailments."* **5:23.**

16. **Religious contentment.** *"There is great gain In godliness with contentment; for we brought nothing into the world, and we cannot take anything out of the world; but if we have food and clothing, with these we shall be content."* **6:6-8.**

17. **Love of money.** *"For the love of money is the root of all evils."* **6:10.**

## 2 TIMOTHY

18. **Spiritual endowment.** *"God did not give us a spirit of timidity but a spirit of power and love and self-control,"* **1:7.**

19. **Life and immortality.** *"And now has manifested through the appearing of our Savior Christ Jesus, who abolished death and brought life and immortality to light through the gospel."* **1:10.**

20. **Dedication.** *"No soldier on service gets entangled in civilian pursuits, since his aim is to satisfy the one who enlisted him."* **2:4.**

21. **Skilled workmen.** *"Do your best to present yourself to God as one approved, a workman who has no need to be ashamed, rightly handling the word of truth."* **2:15.**

22. **High aims.** *"Shun youthful passions and aim at righteousness, faith, love, and peace, along with those who call upon the Lord from a pure heart. Have nothing to do with stupid, senseless controversies; you know that they breed quarrels,"* **2:22, 23.**

23. **The last days.** *"In the last days there will come times of stress. For men will be lovers of self, lovers of money, proud, arrogant, abusive, disobedient to their parents, ungrateful, unholy, inhuman, implacable, slanderers, profligates, fierce, haters of good, treacherous, reckless, swollen with conceit, lovers of pleasure rather than lovers of God, holding the form of religion but denying the power of it. Avoid such people,"* **3:1-5.**

24. **Persecution.** *"All who desire to live a godly life in Christ Jesus will be persecuted."* **3:12.**

25. **Inspiration of scripture.** *"All scripture is inspired by God and profitable for teaching, for reproof, for correction, and for training in righteousness, that the man of God may be complete, equipped for every good work."* **3:16, 17.**

26. **False teachers.** *"For the time is coming when people will not endure sound teaching, but having itching ears they will accumulate for themselves teachers to suit their own likings, md will turn away from listening to the truth and wander into myths."* **4:3,4.**

27. **The final reward.** *"I have fought the good fight, I have finished the race, I have kept the faith."* **4:7.**

## TITUS

28. **Qualifications for elders.** *"Men who are blameless, married only once, whose children are believers and not open to the charge of being profligate or insubordinate."* **1:6.**

29. **Spiritual purity.** *"To the pure all things are pure, but to the corrupt and unbelieving nothing is pure; their very minds and consciences are corrupted."* **1:15.**

30. **The Christian life.** *"Bid the older men be temperate, serious, sensible, sound in faith, in love, and in steadfastness. Bid the older women likewise to be reverent in behavior, not to be slanderers or slaves to drink; they are to teach what is good, and so train the young women to love their husbands and children, to be sensible, chaste, domestic, kind, and submissive to their husbands, that the word of God may not be discredited."* **2:2-5.**

31. **The civil life.** *"To speak evil of no one, to avoid quarreling, to be gentle, and to show perfect courtesy toward all men."* **3:2.**

32. **The reward.** *"So that we might be justified by his grace and become heirs in hope of eternal life."* **3:7.**

# Philemon

1. This is the story of a converted runaway slave—his conversion and return to his master.

2. This is one of the shortest books of the Bible, and the only one dealing wholly with the affairs of one individual.

3. Paul wrote to Philemon, the master of the slave Onesimus, tactfully pleading for forgiveness.

4. This letter was probably written from Rome, about A.D. 59-61.

5. Onesimus carried the letter to Philemon and was accompanied by Tychicus who also carried Paul's letter to the Colossians.

6. It appears that Paul sought forgiveness for the runaway slave and hoped that his master would send him back to be with Paul.

7. We do not know whether or not the slave was returned to Paul.

8. Early in the second century Ignatius writes about one Onesimus, bishop of Ephesus. There is every reason to believe that this bishop was the runaway slave.

9. It seems strange that nowhere does Paul make a frontal attack upon Roman slavery.

10. In those days slavery was very different as compared with later centuries. Many able persons often found themselves enslaved.

# HEBREWS

## I. OUTLINE

## II. AUTHORSHIP

1. Hebrews was not attributed to Paul until the end of the second century. In A.D. 225 Origen thought that Paul was the author of the material, but that someone else put it in written form. He said: "The thoughts are those of the apostle, but the diction and phraseology are those of someone who remembered the apostolic teachings."

2. Other suggested authors: Barnabas, Timothy, Aquila, Priscilla, Luke, Clement, and Apollos.

3. Some have thought Paul's friend Silvanus (Silas) wrote Hebrews.

4. There is some literary resemblance to 1 Peter, which Silvanus might also have written.

5. The author was familiar with the teachings of Plato, Philo, and Paul.

6. The last chapter is like Paul's writings.

7. The book has been dated from A.D. 85 to 110.

8. 1 Clement, written A.D. 96, quotes from Hebrews. Some think Hebrews was written in the late seventies.

9.   In all probability the book was written in Italy.

10.  Several of Paul's doctrines, like "justification by faith," are not found in Hebrews.

11.  Paul does not present Christ as priest in any of his writings, but Hebrews does.

12.  Hebrews is one of the most erudite books of the Bible.

13.  We are forced to conclude that Hebrews was rewritten one or more times. It may have originated as a Pauline letter to one of the churches and then, like Ephesians, was subjected to much editorial rewriting.

14.  The Council of Trent (1546) included Hebrews among the letters of Paul.

15.  *The Urantia Book* speaks of Paul as author—p. 539. On p. 1024 Paul is referred to as "one of the authors." Quotations from Hebrews are ascribed to Paul on pages 539 and 542 in *The Urantia Book*.

## III. GENERAL CONSIDERATIONS

1.   Hebrews begins like a treatise and ends like a letter.

2.   This so-called epistle to the Hebrews is the least Hebrew of all New Testament writings.

3.   Hebrews is in many ways the most "modern" of all New Testament writings.

4.   An outstanding feature is the discussion of Melchizedek, original with this author. Nowhere else in all the New Testament do we find such allusions.

5.   Jesus as "the pioneer and perfecter of our faith" is the theme of Hebrews.

6.   The purpose was to prevent Jewish Christians from backsliding—so they would not *"fall away from the living God."***3:12**.

## IV. THEOLOGY OF HEBREWS

1.   Christ is the final and complete revelation of God.

2.   The dominant idea: "We have such a high priest at the right hand of the throne of the Majesty in heaven."

3.   And all this is "the new and living way."

4.   The idea of making Christ a priest is unique—the only book in the New Testament to do so. This priesthood concept presents a new and unique philosophy of Christology.

5.   The Melchizedek idea is the essence of the author's philosophy, faith has to do with "things hoped for" and "things not seen."

6.  Philo equates Melchizedek with the Logos; Hebrews compares it to the eternal mediatorship of the glorified Christ.

7.  There is close kinship to the thinking of Philo of Alexandria.

8.  Christian convictions are presented in an atmosphere of Platonic idealism.

9.  Hebrews utterly ignores the whole idea of the Messiah.

10. Hebrews is like Paul's writing in that it avoids use of the title "Son of Man" for Christ.

11. For some reason but little is said about the resurrection and the sacraments.

12. Hebrews is sound doctrine in the equal recognition of the humanity and divinity of Jesus.

13. "He was tempted in all points" as we are—yet without sin.

14. But we miss Paul's concept of the "radical change" by the Spirit— conversion.

## V. SELECTED TEXTS

1.  **Attributes of the Son.** *"He reflects the glory of God and bears the very stamp of his nature, upholding the universe by his word of power."* **1:3.**

2.  **Ministering spirits.** *"Are they not all ministering spirits sent forth to serve, for the sake of those who are to obtain salvation?"* **1:14.**

3.  **Man's status.** *"'What is man that thorn art mindful of him, or the Son of man, that thou earest for him? Thou didst make him for a little while lower than the angels, thou has crowned him with glory and honor.'"* **2:6,7.**

4.  **Christ's humanity.** *"Therefore he had to be made like his brethren in every respect, so that he might become a merciful and faithful high priest in the service of God."* **2:17.**

5.  **Understanding high priest.** *"For we have not a high priest who is unable to sympathize with our weaknesses, but one who in every respect has been tempted as we are, yet without sinning."* **4:15.**

6.  **Melchisedek priesthood.** *"As he says in another place, 'Thou art a priest for ever, after iae order of Melchizedek.'"* **5:6.**

7.  **Learning obedience.** *"Although he was a Son, he learned obedience through what he suffered."* **5:8.**

8.  **High priest ministry.** *"A hope that enters into the inner shrine behind the curtain, where Jesus has gone as a forerunner on our behalf, having become a high priest for ever after the order of Melchizedek."* **6:19,20.**

9. **Melchizedek's relationship.** *"He is without father or mother or genealogy, and has neither beginning of days nor end of life, but resembling the Son of God he continues a priest for ever."***7:3.**

10. **The new covenant.** *"This is the covenant that I will make...I will put my laws into their minds, and write them on their hearts.'"***8:10.**

11. **Missions of Christ.** *"So Christ, having been offered once to bear the sins of many, will appear a second time, not to deal with sin but to save those who are eagerly waiting for him."***9:28.**

12. **Provoking virtue.** *"Let us consider how to stir up one another to love and good works."***10:24.**

13. **Presumptuous sin.** *"For if we sin deliberately after receiving the knowledge of the truth, there no longer remains a sacrifice for sins."***10:26.**

14. **Judgment.** *"It is a fearful thing to fall into the hands of the living God."* **10:31.**

15. **What is faith?** *"Now faith is the assurance of things hoped for, the conviction of things not seen."***11:1.**

16. **The heavenly city.** *"For he looked forward to the city which has foundations, whose builder and maker is God."***11:10.**

17. **The saving race.** *"Therefore, since we are surrounded by so great a cloud of witnesses, let us also lay aside every weight, and the sin which clings so closely, and let us run with perseverance the race that is set before us, looking to Jesus the pioneer and perfecter of our faith."***12:1,2.**

18. **The goal of living.** *"Strive for peace with all men, and for the holiness without which no one will see the Lord."***12:14.**

19. **Hospitality.** *"Let brotherly love continue. Do not neglect to show hospitality to strangers, for thereby some have entertained angels unawares."* **13:1,2.**

20. **Avoid love of money.** *"Keep your life free from love of money, and be content with what you have."***13:5.**

# JAMES

## I. OUTLINE

## II. AUTHORSHIP

1. For many reasons it is difficult to accept James, the Lord's brother, as the author of this epistle.

2. Jesus' brothers were slow to accept his divine mission; at the crucifixion he committed his mother to the care of the apostle John.

3. Nothing in this epistle even hints at an intimate association of the author with Jesus.

**Note:** If James did write it, it may be that he was hesitant to refer to the family relationship with Jesus because of the peculiar circumstances of the aborted meeting of the family with Jesus at Capernaum—when Jesus uttered those words which so shocked his family—"I have no mother; I have no brothers." (*The Urantia Book*, p. 1722)

4. This book of James was written by a learned writer—it is high class Hellenistic literature.

5. This epistle was written in Greek. James was probably proficient only in Aramaic.

6. There is one item of evidence which demands attention. Many of the 230 words used by James in **Acts 15:13-30** do appear in the epistle of James.

7. The early fathers assigned the book to James—the Lord's brother.

8. If James wrote it, then the epistle is among the early writings—since James was martyred in A.D. 62.

9. One theory is that it was written by an unknown Christian teacher about A.D. 90.

10. It is doubtful if James can be dated before A.D. 80. It might be even as late as 100.

11. James was written after Romans, because it refers to **Rom. 4**. (The probable date for Romans is A.D. 58.)

12. The sum of all the evidence would suggest that this book was not written by James, the Lord's brother, and the original was probably most thoroughly rewritten.

## III. JEWISH CHRISTIANITY

1. While early Christianity had its center in the Jerusalem council of which James was chairman, Paul refused to recognize it as a *final* authority.

2. But James and the elders regarded themselves as inheritors of "apostolic authority."

3. When Paul wrote that "*Christ is the end of the law*"(**Rom. 10:4**), he taught what Peter said was something "*hard to understand.*"**2 Peter 3:16**.

4. Their trouble arose from failure to distinguish the two laws—moral law, like the Ten Commandments, and the whole mass of ceremonial law, regarding sacrifices, foods, and scores of other trifling details of living.

5. James seems to have been written to provide a middle-of-the-road document— avoiding Paul's extreme "justification by faith" and the Jewish teaching of "obedience to the law."

6. For twenty years James did preside as head of the church at Jerusalem. It is difficult to understand his addressing this epistle to the 12 tribes.

7. The author is influenced by two apocryphal books—Ecclesiasticus and the Wisdom of Solomon.

8. The epistle seems to teach that action is more important than faith. It is mildly controversial as regards Paul's "justification by faith."

## IV. SPECIAL NOTES

1. The sources of James are more Jewish than Christian. Some editor has made it more Christian than it was in the original.

2. Admonitions are given to most of the 12 sons of Jacob to carry out the "scheme" of the epistle.

3. In many early versions of James, it appears as a "letter to Jacob."

4. In the third century both Origen and Eusebius recognized James as "scripture."

5. Church organization was well advanced when James was written. But the elders had not become priests.

6. James presents a definite plan for "anointing the sick," This is the former practice of the disciples of John the Baptist. (See *The Urantia Book*, p. 1678.)

7. This anointing of the sick with pure olive oil is still practiced by a branch of the Greek Orthodox Church.

8. Most likely it was from this "unction" of anointing the sick that the later rite of anointing the dying—"extreme unction"—was derived.

9. Even today many "divine healers" anoint their subjects with oil.

## V. SELECTED TEXTS

1. **Getting wisdom.** *"If any of you lacks wisdom, let him ask God who gives to all men generously and without reproaching, and it will be given him."* **1:5.**

2. **Gaining the crown.** *"Blessed is the man who endures trial, for when he has stood the test he will receive the crown of lire which God has promised to those who love him."* **1:12.**

3. **Nature of temptation.** *"But each person is tempted when he is lured and enticed by his own desire."* **1:14.**

4. **Good endowments.** *"Every good endowment and every perfect gift is from above, coming down from the Father of lights with whom there is no variation or shadow due to change."* **1:17.**

5. **Speech control.** *"If any one thinks he is religious, and does not bridle his tongue but deceives his heart, this man's religion is vain."* **1:26.**

6. **Heirs of the kingdom.** *"Has not God chosen those who are poor in the world to be rich in faith and heirs of the kingdom which he has promised to those who love him."* **2:5.**

7. **Faith and works.** *"What does it profit, my brethren, if a man says he has faith but has not works? Can his faith save him?"* **2:14.**

8. **Dead faith.** *"So faith by itself, if it has no works, is dead."* **2:17.**

9. **Faith and works.** *"But some one will say, 'You have faith and I have works.' Show me your faith apart from your works, and I by my works will show you my faith."* **2:18.**

10. **Justified by works.** *"You see that a man is justified by works and not by faith alone."* **2:24.**

11. **Dead faith.** *"For as the body apart from the spirit is dead, so faith apart from works is dead."* **2:26.**

12. **Untamable tongue.** *"But no human being can tame the tongue—a restless evil, full of deadly poison."* **3:8.**

13. **Wisdom.** *"But the wisdom from above is first pure, then peaceable, gentle, open to reason, full of mercy and good fruits, without uncertainty or insincerity."* **3:17.**

14. **Submission to God.** *"Submit yourselves therefore to God. Resist the devil and he will flee from you."* **4:7.**

15. **True humility.** *"Humble yourselves before the Lord and he will exalt you."* **4:10.**

16. **What is sin?** *"Whoever knows what is right to do and fails to do it, for him it is sin."* **4:17.**

17. **Patience.** *"You also be patient. Establish your hearts, for the coming of the Lord is at hand."* **5:8.**

# PETER

## I. OUTLINE

## II. AUTHORSHIP

1. There can be little doubt that Peter wrote this letter. Verse 12 of Chapter 5 suggests that Silas (Silvanus) might have written as Peter dictated. This would account for the classic Greek style.

2. Polycarp, Eusebius, and Irenaeus all ascribed the authorship to Peter.

3. This letter shows knowledge of both Ephesians (A.D. 59-60) and Romans (A.D.58).

4. The letter was written from Rome, but Peter used "Babylon" to so disguise it that hostile authorities would not be aroused.

5.  The allusion to "feeding the flock" is reminiscent of Jesus' instruction to Peter. **John 21:17.**

6.  The date is somewhere between A.D. 62 and 65—certainly before 67.

## III. IN GENERAL

1.  The epistle is a gem of both doctrine and ethics.

2.  This epistle is one of the finest pieces of work in all of the New Testament. It is profound in both its courage and its piety.

3.  The passage (**3:19-22**) about preaching to the spirits in prison is a reference to a story in the Book of Enoch. This, with the reference to preaching to them that are dead (**4:6**), constitutes the most difficult of all New Testament writings to comprehend. It was, an early belief that Jesus preached in Hades between his death and resurrection.

4.  The Apostles' Creed alludes to this passage—"He descended into hell."

5.  *The Urantia Book* alludes to the activities of Jesus during the time of the tomb—see p. 2015.

6.  This epistle seems to be sort of a circular letter—like Ephesians—addressed to a group of churches.

7.  Peter discusses Christian duties, civic life, married life, and the trials of Christian living.

8.  The epistle breathes the spirit of the exuberant Simon Peter.

## IV. THEOLOGY

1.  The doctrine is the theology of primitive Christianity.

2.  The theology of Peter:

    A.  Old Testament promises are fulfilled.
    B.  The Messiah has come.
    C.  He is Jesus of Nazareth.
    D.  He went about doing good.
    E.  He was crucified.
    F.  He was raised from the dead.
    G.  He was elevated to God's right hand.
    H.  He will come again in judgment.

3.  The book teaches Paul's atonement.

4.  These teachings are parallel with the Gospels:

    A.  1:13 ................................................. **Luke 12:35**
    B.  1:17 ................................................. **Luke 11:2**

    C.  2:12 ................................................. **Matt. 5:16**
    D.  3:9 .................................................. **Luke 6:28**
    E.  3:14 ................................................ **Matt. 5:10**
    F.  4:5 ............................................. **Matt. 12:36**
    G.  4:14 ............................................ **Matt. 5:11**
    H.  5:6 ............................................. **Luke 14:11**
    I.  5:7 ............................................. **Matt. 6:25**

5.  The doctrine of God is modern—Creator, Father, and Judge.

6.  The doctrine of Christ is thoroughly Pauline.

7.  The doctrine of the Spirit is according to the times.

8.  The second coming and heaven are also Pauline.

## V. SELECTED TEXTS

1.  **The imperishable inheritance.** *"And to an inheritance which is imperishable, undefiled, and unfading, kept in heaven for you, who by God's power are guarded through faith for a salvation ready to be revealed in the last time."* **1:4,5.**

2.  **Saving joy.** *"Without having seen him you love him; though you do not now see him you believe in him and rejoice with unutterable and exalted joy."* **1:8.**

3.  **Controlled minds.** *"Therefore gird up your minds, be sober, set your hope fully upon the grace that is coming to you at the revelation of Jesus Christ."* **1:13.**

4.  **Holiness.** *"'You shall be holy, for I am holy.'"* **1:16.**

5.  **Spiritual nutrition.** *"Like newborn babes, long for the pure spiritual milk, that by it you may grow up to salvation; for you have tasted the kindness of the Lord."* **2:2,3.**

6.  **God's own people.** *"But you are a chosen race, a royal priesthood, a holy nation, God's own people, that you may declare the wonderful deeds of him who called you out of darkness into his marvelous light."* **2:9.**

7.  **The sacrifice.** *"By his wounds you have been healed."* **2:24.**

8.  **The divine oversight.** *"'For the eyes of the Lord are upon the righteous, and his ears are open to their prayer."* **3:12.**

9.  **Spirits in prison.** *"Being put to death in the flesh but made alive in the spirit; in which he went and preached to the spirits in prison."* **3:18,19.**

10.  **Grace to the humble.** *"'God opposes the proud, but gives grace to the humble.'"* **5:5.**

# PETER

## I. OUTLINE

## II. AUTHORSHIP

1. Style and every other criterion suggest that Peter did not write this epistle.

2. Second Peter really belongs with such other books as "Gospel of Peter," "Acts of Peter," "Teaching of Peter," and the "Preaching of Peter."

3. The author knew about the four Gospels and Paul's letters. He knew about Jude and 1 Peter.

4. He knew about the false gospels of Marcionism and Gnosticism.

5. The date is uncertain, but may be well into the second century.

6. It was written from Rome.

## III. PURPOSE

1. To combat false teachings; to uphold the adventist doctrine.

2. To keep free from all "worldly pollutions."

3. "Knowledge" is the key word of this epistle.

4. Stress is put upon the very great and precious promises. **1:4.**

5. The keynote is to arouse faith in the immediate second coming of Christ.

# IV. SELECTED TEXTS

1. **Growth in grace**. *"Make every effort to supplement your faith with virtue, and virtue with knowledge, and knowledge with self-control, and self-control with steadfastness, and steadfastness with godliness, and godliness with brotherly affection, and brotherly affection with love."* **1:5-7.**

2. **Inspiration**. *"No prophecy ever came by the impulse of man, but men moved by the Holy Spirit spoke from God."* **1:21.**

3. **False liberty**. *"They promise them freedom, but they themselves are slaves of corruption; for whatever overcomes a man, to that he is enslaved."* **2:19.**

4. **The advent faith**. *"And saying, 'Where is the promise of his coming? For ever since the fathers fell asleep, all things have continued as they were from the beginning of creation.'"* **3:4.**

5. **Length of one day**. *"With the Lord one day is as a thousand years, and a thousand years as one day."* **3:8.**

6. **The divine grace**. *"The Lord is not slow about his promise as some count slowness, but is forbearing toward you, not wishing that any should perish, but that all should reach repentance."* **3:9.**

7. **The day of the Lord**. *"But the day of the Lord will come like a thief, and then the heavens will pass away with a loud noise, and the elements will be dissolved with fire, and the earth and the works that are upon it will be burned up."* **3:10.**

8. **New heavens**. *"But according to his promise we wait for new heavens and a new earth in which righteousness dwells."* **3:13.**

9. **Grow in grace**. *"Grow in the grace and knowledge of our Lord and Savior Jesus Christ."* **3:18.**

# JOHN

## I. OUTLINE
### 1 JOHN

## II. AUTHORSHIP

1. *The Urantia Book* (p. 1342) says 1 John was a covering letter for the Gospel of John, written by Nathan.

2. Most critics agree that the three epistles have the same author.

3. There is little doubt that the three letters were written by the apostle John around the turn of the first century, from a province in Asia.

4. The style, in general, is that of the fourth Gospel.

5. Slight differences between the epistles and the Gospel of John may be explained by the fact that the epistles were personal letters written by John, while the Gospel of John was really written by Nathan at John's direction.

## III. BACKGROUND AND MESSAGE

1. The epistles are distinct from both Jewish Christianity and Paulinism.

2. All of John's writings are to safeguard the "incarnation" from Docetic error—that Jesus was not to be identified with Christ.

3. There is a distinction between the "world" and the "new life" in Christ.

4. The theme song of the three epistles is "fellowship."

5. The epistles combat heresy—Docetic and Gnostic.

6. The heart of the first epistle is "God is love," 1 **John 4:8**.

## IV. SELECTED TEXTS
## *1 JOHN*

1. **The message**. *"This is the message we have heard from him and proclaim to you, that God is light and in him is no darkness at all."* **1:5**.

2. **Certain forgiveness**. *"If we confess our sins, he is faithful and just, and will forgive our sins and cleanse us from all unrighteousness,"* **1:9**.

3. **Love not the world**. *"Do not love the world or the things in the world. If any one loves the world, love for the Father is not in him."* **2:15**.

4. **Abiding life**. *"The world passes away, and the lust of it; but he who does the will of God abides for ever."* **2:17**.

5. **Eternal life**. *"And this is what he has promised us, eternal life."* **2:25**.

6. **Sons of God**. *"See what love the Father has given us, that we should be called the children of God."* **3:1**.

7. **Our future**. *"Beloved, we are God's children now; it does not yet appear what we shall be, but we know that when he appears we shall be like him for we shall see him as he is."* **3:2**.

8. **Brotherly love**. *"We know that we have passed out of death into life, because we love the brethren."* **3:14**.

9. **Testing the spirits**. *"Do not believe every spirit, but test the spirits to see whether they are of God."* **4:1**.

10. **Brotherly love**. *"Let us love one another; for love is of God."* **4:7**.

11. **God is love**. *"He who does not love does net know God; for God is love."* 4:8. *"God is love."* **4:16.**

12. **Perfect love.** *"There is no fear in love, but perfect love casts out fear."* **4:18.**

13. **Motivation**. *"We love because he first loved us."* **4:19.**

14. **Obedience**. *"For this is the love of God, that we keep his commandments."* **5:3.**

15. **Victorious faith**. *"And this is the victory that overcomes the world, our faith."* **5:4.**

16. **Eternal life**. *"God gave us eternal life, and this life is in his Son."* **5:11.**

## 2 JOHN

17. **Orthodoxy**. *"If any one comes to you and does not bring this doctrine, do not receive him into the house or give him any greeting."* **v.10.**

## 3 JOHN

18. **Good health**. *"Beloved, I pray that all may go well with you and that you may be in health; I know that it is well with your soul."* **v.2.**

# JUDE

## I. OUTLINE

## II. AUTHOR AND THE TIME

1. Jude is a letter designed to combat heresy.

2. The author of 2 Peter knew Jude and quoted him.

3. This Jude claims kinship with James. Some authorities believe he was a brother of Jesus—a son of Joseph and Mary.

4. Jude quotes from the apocalyptic books of Enoch and the Assumption of Moses.

5. The trouble with Jude (the brother of Jesus) as the author is that he could hardly have lived to the times of the heresies he combats.

6. The date of writing was perhaps around A.D. 125.

7. The book of Jude was probably written from Rome.

## III. THE MESSAGE

1. Defense of the faith once delivered to the saints.

2. Denunciation of the deceptive teachings of ungodly persons.

3. An appeal to return to the early apostolic teachings.

## IV. SELECTED TEXTS

1. **True faith.** *"To contend for the faith which was once for all delivered to the saints."* **v.3**.

2. **Troublemakers.** *"'In the last time there will be scoffers, following their own ungodly passions.'"* **v.18**.

3. **Eternal security**. *"Now to him who is able to keep you from falling and to present you without blemish before the presence of his glory with rejoicing,"* **v.24**.

# REVELATION

## I. OUTLINE

## II. AUTHORSHIP

1. *The Urantia Book* says the apostle John wrote Revelation, but that it has suffered many revisions and rewritings. p. 1555.

2. The following Revelation references are assigned to John by *The Urantia Book*. p. 608 (**Rev. 12:4**), p. 599 (**Rev. 21:1,2**), p. 378 (**Rev. 4:4-6**), and p. 539 (**Rev. 15:2**).

3. Original Revelation had much of John—even more than the Gospel of John written by Nathan.

4. The astrology of Revelation was not the work of John, but the addition of the third reviser of Revelation.

5. Of all New Testament books, the text of Revelation is the most confused.

6. Among different manuscripts of Revelation there are 1,650 variants.

7. Biblical authorities believe there was one author, but probably not the same as the author of the Gospel of John. They are uncertain as to who it was and when the book was written.

8. The early Christian fathers regarded the apostle John as author of Revelation.

9. Revelation was late in being accepted as canonical.

10.  It was written during the latter part of the first century.

11.  The present form of Revelation probably dates from the third or fourth century.

## III. IN GENERAL

1.  The book was written at a time of fiery persecution.

2.  Revelation is one of the most difficult of all the books of the Bible to decipher.

3.  Revelation depicts the origin, history, and end of evil.

4.  The author thought the end of the world was impending.

5.  Revelation presents the sudden and dramatic end of the present evil age—the rule of Satan.

6.  The new Jerusalem comes down to earth from heaven.

7.  The term Babylon always refers to Rome.

8.  The chronology of Revelation:

> War in heaven.
> Satan cast down to earth.
> Garden of Eden.
> Present evil age.
> Rule of Antichrist.
> End of the age.
> Millennium—1,000 years.
> > Satan bound.
> The eternal age.
> > New Eden—Christ's rule.
> > Saints rule with Christ.
> > Second resurrection.
> Final judgment. Satan destroyed.
> The new and eternal age.

## IV. SELECTED TEXTS

1.  **The second advent.** *"He is coming with the clouds, and every eye will see him."* **1:7.**

2.  **Safe in Paradise.** *"To him who conquers I will grant to eat of the tree of life, which is in the paradise of God."* **2:7.**

3.  **The new name.** *"I will give him a white stone, with a new name."* **2:17.**

4. **Conquerors**. *"He who conquers, I will make him a pillar in the temple of my God."***3.12.**

5. **The lukewarm**. *"So, because you are lukewarm, and neither cold nor hot, I will spew you out of my mouth."***3:16.**

6. **Standing at the door**. *"Behold, I stand at the door and knock; if any one hears my voice and opens the door, I will come in to him and eat with him, and he with me."***3:20.** (*The Urantia Book*, p. 1765, 1829)

7. **Paradise broadcasts**. *"From the throne issue flashes of lightning, and voices and peals of thunder, and before the throne burn seven torches of fire, which are the seven spirits of God."***4:5.** (*The Urantia Book*, p. 378)

8. **Twenty-four elders**. *"The twenty-four elders fall down before him who is seated on the throne and worship him who lives for ever and ever."***4:10.**

9. **The harps**. *"The twenty-four elders fell down before the Lamb, each holding a harp."***5:8.**

10. **The seven trumpets**. *"Now the seven angels who had the seven trumpets made ready to blow them."***8:6.**

11. **The seventh trumpet**. *"Then the seventh angel blew his trumpet, and there were loud voices in heaven, saying, 'The kingdom of the world has become the kingdom of our Lord and of his Christ, and he shall reign for ever and ever.'"***11:15.**

12. **War in heaven**. *"Now war arose in heaven, Michael and his angels fighting against the dragon; and the dragon and his angels fought, but they were defeated and there was no longer any place for them in heaven."* **12:7,8.** (*The Urantia Book*, p. 606)

13. **The blessed dead**. *"'Blessed are the dead who die in the Lord henceforth.' ... 'that they may rest from their labors.'"***14:13.**

14. **The harps of God**. *"And those who had conquered the beast and its image and the number of its name, standing beside the sea of glass with harps of God in their hands."***15:2.** (*The Urantia Book*, p. 539)

15. **Binding Satan**. *"Then I saw an angel coming down from heaven, holding in his hand the key of the bottomless pit and a great chain. And he seized the dragon, that ancient serpent, who is the Devil and Satan, and bound him for a thousand years, and threw him into the pit, and shut it and sealed it over him, that he should deceive the nations no more, till the thousand years were ended."***20:1-3.**

16. **The end of Satan.** *"And when the thousand years are ended, Satan will be loosed from his prison and will come out to deceive the nations which are at the four corners of the earth, that is, Gog and Magog, to gather them for the battle...but fire came down from heaven and consumed them."* **20:7-9.**

17. **The new heavens.** *"Then I saw a new heaven and a new earth; for the first heaven and the first earth had passed away, and the sea was no more. And I saw the holy city, new Jerusalem, coming down out of heaven from God."* **21:1,2.** *(The Urantia Book,* p. 599)

18. **Paradise light.** *"And the city has no need of sun or moon to shine upon it, for the glory of God is its light."* **21:23.**

19. **The tree of life.** *"On either side of the river, the tree of life with its twelve kinds of fruit...and the leaves of the tree were for the healing of the nations."* **22:2.**

20. **The water of life.** *"And let him who is thirsty come, let him who desires take the water of life without price."* **22:17.**

Printed in the United States
1498100004B/175-198

# THE URANTIA BOOK WO

## Volume Six

*Bible Study*

$7.49

868061
AO —
291 — G

No Exchange
Books
Religion & Spirituality
value village

*O*riginally published in the 1950s and ~~~~~~~~~~ *History of The Bible* and *A Study of the Books of The Bible*, these study aids were authored by some of the first readers of *The Urantia Book* to serve as texts to train teachers and leaders of the fifth epochal revelation. Urantia Foundation is bringing these study aids into the twenty-first century to assist the next generation of *Urantia Book* students in their continuing quest for truth.

*" As they thus tarried before embarking on their active public preaching, Jesus and the seven spent two evenings each week at the synagogue in the study of the Hebrew scriptures."*

—The Urantia Book, p. 1535.

Central Office: Urantia Foundation
533 W. Diversey Parkway, Chicago, Illinois 60614, USA
E-mail: urantia@urantia.org • Web site: http://www.urantia.org
Phone: +1-773-525-3319 • Fax: +1-773-525-7739

Philosophy • Cosmology • History • Religion
The Urantia Book © 1955 Urantia Foundation
The Urantia Book Workbooks Volume VI: Bible Study
© 1961, 1962, 1963, 2003 Urantia Foundation
All Rights Reserved   ISBN 0-942430-94-8

ISBN 0-942430-94-8

52995

9 780942 430943